The Business of Projects

The Business of Projects breaks new ground by showing how leading businesses create and implement projects to drive strategy and innovation. Projects are used to coordinate activities with customers and suppliers and ensure that organisations become more dynamic and adaptable. The book extends the resource-based view of the firm to focus on the business lessons learned from the design and production of high-value complex products and systems (CoPS) which have always been project-based. As well as new frameworks and management tools, it provides case studies of high-technology industries – such as telecommunications, flight simulation and medical devices – to show how projects are used to achieve strategic objectives, perform systems integration, organise productive activities, manage software, achieve organisational learning and deliver solutions for customers.

This book is essential reading for project professionals, academics, students, engineers, managers and policy makers seeking a business strategy and innovation management perspective on projects.

DR ANDREW DAVIES is a Principal Research Fellow at the Innovation Studies Centre, Tanaka Business School, Imperial College London. He was previously Senior Fellow at SPRU and Deputy Director of the Complex Product Systems Innovation Centre at the University of Sussex.

PROFESSOR MICHAEL HOBDAY is Co-Director of the Complex Product Systems Innovation Centre at SPRU, University of Sussex and Professor of Innovation at CENTRIM (Centre for Research in Innovation Management), University of Brighton.

The Business of Projects

Managing Innovation in Complex Products and Systems

ANDREW DAVIES AND MICHAEL HOBDAY

CAMBRIDGE
UNIVERSITY PRESS

CAMBRIDGE UNIVERSITY PRESS
Cambridge, New York, Melbourne, Madrid, Cape Town, Singapore, São Paulo

CAMBRIDGE UNIVERSITY PRESS
The Edinburgh Building, Cambridge CB2 2RU, UK

Published in the United States of America by Cambridge University Press, New York

www.cambridge.org
Information on this title: www.cambridge.org/9780521843287

First published 2005

Printed in the United Kingdom at the University Press, Cambridge

A catalogue record for this book is available from the British Library

ISBN-13 978-0-521-84328-7 hardback
ISBN-10 0-521-84328-6 hardback

Contents

Figures

Tables

Foreword

The Business of Projects is a highly original book in what we have hitherto considered a crowded market.

Most books about projects deal with how to manage them 'from the inside' – what tools and techniques to apply in order to deliver the project 'on time, in budget, to scope'. This is the reality faced by many thousands of project management practitioners who are tasked with doing just this. Increasingly, however, it is being recognised that such an orientation has its limits: there are whole areas which typically are barely addressed in many if not most of the traditional project management texts. Much of the early project developmental work for example is barely discussed. The linkage with enterprise strategy is hardly covered (nor indeed is the whole subject of project strategy itself). There is often scant information on dealing with commercial issues such as procurement (which may even be treated as separate and distinct from project management) and contract management. Technology issues – requirements management, testing, information management and configuration management – may similarly be seen as somehow not part of project management. The hugely important area of people – perhaps *the* most important area of all – is generally poorly handled. Little encouragement may be given to thinking about the benefits that the project is to deliver, or how to measure them or how to optimise the value that the project represents.

These broader areas are progressively being chiselled away at, however. Gradually their role in the management of projects is being formalised. The 5th edition of the Association for Project Management's *Body of Knowledge* is perhaps a real milestone in this regard. This book is certainly a major contributor to this developing new view of the discipline.

But what Davies and Hobday have done is more than this: they have catapulted the subject into a new orbit. Davies and Hobday analyse the role of projects, and the actions of managers within them, from two particular viewpoints: one is that of complex products and systems as a particular class of undertaking; the other is the role of projects in stimulating and effecting innovation. Their insights on both topics are many and telling. For example they lay the myth, so often asserted in the literature, that all projects are 'unique', pointing out that there are production routines in many projects. They show how projects are used in different ways strategically to adapt and innovate, as for example in their discussion on value-led strategies for diversification of project-based services. They develop a strategic perspective on how organisational learning can be project-led and, by skirting the traditional focus on learning about how to manage projects better, provide a new and thoroughly original contribution to the literature.

Indeed, a great strength of the book is its strong literature base: one of the real services it will give to scholars and to students is the way it so carefully and systematically summarises the relevant literature in each of its carefully organised chapters. In doing so, it becomes one of the few books in the business to bridge the gap between the disciplines of technology and social science; one of those rare scholarly treatises to be able to argue a managerialist viewpoint without sounding trite.

The chapters on systems integration and software projects are good examples. The historical overview on project management and systems integration is outstanding. The chapter on software is especially insightful, bringing out clearly the challenge of when and when *not* to apply project management rules (rational-soft project management) building on the work of Brown and Duguid and reminding us of the insights of Burns and Stalker. Too often advocates of project management promote tools and techniques while critics point out their apparent ineffectiveness, given the persistently high failure rate of projects generally, and IT projects in particular. Davies and Hobday's conclusion, which I believe to be correct, is that *both* the rational and the soft approaches are required. Crucially, they go on to underline the importance of personalities in getting this mixture right – something which, despite the increased recognition now given to 'people' factors – is almost entirely missing from the literature. As they say, 'it is the manner in which [rational processes] are created, valued, perceived and implemented which determines their usefulness or otherwise'.

There are limitations. Interestingly programmes and programme management, approaches already in the literature on innovation and now increasingly popular in the practitioner community, are less fully explored. The perspective is very much one of suppliers (with bidding distinguished from project management, which the more holistic 'management of projects' view of the discipline would argue against). The broader client, or sponsor's, role, so important in projects and programs, is underplayed. But I don't doubt that these and other points will be addressed by Davies and Hobday and their colleagues at CoPS in future work as part of their on-going research agenda.

This is research of high calibre. Thoroughly grounded in the literature; based on solid empirical evidence; practical and intellectually coherent; suggesting fresh insights and new avenues.

Peter Morris
Professor of Construction and Project Management
University College London

Acknowledgements

We are grateful to the Economic and Social Research Council's (ESRC) Complex Product Systems (CoPS) Innovation Centre at the Universities of Sussex and Brighton and the Engineering and Physical Sciences Research Council (EPSRC) for funding the research within this book.

We want to thank all our colleagues in SPRU, CENTRIM and the CoPS Innovation Centre who helped to shape the whole idea of the project business, attended seminars and workshops on these topics, and participated in the research projects referred to in the book. Two people were indispensable to this book. Tim Brady commented extensively on various drafts of the book and, as co-author of several articles which form the basis of some of our chapters, contributed greatly to the formulation of key ideas presented in the book. Howard Rush, who as co-founder and co-Director of the CoPS Innovation Centre helped to put CoPS on the map of innovation studies, contributed extra effort in the final stages to sharpen our argument. Andrea Prencipe and Paul Nightingale read and commented on different versions of the chapters. The book's main arguments were submitted to rigorous scrutiny in seminar discussions, essays and dissertations by post-graduate students in SPRU and at several Swedish universities that took the course on 'Managing Innovation in Complex Products and Systems'.

We would like to thank Jenny Newton in SPRU for preparing the manuscript and Katy Plowright for encouraging us to publish a book on the project business.

Glossary

1G	1st Generation – mobile communications systems technology
2G	2nd Generation – mobile communications systems technology
3G	3rd Generation – mobile communications systems technology
ABB	Global supplier of power and automation technologies, formerly ASEA Brown Boveri
ADA	A programming language created by the DoD, christened ADA in honour of Lady Ada Lovelace, daughter of Lord Byron and assistant to the mathematician Charles Babbage
AIM	Advise, Integrate and Manage
ANSER	Analytical Services Inc.
APL	Applied Physics Laboratory
AT&T	Global telecommunications operator, formerly American Telephone and Telegraph
BAA	Owner and operator of airports in the UK and abroad, formerly British Airports Authority
BAE Systems	International supplier of defence and aerospace systems, formerly British Aerospace Systems
BN	Business Networks – Cable & Wireless division
BP	International supplier of energy products and services, formerly British Petroleum
BSC	Base station controller
BT	Global telecommunications operator, formerly British Telecommunications
C&W	Cable & Wireless, a global telecommunications operator
CASE	Computer-aided software engineering
CCC	Concurrent Computer Corporation

CDMA	Code Division Multiple Access – mobile communications standard
CEO	Chief executive officer
CFU	Customer-facing unit
CMM	Capability Maturity Model
CoPS	Complex products and systems
DoD	Department of Defense
EPSRC	Engineering and Physical Sciences Research Council
ERP	Enterprise resource planning
ESRC	Economic and Social Research Council
ETL	Ericsson Telecommunication Limited
FMO	Functional matrix organisation
FOA	First Office Application
FORTRAN	FORmula TRANslation – high-level program language
GE	General Electric, a diversified, global supplier of products and services (e.g. aircraft engines, power generation, financial services, plastics and medical imaging)
GKN	Global supplier to the world's automotive and aerospace manufacturers (now only known as GKN)
GM	Global Markets (previously Business Networks), a division of Cable & Wireless
GMR	Giant magneto-resistive
GSK	GlaxoSmithKline, world leading research-based pharmaceutical company
GSM	Global System for Mobile communications – EU's 2G standard for mobile communications
GTE	Formerly a US telecommunications operator which merged with Bell Atlantic in 2000 to form Verizon Communications
HDD	Hard disk drive
HVAC	Heating, Ventilation, Air Conditioning, and Refrigeration
IBM	International Business Machines, a global supplier of advanced IT, including computer systems, software, storage systems and microelectronics.
ICBM	Intercontinental ballistic missile

ICE	In-Circuit Emulator
ICT	Information and communications technology
ICV	Internal corporate venturing
ILS	Integrated Logistics Support (standard SLIC-2B)
IMVP	International Motor Vehicle Programme
IP	Internet protocol
ISO	International Organisation for Standardisation – technical standards
IT	Information technology
KIBS	Knowledge-intensive business services
LG	Formerly Lucky-Goldstar, a major Korean electronics equipment supplier
MoD	Ministry of Defence
MIT	Massachusetts Institute of Technology
MITRE	Non-profit corporate organisation providing systems engineering and technical services to the US Federal government (not an acronym)
MNS	Managed network services
MR	Magnito-resistive
MRP	Manufacturing Resource Planning
MSA	Pseudonym given to worldwide corporate toolbook (name changed to protect confidentiality)
MSC	Mobile switching centre
MU	Market unit
NATS	National Air Traffic Services – provider of air traffic control services in the UK airspace and over the eastern part of the North Atlantic
NAVAIR	Naval Air Systems Command
NAVSEA	Naval Sea Systems Command
NMT	Nordic Mobile Telephone – 1G mobile communications standard
NPD	New product development
O2O	One-2-One – UK mobile phone operator, now part of T-Mobile
OECD	Organisation for Economic Cooperation and Development
OEM	Original equipment manufacturer
PBO	Project-based organisation

PCB	Project capability building
PDM	Product data management
PE	Project engineer
PERT	Program Evaluation and Review Technique
PFI	Private Finance Initiative
PLC	Product life cycle
PM	Project manager
PPP	Public–Private Partnership
PPR	Post-project review
PROPS	Ericsson's general model of project management (not an acronym)
R&D	Research and development
RBS	Radio base station
RBU	Regional business unit
RFP	Request for Proposal
SAIC	Formerly Science Applications Incorporated, now known as SAIC
SLA	Service level agreement
SLIC-2B	Systems and logistics integration capability
SME	Small and medium-sized enterprise
SPAWAR	Systems Center and the Naval Air Warfare Center
SPC	Statistical process control
SYNTEK	Founded in 1994, BMT Syntek Technologies Inc. is a technical and engineering professional services firm based in Arlington, Virginia, USA (SYNTEK is a wholly owned subsidiary of British Maritime Technology)
TQM	Total quality management
TRW	A global manufacturing and services company headquartered in Cleveland, Ohio, USA (originally Thompson Ramo Wooldridge, today TRW Inc.)
TS4i	Total Solutions for Industry
TT&S	Thales Training and Simulation, a business group of Thales, a global electronics supplier serving aerospace, defence and IT markets
WBS	Work Breakdown Structure

1 | Introduction

Between firms and markets

PROJECTS are becoming key to the growth, profitability and survival of the firm in an increasingly competitive and global business environment. Consultancy organisations, film makers, defence contractors, civil engineering companies, oil and gas producers, advertising agencies, and manufacturers of trains, aerospace and telecoms systems are all project businesses. They use projects to handle most of their internal needs as well as customer-facing activities such as product or process innovation, delivering major capital projects, promoting organisational renewal, and exploring new technology and market opportunities.

Today, firms in all types of industries are finding that traditional organisations, including functional departments, business units and divisions, are stifling innovation. Set up as permanent or semi-permanent structures, these organisational forms are suited to maintaining high-volume throughputs of standardised products and services and to making repetitive decisions in a relatively stable technological and market environment. But in a rapidly changing, uncertain and often turbulent environment, firms face many one-off opportunities and unique problems that cannot be dealt with easily by permanent or semi-permanent organisations. They are discovering that a one-off temporary problem or opportunity requires a one-off or temporary project organisation to resolve it.[1]

In contrast to the hierarchical and mechanistic management structures used in functional organisations, a project brings people together in an organic, adaptive and flatter structure (Bennis, 1966; Bennis and

---

[1] As Toffler pointed out, 'It is obviously inefficient to build a full, permanent structure to deal with a problem that will not be there after a fixed interval of time' (Toffler, 1985: 120). Indeed, as we show in this book, the project is able to counter the anti-innovation bias of the typical large firm departmental structure.

1

Slater, 1968) – or adhocracy, a term popularised by Alvin Toffler (1970) – that is able to innovate around specific customer needs in fast-changing conditions.[2] Whereas functional organisations focus inwardly on increasing performance by perfecting standardised processes and outputs, project structures focus outwardly on solving customer problems and encouraging innovation. Mintzberg (1983) recognised that the project form is used to organise new product development in consumer goods and appears repeatedly in the low-volume and highly customised production systems: 'A number of organisations are drawn to adhocracy because of the dynamic conditions that result from very frequent product change. The extreme case is the *unit producer*, the manufacturing firm that custom-makes each of its products to order, as in the case of the engineering company that produces prototypes ... [E]ach customer order constitutes a new project' (Mintzberg, 1983: 270, original emphasis). Building on the work of these early studies that drew attention to this new species of organisation (including Lawrence and Lorsch, 1967; Galbraith, 1973; Mintzberg, 1979 and 1983),[3] this book provides the first in-depth examination of the ways in which project businesses survive, compete, grow and transform themselves in today's dynamically changing technology and market conditions.

As the pace of change accelerates, some argue that the project is becoming 'the wave of the future in global business' (Pinto and Kharbanda, 1995). Project management and project modes of organising are used to cope with ever-increasing flows of new and more complex business opportunities and problems, rapid technological obsolescence, shortening product life cycles, and cross-functional

---

[2] Mintzberg (1983) showed that adhocracies refer to a whole spectrum of organisations, including space agencies, film companies, manufacturers of complex products, consultancy businesses, petrochemical producers, research-based organisations and non-commercial organisations like UNICEF.

[3] Although they do not specifically discuss project organisations, Burns and Stalker (1961) acknowledge that mechanistic forms of management used in functional organisations are appropriate for stable conditions, but emphasise that organic forms of management are better adapted to rapidly changing technology or commercial conditions. Following Mintzberg (1979 and 1983), many studies now use the term organic to describe the adaptive and responsive features of project structures. Woodward's (1965) classification of production systems is also used by Mintzberg and others to emphasise the importance of project-based activities in low-volume unit and small batch production.

product development.[4] The trend in recent years for large, vertically integrated firms to focus on their core business and to outsource non-core activities is creating opportunities for suppliers to provide individual solutions to each customer's outsourcing needs based on projects. Changes in government procurement policies, such as the UK's Private Finance Initiative (PFI) and Public–Private Partnership (PPP), are encouraging firms to take on the risks and responsibilities for performing long-term public projects, ranging from schools to large infrastructure projects like the Channel Tunnel. The result of all these various changes has been a proliferation in the number of projects and the range of project types. These include single- and multi-firm projects and programmes, national and international consortia and many other kinds of temporary problem-solving organisations. These are typically assembled for the time it takes to complete a particular episodic activity which can extend to several decades in the case of complex military weapons systems.

Internally, large firms are breaking themselves down into less bureaucratic, more adaptable and fluid project-based units (Lindkvist, 2004). They use projects in different ways to achieve organisational change, explore new market opportunities, develop whole new categories of product and solve complex or novel problems such as how to accelerate new product development and shorten times to market. When deployed effectively, projects provide a flexible, efficient and dynamic way of organising a firm's internal resources and capabilities around the needs and priorities of individual customers.

Increasingly, projects extend beyond the boundaries of the individual firm (Gann and Salter, 1998 and 2000; Grabher, 2002a). They include many organisations – such as systems integrators, customers, subsystem and component suppliers, software houses and consultants – working together in temporary coalitions or networks of firms, including strategic partnerships and alliances. Sometimes, large multi-firm projects are established for the sole purpose of delivering the entire range of technologies, products and services required to meet a single customer's business need. When the project ends, the organisation disbands. In this expanding middle ground between firms and markets, *'the actual operating unit becomes the business project enacted by a*

---

[4] The term cross-functional simply means combining different types of engineers, managers and marketing staff (and sometimes clients), usually to respond to fast-changing technologies and new customer needs.

network, rather than individual companies or formal groupings of companies' (Castells, 1996: 177, original emphasis).

The project business

There are many studies of project management as a technical and managerial discipline, specific types of projects (e.g. research and development) and project activities in particular sectors (e.g. information technology, cars, pharmaceuticals and construction).[5] However, as yet, there has been no book which deals with the *business* of projects. This book is the first to explore systematically the ways in which businesses use projects to drive business strategy and innovation. It goes beyond the traditional domain of project management to place projects centre stage in product and process innovation, strategy formulation and implementation, capability building and learning, organisational structure and design, and systems integration (the capability to combine diverse knowledge bases and physical components into a functioning system, such as an aircraft engine or a major e-commerce system).

The absence of a book on the business of projects is surprising. Although the evidence suggests that projects are becoming larger, more complex and increasingly widespread (Miller and Lessard, 2000; Flyvbjerg et al., 2003), they are not a new phenomenon. Many industries, such as aerospace, defence and business computing, have been organised along project lines since the 1940s and 1950s and the competitiveness of some of the world's largest global corporations – such as IBM, General Electric, HP, AT&T, Siemens and ABB – has long depended on their ability to conceive and execute major projects.

This book derives lessons for innovation and strategy from firms and industries that have been organised along project lines for several decades, namely high-value capital goods, which we call complex products and systems (CoPS), such as aircraft, defence systems, flight simulators, information technology (IT) systems, high-speed trains and telecoms networks. CoPS are designed and produced as one-offs or in

---

[5] These range from the early work of Baumgartner (1963) to Buttrick (2000). Also see Morris (1994) for a path-breaking book on why project management as a technical discipline is often inadequate in the real world of complex and changing circumstances. Clark and Wheelright (1992) and Clark and Fujimoto (1991) examine new product development teams in car manufacturing. For a theoretical approach see Stinchcombe and Heimer (1983).

small tailored batches to meet the requirements of large business or government customers. This vital category of low-volume and highly customised business-to-business activity has always been organised on a project basis. Indeed, early innovations in the project form and project management techniques were pioneered by the US defence industry in the middle of the twentieth century (Hughes, 1998). During the 1960s, such project innovations began to diffuse from the US military into the other industries (Gaddis, 1960; Middleton, 1967), such as telecoms and construction, and beyond into public-sector and other spheres of society (Morris, 1994).

Much can be learned from the histories of these pioneering firms and the experiences of today's CoPS suppliers by all types of firms that seek to master the challenge of managing innovation and achieving strategic advantage through projects. Many other firms and industries, such as consumer goods and services, are undertaking projects as a growing part of their research and development activities although their primary productive activity is volume-based or operations-oriented (Keegan and Turner, 2002). In some project-based firms and industries, such as professional services, film making, advertising and construction, the majority of the products and services produced are organised in projects (Gann and Salter, 1998 and 2000; DeFillippi and Arthur, 1998; Grabher, 2001).

In this book we use the term project business to refer to organisations – which may be entire firms or units within firms – that deploy projects to achieve major business objectives, including all firms which design and produce CoPS. These project businesses consist of a variety of organisational forms ranging from small projects conducted within a firm to large multi-firm alliances (e.g. the Channel Tunnel Rail Link consortium). The activities of a firm may be entirely project-based such as Bechtel and Arup in construction and Accenture and McKinsey in management consulting. But in many cases project businesses are individual departments, business units or divisions set up to supply CoPS within large diversified firms – such as General Electric, IBM and Nokia – which may also provide a range of mass-produced consumer goods and services.

The aim of this book

The aim of this book is to show how major international firms make a business out of projects. It does this by analysing concrete examples of innovation and business strategy in CoPS. The evidence presented is of value to a wide business and academic audience and draws extensively from the field of innovation and technology management. This field is an increasingly important area of multi-disciplinary research and teaching which overlaps with business strategy, management and organisational studies as well as economic history and technology policy. Using detailed case study evidence, the book shows how and why the nature and dynamics of innovation in CoPS differ from non-project-based industries, especially standardised consumer goods and services produced in volume for mass consumption. It provides systematic guidance on business strategy and innovation management by explaining how firms deploy projects as part of an integrated corporate strategy to meet today's increasingly complex business problems and opportunities. The book introduces new concepts, frameworks and management tools, supported by empirical evidence, which account for successes and failures in project business practices. The aim is to show how firms can:

- respond strategically to opportunities to diversify into new technology and market positions through a process of project capability building, both within and beyond the firm's boundaries;
- improve company efficiency and effectiveness by capturing the learning and usable experience about successes and failures from one project and transferring them to subsequent projects and to the wider business organisation;
- select the appropriate project organisational form – which varies widely from pure project to matrix structures – to match the complexity, scale and novelty of the problem or opportunity;
- manage the wider business challenges and opportunities of developing software-intensive products and systems, performing systems integration and implementing strategies to move base into high-value service-intensive solutions.

What are complex products and systems?

CoPS are high-technology, high-value capital goods.[6] They are defined as high-cost, engineering- and software-intensive goods, systems,

---

[6] We use the term CoPS because the more conventional term capital goods fails to capture or convey the specific characteristics, diversity and importance of these products to modern economies. We recognise that while not all capital goods are complex, all of the products and systems discussed under the term CoPS in this book are capital goods. Throughout the book we use the term CoPS to distinguish

networks, infrastructure and engineering constructs and services, many of which are vital to industrial growth and the modern economy. Table 1.1 provides a list of CoPS produced in the UK and in other industrially advanced nations. As major items of fixed capital, CoPS underpin both the 'old' and 'new' economy and form the critical infrastructures that allow the flow of goods, services, energy, transportation, information and knowledge in both advanced and developing economies.

Our research shows that CoPS produced in the UK account for around 21 per cent of gross value added of manufacturing and construction, approximately £133 billion in output, and roughly 1.4 million in employment (Acha et al., 2004). Although many are produced within the economy for domestic consumption, CoPS consistently account for around 15 per cent of international trade over the past 30 years or more (Hobday and Laursen, 2003). These project-based CoPS businesses represent a significant proportion of the gross value added of all advanced industrialised countries and they are a major source of competitive advantage. However, the competitive advantage enjoyed by the advanced OECD (Organisation for Economic Cooperation and Development) countries over other parts of the world, including the rapidly developing East and South East Asian economies, cannot be taken for granted. Japan, Korea, China and others are making huge efforts to master the development and production of high-technology CoPS such as high-speed trains, intelligent buildings, aircraft and third-generation mobile communications because they are essential to their future growth.

In the UK, recent changes in government policy (e.g. PFI, PPP and smart procurement) have raised awareness of the importance of large capital projects and the CoPS which underpin them. However, recent high-profile project failures – such as the Swanwick air traffic control centre, the Channel Tunnel Rail Link, the UK passport issuing office, the London Ambulance Service, the London Stock Exchange and high-profile government IT and military projects – illustrate the difficulties involved in successfully managing project businesses and reveal the lack of business understanding and effective management tools in this area.

complex high-technology capital goods from standard, mass-produced consumer goods and routinely produced and low-technology capital goods.

*Table 1.1: Examples of complex products and systems**

Air-traffic control systems	Nuclear decommissioning systems
Aircraft carriers	Nuclear fusion research facilities
Aircraft engines	Nuclear power plant
Armoured fighting vehicles	Nuclear waste storage facilities
Avionics equipment	Ocean-drilling vessels
Baggage-handling systems	Offshore oil production platforms
Banking automation systems	Oil-refining equipment
Base stations for mobile comms	Oil tankers
Battleships	Passenger aircraft
Bridges	Port loading/unloading systems
Bulk carriers (ships)	Process control systems for oil
Business information networks	refining
Chemical plant	Production systems (automated)
Clean rooms for semiconductors	Racing cars (e.g. Formula 1)
Combined-cycle gas turbines	Racing power boats
Cruise liners	Radio towers (large)
Dams	Rail signalling/control systems
Docks and harbours	Rail transit systems
Electricity network control systems	Refuelling aircraft and systems
Electronic commerce systems (e.g.	Remote nuclear decommissioning
internet systems)	units
Electronic retail networks	Road systems/flyovers
Flexible manufacturing systems	Road traffic management systems
Flight simulators	Robotics equipment
Frigates	Rollercoaster equipment
Ground to air missile control units	Runways for aircraft
Helicopters	Satellite systems
High-speed trains	Semiconductor fabrication
	equipment
Hovercraft	Sewage treatment plant
Integrated mail-processing systems	Software packages
Integrated tram systems	Space launch vehicles
Intelligent buildings	Space observatories
Intelligent warehouses	Space stations
Jet fighters	Strategic bombers
Mainframe computers	Submarines
Maritime communication systems	Supercomputers
Mine hunters (and other large	Superserver networks
military ships)	Synchrotron particle
Missile systems	accelerators

Tank communication systems (battlefield and tactical)	Telecommunications repeater systems
Tanks (e.g. main battle)	Training jets
Telecommunications exchanges	Water filtration/purification plant
	Water supply systems
Telecommunications network management systems	Wide area networks
	Yachts (e.g. 12-metre racing)

* These products include various kinds of capital goods, networks, systems, subsystems, and engineering constructs (e.g. intelligent buildings).
Source: Hobday (1998: 697).

Why industry differences matter

Although almost all major firms now use projects to drive parts of their business, firms and managers have to differentiate between strategies and practices appropriate for large-scale, standardised activities (e.g. volume manufacturing) and those which are project-based and customised (e.g. CoPS). These differences are all important in strategy formulation, day-to-day management and, ultimately, business success. The evidence from CoPS firms and industries provides rich insights into the challenges facing project business in general and the differences between project and volume business operations.

One of the key differences is that, in contrast to consumer goods, CoPS are never mass produced for final consumers. Instead, they are designed and produced on a project basis as one-offs or sometimes in small tailored batches for large professional business, government and institutional customers. Unlike the final consumer, these intermediate customers are usually intimately involved in the innovation process throughout the life cycle of the project. Indeed, the innovation idea often originates with the customer. Increasingly, as this book shows, complex services, such as consultancy, finance and training, are now also an essential part of the successful project business, as clients demand complete solutions to their business needs.

In some respects, today's producers of high-volume consumer goods face similar project business challenges. They have to rapidly deploy major capital goods in new interconnected plants around the globe to supply new products. They too need to execute major projects to develop the new product designs and prototypes essential for future business success. Like capital goods producers, consumer goods firms – such as personal computers, consumer electronics and car manufacturers – are quickly learning that there are more sustainable revenue streams from intangible service-based activities than from the supply of physical products. Increasingly, consumer goods suppliers need to involve customers in new designs in order to keep abreast of their changing needs. Even in volume-based manufacturing, many firms have developed extensive in-house project management capabilities to meet their on-going internal needs for major capital equipment, such as assembly plant and IT systems. Perhaps most importantly, new business projects are essential to the revitalisation of mature businesses and especially the efforts of firms to move out of low-margin, low-growth businesses into higher value-added, more profitable activities.

Such inter-industry differences matter also because many leading US and European firms, including General Electric, IBM, LogicaCMG, BT, BAE Systems, Ericsson and Rolls-Royce, across diverse CoPS industries, have maintained or increased their dominance during the recent phase of intensified global competition. As this book shows, a core capability and source of competitive advantage for these firms is their ability to organise a growing proportion of their internal and external activities on a project basis.

Suppliers of consumer goods, by contrast, experienced an onslaught of Asian competition during the 1980s and 1990s. Consumer products, such as household appliances and consumer electronics, are becoming commoditised, offering low margins in slow-growth markets. Even in fast-growing areas such as personal computers and mobile handsets, US and European firms that previously enjoyed leadership positions can no longer match the competitive advantages of high-volume Asian manufacturers such as Samsung, LG and Sony. However, US and European firms retain an impressive lead in project business and supply a large proportion of the complex high-value capital goods needed by the Asian economies. As mentioned above, without a continuous and deliberate improvement in the management of innovation in project business, this lead is likely to slip away in the next decade or two.

Rethinking innovation management

A central theme of this book is that firms managing projects must rethink traditional management processes and best practices that typically have originated from the volume-produced consumer goods sectors. Successful innovation in project business cannot be understood or achieved using the conventional concepts, frameworks and models of innovation developed from high-volume consumer goods. However, firms across diverse manufacturing and service sectors can learn from the successes and failures of project businesses in CoPS. By highlighting the distinctive characteristics of innovation in low-volume, project-based business, this book offers new insights for innovation scholars and managers alike by pointing to the inadequacies of mainstream approaches and, more importantly, by providing the evidence, frameworks and tools needed to understand and manage project-based business.

Many of the best practice tools and techniques for innovation and management (e.g. process-based competition, continuous improvement, organisational learning mechanisms, business process re-engineering, single firm strategy, lean production, agile manufacturing, total quality management, enterprise resource planning, manufacturing resource planning and mass customisation) have been developed for mass-produced goods and, as such, are either inappropriate or at the very least need substantial modification for project business. There are considerable gaps in best management practices and tools available for project business because of the traditional focus of the management field.

For example, most work on business concentrates on the individual firm as the unit of analysis (e.g. Hamel, 2000; Teece and Pisano, 1994; Mintzberg, 1979; Porter, 1985; Barney, 1991). As we have seen, however, the project business involves more than one firm, and sometimes large groups of firms, working in collaboration on single products with their clients. Here, the main challenge is to manage and reconcile sometimes conflicting corporate cultures, goals and business systems as the project unfolds. While standard strategy and management tools fail to deal with this central aspect of project business, many of the management tools relevant for CoPS deal directly with managing multi-firm alliances. As we show below, some tools have good track records, others not so good. They include tools for learning from project to project, methods for managing uncertainty in complex multi-task environments, benchmarking for one-off and routine projects, designing project-based organisational structures, mastering systems integration and moving downstream from hardware to service-intensive 'solutions'. Each of these management techniques, including their advantages and disadvantages, is presented in the book, alongside concrete case examples of how to apply them and how to avoid the common pitfalls.

Research approach

Rather than focusing solely on the firm, as most innovation and management texts do, we work with the three main units of analysis central to project business in general and CoPS in particular:

- the product, to explore the relationship between product characteristics and the form of production, focusing on the project as the key organisational unit for producers and their partners;
- the project, to identify how projects are organised in ways that both are internal to firms and cut across firm boundaries, involving temporary multi-firm alliances;
- the firm, to identify the core organisational capabilities required to set up and execute projects, improve project performance and learning and shift into new areas of technology or market.

Typically, CoPS firms are prime contractors or systems integrators, responsible for managing large, multi-firm projects involving customers and numerous component and subsystems suppliers. The book examines how these firms, through their projects, are responding to changes in the business environment, such as intensifying competition, shortening product life cycles, liberalisation of markets, private–public partnerships and other forms of government involvement. The ways in which leading CoPS firms have responded to intensifying pressure is of considerable interest to other firms engaged in major projects.

Although it has long been recognised that the nature of innovation differs across industries (Pavitt, 1994), much of the writing on innovation continues to be preoccupied with explaining the evolutionary dynamics of high-volume standard or mass-customised consumer goods. Indeed, the academic literature often assumes that innovation models and concepts apply universally across all firms and sectors. For example, the highly influential product life cycle explanation of the dynamics of innovation originally developed by Utterback and Abernathy (1975), mostly from studies of consumer goods, is often presented as a generic model that can explain innovation patterns across industries (Klepper, 1996). While the life cycle model has proved to be an extremely useful tool for analysing the evolution of mass-production industries such as consumer electronics, cars and household goods, it cannot explain how innovation occurs in capital goods or other project businesses. In the case of complex capital goods this is because they are a low-volume, customised project activity where product innovation is all important, but high-volume process innovation is seldom, if ever, relevant to competitive advantage because the mass-production, process-intensive phase does not and cannot occur.

The book benefits from previous research which has attempted to deal with topics related to high-technology capital goods business. Rosenberg (1963) emphasises the pivotal role of capital goods in driving technological innovation and economic growth. Some of the literature on major projects (notably Morris, 1994) has improved our understanding of the challenges of managing large, complex projects. Historical studies have helped to explain the evolution of large technical systems and capital goods projects (e.g. Hughes, 1983 and 1998; Sapolsky, 1972). As yet, none of these contributions has attempted to provide a systematic analysis of how innovation can be understood and managed in the supply of CoPS. Nor have they applied their insights into the realm of project business in general.

The book draws upon insights from disciplines such as organisational science, economics and the history of technology, but it is based primarily on two main intellectual foundations. First, it engages with main themes in the literature on the dynamics of innovation, particularly product life cycle theory and related concepts of dominant designs and technological discontinuities. Second, we draw upon the resource-based theory of the firm inspired by the work of Edith Penrose (1959) and, more recently, David Teece (1996). The resource-based theory is particularly useful in identifying the core capabilities required by CoPS and how they are moving from their established positions into new technologies and markets.

Whereas most books on project management concentrate on operational rather than higher-level strategic issues, books on strategic management often fall into the opposite trap of emphasising strategy at the expense of project or functional practices. This book clarifies the vital link between top-down strategy development and bottom-up project capability building and learning. It also avoids the dangers of analysing and interpreting the project business from the narrow perspective of traditional academic disciplines. Mintzberg (2004) recently pointed out that teaching and research done in business schools take place in terms of specialised functions. Teaching about material that cuts across the specialised functions such as project teamworking or new product development does occur, but it is undertaken within university departments separated by discipline, such as organisational behaviour or marketing. In other words, as 'businesses work valiantly to bust down the walls between their "silos", business schools work valiantly to reinforce them' (Mintzberg, 2004: 32). We suggest that a new interdisciplinary approach to teaching and research about the project organisation, project management and associated cross-functional thinking should be incorporated into the core of business education and practice.

In making the claim that a major rethink of innovation management studies is needed to explain project business the authors draw on a decade or so of detailed empirical research into CoPS carried out in SPRU (University of Sussex) and CENTRIM (University of Brighton) where the Complex Product System Innovation Centre is located. Core funding for the centre is provided by the UK Economic and Social Research Council. The book also draws on three major Engineering and Physical Sciences Research Council-funded projects undertaken by SPRU and CENTRIM jointly between 1994 and 2003. This research allowed us to engage in long-term collaborations with leading global suppliers of CoPS. Each project addressed a particular challenge facing suppliers, including managing the project business to create innovation and achieve corporate advantage, capturing and transferring knowledge from project to project and to the wider business organisation, and developing the systems integration and service capabilities essential for project business.

The structure of the book

The Business of Projects has its intellectual foundations in research conducted by the CoPS Innovation Centre over the past decade. Specifically, its main stimulus was a Masters course taught at SPRU on the subject of 'Managing Innovation in Complex Products and Systems'. From our collaborative research with managers in leading firms and the many project case studies produced by the CoPS Centre, we and our students discovered that managers in many firms are convinced they need to understand how to use projects to improve the management of innovation and achievement of their strategic objectives.

The book has been structured to take researchers, students and managers through the field step by step. Each chapter addresses questions vital to managing innovation in today's project business, providing specific tools and evidence for practising managers and researchers. Those learning about project business for the first time or those teaching project business courses may wish to go through each chapter one at a time. The book's main theoretical and conceptual arguments are laid out in Chapter 2 (project-based innovation). Chapters 3 (project capability) and 4 (systems integration) identify and explain the core capabilities of the project business. Some of the rich empirical research that we and our colleagues in the CoPS Centre have conducted over the years is presented in Chapters 5 (on organisational structure), 6 (on software and IT), 7 (on project and business-led learning), 8 (on services and integrated solutions) and 9 (on strategic lessons). We also provide strategic and cross-industry views of key trends and challenges in CoPS that we have observed in recent years, showing how leading firms have dealt with these challenges. Those wishing to solve particular problems may wish to jump in at the particular chapter which deals with the topic. Below is a short summary of the subjects covered in each chapter.

Chapter 1: Introduction

In this (the current) chapter, we have laid out the main aims and arguments of the book. Although the importance of the project has been recognised by many in the past (e.g. in the project management and new product development areas), what is missing is a treatment of projects as a core, strategic business activity and an understanding of the way suppliers of CoPS manage innovation in the project business.

Chapter 2: The dynamics of innovation in complex products and systems

This chapter shows the importance of CoPS and how they can be used as key examples of project business in general. Because every CoPS is different we provide a taxonomy of projects based on system scope and innovativeness. The chapter shows that the nature of the specific product or system is an important determinant of the type of business project adopted by the organisation. It discusses some of the critical dimensions of product complexity, such as customisation of the product and its components, involvement of users, the complexity of component interfaces, and the wide range of knowledge and skills required for production. The nature of the product implies that a project-based unit is the most appropriate production form. The chapter argues that innovation in CoPS cannot be understood using conventional models and concepts, such as technological discontinuities and product life cycle approaches. As in other chapters, the arguments are highlighted through comparison with consumer goods.

Chapter 3: Business strategy and project capability

This chapter shows that project capability is a vital source of competitive advantage in CoPS and in project business in general. Previous research (e.g. Chandler, 1962 and 1990) emphasises the strategic and functional capabilities required to obtain economies of scale and scope in high-volume production, especially in consumer goods. In CoPS, by contrast, such cost advantages are not achievable because production is confined to low volumes, typically one-off and small batches. Suppliers of CoPS achieve operational improvements by developing the project capabilities necessary to prepare major proposals and execute different types of projects (research, development and implementation) in a particular industry or market context. The chapter draws upon resource-based theories of the firm (Penrose, 1959; Nelson and Winter, 1982; Teece and Pisano, 1994) to develop a framework for analysing how firms use projects to improve their operational performance and achieve their strategic objectives. It shows that firms develop and use project capability to: (1) realise cost advantages by exploiting the economies of repetition (i.e. by developing routine and standardised bid and project processes) and economies of recombination (i.e. by creating reusable product and service modules); and (2) explore strategic moves into new technology or market positions, by setting up base-moving projects.

Chapter 4: Systems integration and competitive advantage

This chapter shows how, across a wide range of CoPS and other high-technology industries including cars and hard disk drives, projects are used as a method of organising networks of industrial activity across firm boundaries. It focuses on systems integration as an emerging model of industrial organisation and as a strategic capability. Systems integrator firms are responsible for integrating various kinds of technology, knowledge, hardware, software and services across various supplier firms. Manufacturing firms traditionally provided these core inputs from in-house divisions. Increasingly they now integrate the products and systems of other firms, moving from a model of vertical integration to one of systems integration. To do this, these firms specialise in being able to design and integrate key strategic components, products and services supplied by external manufacturers. Projects are used to develop long-term partnerships with customers as well as with suppliers of critical components, technologies and knowledge. The evidence shows that systems integration is fast becoming a generic strategic capability of the project-based enterprise and a powerful source of competitive advantage.

Chapter 5: The project-based organisation

This chapter examines the effectiveness of producing CoPS in a project-based organisation as compared with the more traditional functional and matrix organisations. Using evidence from the medical and scientific equipment industry, a simple model is developed to show how a project-based organisation compares with other types of organisational structures. This tool can be used to help with the design of any business organisation involved in major projects and case evidence is used to identify the strengths and weaknesses of the project-based enterprise. The project-based organisation is able to cope with changing customer needs and emerging properties in design, but it is inherently weak in performing routine tasks, achieving economies of scale and scope, enabling firm-wide learning and allowing overall business coordination. The chapter shows how leading firms have adopted mechanisms to overcome these weaknesses and how 'project-led organisations' are able to overcome some of the difficulties encountered.

Chapter 6: Managing software-intensive projects

Increasingly, the core transformative technology for a CoPS business is software and information technology. In a wide range of CoPS and in some modern consumer goods (e.g. cars, camcorders and lap-top computers), embedded software has become a major technical challenge. Producers have to acquire strong capabilities in software engineering and manage large, complex software projects. In addition, IT-based management tools are now widely used to assist in the management of software and IT projects. Using a study of a flight simulator producer, the chapter tracks the deployment of the capability maturity model (CMM) developed by the Carnegie-Mellon Software Engineering Institute to improve software development. However, the evidence shows that CMM alone is insufficient to improve the quality of software because it does not adequately address the human or 'soft' side of an organisation's capability. The CMM approach to software development emphasises engineering discipline, rigorous business processes, working procedures and management toolkits. The soft approach recommended in this chapter accepts the need for efficient procedures but also draws attention to the human factors, stressing leadership, motivation, good communications and teamwork in project success. In any complex working environment these soft factors can make or break major projects.

Chapter 7: Learning in the project business

One of the key challenges facing project business is that of continually improving efficiency by learning from project to project and then transferring this learning to the wider business organisation. Using case studies of two leading corporations, Ericsson and Cable & Wireless, this chapter shows that the initial move into a technology or market base is characterised by exploratory learning when the firm experiments with the new bid and project practices required to cope with unfamiliar activities. Over time, the emphasis switches to exploitative learning as the learning gained is used to develop the company-wide capabilities, resources and routines needed to provide a growing volume of projects. A new model of project capability building is presented which has wide industrial applicability. It consists of two interacting levels of learning: the bottom-up, project-led phases of learning that occur when a firm moves into a new base, and the business-led learning that occurs when top-down strategic decisions are taken to create and exploit company-wide resources and capabilities as projects expand and become increasingly routine.

Chapter 8: Integrated solutions for customers

Many CoPS suppliers as well as leading producers of cars, household goods and consumer electronics are moving beyond the supply of physical products into high-value services. In CoPS, firms are developing new business models to provide complete integrated solutions for their customers. Building on their core capabilities as systems integrators, these solutions providers are offering a range of services including operational and maintenance services, consultancy advice and financial support. The goal is to increase profits by competing in service activities as manufacturing becomes increasingly a low-profit, routine task. Using case study research on five companies operating in mobile phone systems, corporate telecoms networks, flight simulators, railways and the built environment, we show precisely how leading suppliers are making this transition. The chapter presents a conceptual framework to show how project-based firms are moving into integrated solutions by occupying new positions in the industry value stream, building additional capabilities and creating customer-facing organisations.

Chapter 9: Lessons for the project business

The concluding chapter shows how the experience of CoPS suppliers is of great significance to project business in general, providing a new model of industrial organisation centred on the project. Many businesses are using projects to create competitive advantage, enable organisational transformation and build entirely new markets. The chapter shows how the insights, tools, positioning frameworks and best practices drawn from our research on CoPS provide important strategic and operational lessons for the project business of the future. The business of projects differs fundamentally from traditional mass-production activities. However, as manufacturing production processes become routine and standardised, new projects are increasingly becoming a source of competitive advantage for all kinds of firms, including volume producers. The chapter identifies seven strategic lessons that organisations must learn to create dynamic and innovative project business, and shows that project business represents a fascinating vision of our industrial future.

2 | *The dynamics of innovation in complex products and systems*

T
HIS chapter examines the importance of high-technology CoPS to the economy and describes their innovation dynamics, showing that management practices and challenges differ fundamentally from those of mass-produced consumer goods.[1] CoPS, like consumer goods, are not 'all the same', so we develop a simple taxonomy of complex products and projects based on their system scope and intensity of innovation. Underlining a major theme of this book, the chapter shows how and why a firm's core productive organisation, management structures and capabilities are shaped by the complexity of the product that it produces.

In discussing the critical dimensions of product complexity we focus on the value and cost of the products and their degree of customisation for the buyer and user. The nature of the component inputs, complexity of component interfaces, range of knowledge and skills involved, and intensity of user involvement together determine the overall complexity of the product and the type of project needed to produce it. In this and subsequent chapters where the issues are explored in more depth, we show that the need to produce CoPS in low volumes to unique customer requirements calls for strong capabilities in the management of projects and integration of systems rather than volume production and mass marketing as in high-volume consumer goods. We also show that the project organisation is ideally suited for performing such one-off or temporary assignments, rather than the traditional functional organisations used to perform standardised and recurring activities. In reviewing the evidence and literature on the dynamics of innovation in CoPS compared with high-volume consumer goods, this chapter also draws initial implications for project business in general which we follow up in subsequent chapters.

---

[1] This chapter draws heavily from Hobday (1998).

20

The nature and importance of complex products and systems

The links between product and project

The idea that a whole category of industrial products can be defined as 'complex' draws on the military systems literature (Walker et al., 1988), work on the measurement of complexity of systems (Kline, 1990) and research on large technical systems (Hughes, 1983). Historians of technology and evolutionary scholars such as Nelson and Rosenberg (1993) mention complex systems in passing but neither define them nor treat them as a distinct industrial category. Individual industries such as aircraft are studied but this is usually in isolation rather than as one of a generic group (e.g. Mowery and Rosenberg, 1982a and 1982b).

As indicated in Chapter 1, CoPS can be defined as any high-cost, engineering-intensive product, subsystem, system, network, software system, high-technology service, capital good or construct supplied by a unit of production (i.e. a single firm, production unit, group of firms or temporary project-based organisation). Some elements of new knowledge are usually involved in complex product development and as Rosenberg (1976) argues, these capital goods are a key point of entry of technology into the economic system. Complex products are typically purchased by one or more business or government users, usually under one (or more) formal contracts within a recognisable, single project.

The complexity of the artifact and its process of manufacture (usually a major project) are inextricably entwined and the definition of one makes most sense in relation to the other. The chief units of analysis for innovation purposes are (a) the project and (b) its output (or product) and (c) the links between them.

Our focus on the supply and development of complex capital goods differs from the approach used by historians of large technical systems such as Hughes (1983), Mayntz and Hughes (1988) and Summerton (1994) who analyse the historical evolution of networks and systems. Large technical systems are, in fact, made up of individual complex products (and other inputs) at the subsystem level and the wider technical systems deeply influence the innovation trajectories of individual subsystems and components and *vice versa* (Davies, 1996 and 1997b).

The project represents a clearly defined supply task which is undertaken within a certain timescale with given resources and the specific needs of one or more customers in mind. The project can be a temporary coalition of organisations which extends beyond the boundary of the single firm. But many projects are undertaken entirely in-house within a single firm. Projects normally involve a series of phases including pre-production bidding, conceptual and detailed design, fabrication, delivery and installation, post-production innovations, maintenance, servicing and, eventually, de-commissioning.

Within the project management field, the production of CoPS can be viewed as a subset of projects concerned with the development, manufacture and delivery of complex capital goods. The field of project management spans all types of industry and services and many different projects. In fact, only recently has the project management literature begun to focus in on the differences between various types of projects. Usually, projects tend not to be disaggregated according to type and instead are treated as fundamentally similar and subject to similar rules, systems and procedures: 'a project is a project is a project.'[2]

The scope of complex products and systems

As noted in Chapter 1, in the UK CoPS account for a large share of gross value added of manufacturing and construction, industrial output and international trade over the past 30 years or so. CoPS represent a significant proportion of gross value added of all advanced industrialised countries and are a major source of competitiveness of firms based in the UK and other OECD countries.

To show how CoPS relate to the manufacturing and project management fields, it is useful to locate them within (a) the traditional industrial categories of Woodward (1958) and (b) the recent project management framework of Shenhar (1993, 1994a and 1994b) and others. Together they provide insights into the nature of complex systems and subsystems, their technological character and processes of production.

---

[2] Pinto and Covin (1989: 49) cited in Shenhar, 1994: 1308. For a collection of project management papers see Cleland and King (1988). Pinto and Covin (1989) examine the differences between construction and research and development (R&D) projects.

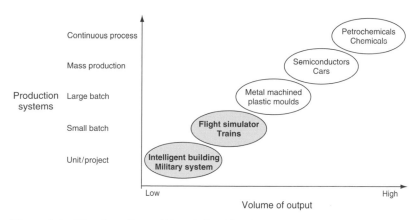

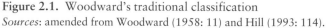

Figure 2.1. Woodward's traditional classification
Sources: amended from Woodward (1958: 11) and Hill (1993: 114).

Figure 2.1 situates CoPS along the traditional spectrum of production processes in the classic framework of Woodward (1958), ranging from (a) project/one-off to (b) small batch to (c) large batch to (d) mass production and (e) continuous process. Complex products include all the high-cost, complex, high-technology networks, service, infrastructural, engineering products contained in categories (a) and (b). Some mature technology systems would not be included (e.g. roadworks and simple building constructs), nor would small low-cost equipment. One way or another, most of the goods produced in categories (c) to (e) also depend on CoPS, such as computer networks, plant, machinery and other infrastructural goods.

As discussed earlier, much of our understanding of innovation and its management has evolved implicitly or explicitly from studies of (c), (d) and (e) and especially mass-produced goods such as cars and semiconductors. Categories (a) and (b) have tended to be treated as special cases rather than as generic categories for research.

Although useful, the Woodward classification lacks a sense of the nature of the product or its technological novelty. These features are captured by Shenhar (1993, 1994a and 1994b) who attempts to show how project management needs to relate to the product under development and especially the technological uncertainty of a product or system.

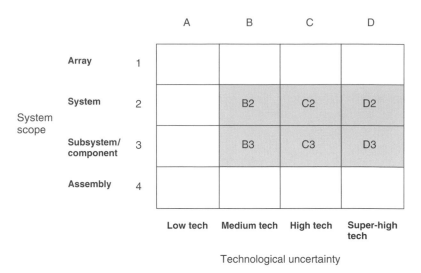

Figure 2.2. Two key dimensions of CoPS projects and products
Sources: amended from Shenhar (1994b: 1312), Hughes (1983) and Walker et al. (1988).

Figure 2.2 relates system scope to technological uncertainty. Scope refers to the physical nature of the products/system and, in particular, the extent of hierarchy contained within it. Shenhar (1994b: 1312–1313) provides a three-part classification (an assembly, a system and an array). In Figure 2.2 a four-part hierarchy is used following Hughes (1983) who emphasises the hierarchical nature of systems. In reality there exists a spectrum of products/systems and, no doubt, considerable overlap between them (Walker et al., 1988). Consequently, definitions used tend to be somewhat arbitrary.

An assembly is usually a mass-produced stand-alone product which performs a single function and does not form part of a wider system (e.g. a shaver, calculator or personal computer) unless it is connected by a network. A component, by contrast, always performs a role in a larger system (e.g. a digital exchange is a component in a telecoms network). Clearly, there exist grey areas between assembly and component. For example, a personal computer could be an assembly or component depending on its use. A system is defined by three characteristics: components, a network structure and a mechanism of control. A system (e.g. an aircraft, a business information system or a weapon system) is organised to perform a common goal. An interesting example is the mobile communications system shown in Figure 2.3 because it consists of components which are mass produced for the final consumer (mobile handsets) and subsystems which are configured for individual mobile phone operators (mobile networks). Finally, an array or 'system of systems' is a collection of distinct but interrelated systems, each performing independent functions but which are organised to achieve a common goal (e.g. airports which consist of aircraft, terminals, runways, air traffic controls and baggage-handling systems). Further examples of CoPS and other types of goods associated with the different levels of system scope are shown in Table 2.1.

Shenhar argues that technological uncertainty (determined by the degree to which new devices, knowledge or techniques are embodied in a product) is a vital consideration in project management. Uncertainty is closely connected to the notion of high and low technology, a concept rarely satisfactorily defined.[3] As Figure 2.2 shows, the uncertainty dimension can be divided into four groups, although again a continuum with no clear boundaries would be more accurate. Type A (low-technology) products rely on well-established technologies (e.g. roads and simple buildings). These can be large or small in value but no new technology is required in production. Type B (medium-technology) products incorporate some new features but most technology is available, as with new models of existing products. Type C (high-technology) products consist of, mostly, recently developed technology. Examples include new supercomputers and intelligent buildings. Type D (super-high-technology) products, which depend on the development of new artifacts, skills and materials, are fairly rare and depend on emerging technologies. They involve extremely high levels of uncertainty, risk and new investment (e.g. spacecraft and intelligent defence systems).

According to this classification, CoPS projects include the components and systems which fall mainly into high-technology groups C2 and C3 and super-high-technology groups D2 and D3 and there may

---

[3] Miller and Cote (1987: 11) operationalise the notion of high technology (in relation to industry) using R&D intensity and the proportions of scientists, engineers and technicians in the workforce. Although useful for some purposes, so-called high-technology industries and products (e.g. electronics) often have a substantial low-technology component to them (e.g. plastics, mechanical engineering, assembly and manual testing) and *vice versa*. The definition and measurement of high technology will often depend on the purpose in question.

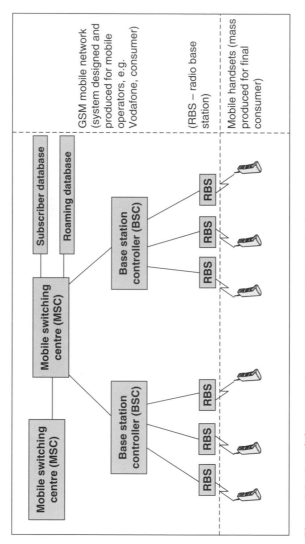

Figure 2.3. A mobile communications system (GSM standard)

Table 2.1: Examples of CoPS

Array	System of systems
	Independent functions with common goal
	e.g. airports (air-traffic control, baggage handling, runways, terminals, etc.)
System	Components, network/structure and control
	Common goal
	e.g. air-traffic control, aircraft, weapon system, telecoms network
Subsystem/ component	Performs a function in larger system
	e.g. telephone exchange, avionics system, signalling system
Assembly	Self-contained or within a larger system
	Often mass produced
	e.g. computer hard disk, CD player, etc.

well be overlap with B2 and B3. However, the definition above would exclude low-technology goods (A1 to A4) and some medium-technology goods (B1 to B4) regardless of cost. Also, arrays comprised of combinations of systems would mostly be excluded from the definition, unless they were supplied under one definable project.

Taken together, system scope and technological novelty provide a starting point for describing the breadth and nature of CoPS. As shown below, innovation in CoPS is concerned with the development and supply of new components, subsystems, control units and systems, contracted for and executed in single projects.

Examples of complex products and systems

In Chapter 1, we presented a selection of CoPS to illustrate their range and variety (Table 1.1). They also include subsystems, such as avionics used in aircraft, as well as complete aircraft. Some of the devices in Table 1.1 overlap with low-technology products. For example, some standard civil engineering projects (e.g. roads and construction) may involve little new knowledge or uncertainty. However, larger civil engineering projects often require the development and application of novel technologies. A modern transit system, for example, could

involve computer-simulated bridge design, advanced structural engineering, an understanding of the latest materials technology and geo-
technics, fire engineering, environmental assessment skills and so on.
Many building projects (e.g. airport terminals, sports facilities and
corporate headquarters) incorporate highly sophisticated information-
technology systems and new materials (Gann, 1993 and 2000).

Innovation processes can be very complex, especially those with a high
software content. The number and complexity of projects worldwide
has risen with economic growth and many now contain an important
core of embedded software. Telecommunications exchanges and flight
simulators, for example, were once electromechanical devices produced
by single large suppliers. Today, a large part of the production task is
software development and many of the subsystems and components are
subcontracted out to specialist suppliers (Miller et al., 1995).

High-value complex services

Many high-technology services such as air, rail and road transportation,
information and communications services and energy provision depend
directly or indirectly on CoPS infrastructure for their development
and provision. Banking services, logistics and retail chains, for example,
rely on complex IT networks. R&D services depend crucially on complex
instrumentation equipment and other capital goods. Telecommunications
services rely on complex products such as software-controlled switching
and transmission systems. Television services form an important part of
the TV network infrastructure (e.g. satellites for transmission and studio
equipment for making programmes).

As shown in Chapter 8, many CoPS suppliers are also major providers of related high-value complex services. Indeed, the supply of
high-technology services by capital goods producers (e.g. Rolls-Royce,
GE and IBM) has increased markedly in recent years and for many
large corporations now represents a substantial proportion of sales.
The professional services supplied by producers of flight simulators,
aircraft engines and large computer networks include design, installation, upgrading, maintenance, software support and training, consultancy and financial deal structuring. Some large capital goods suppliers
(e.g. Boeing) have diversified horizontally into financial services,
increasing still further the proportion of services in their turnover.

The changing innovation environment

Since the 1960s and 1970s, the innovation environment has changed markedly. Technological, policy and financial changes have forced the pace of innovation in key CoPS industries such as telecommunications, energy, railways and aviation. Market growth and the increasing internationalisation of firms have progressed apace, as have new forms of regulation. New mechanisms of financing and deal structuring involving private capital have made ever larger projects possible. The deregulation of sectors such as telecommunications, aerospace, nuclear power and electricity in several countries has created a global market for new capital equipment and services, while large new investments in Eastern Europe and East Asia have changed the market prospects facing suppliers.

In large projects which affect the physical environment such as railways, nuclear power and water treatment plants, a variety of institutional factors, not least outside stakeholders' interests, has to be accounted for before, during and after the project execution stages. New standards of safety and pollution control often need to be built into project planning from the outset. Emerging environmental concerns feed into risk and project management from planning and execution through to operation and de-commissioning. Mechanisms for dealing with feedback from users and other stakeholders form an important part of the management process, especially for larger projects.

CoPS are an important area of competitive advantage for the US and EU over large parts of East Asia. The relatively poor performance of non-Japan East Asia in exporting capital goods compares vividly with their advance in mass-produced goods such as electronics, clothing and footwear (Abegglen, 1994; Hobday, 1995). Even the largest Korean and Taiwanese firms have weaknesses in advanced capital goods and have to import these from Japan, the US and Europe. With the exception of Japan, East Asia is at an earlier stage of development in complex products and firms are investing heavily to catch up both to reduce imports and to capture market shares (e.g. in nuclear plant, telecommunications and aerospace).

Critical product dimensions

To analyse the nature of innovation in CoPS it is helpful to focus in on the critical factors which define the complexity of a product along a

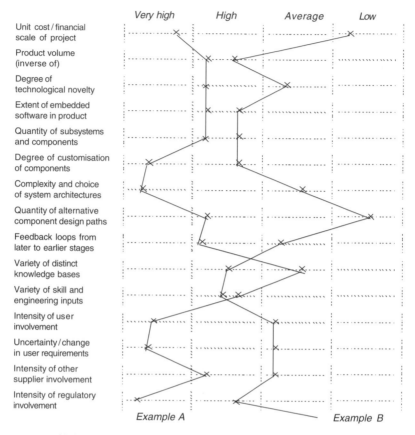

Notional examples 'A' (air traffic control system) and 'B' (flight simulator)

Figure 2.4. Critical product dimensions of complex products and systems

range of dimensions independent of particular products, sectors or industries. These critical product dimensions provide a rough measure of product complexity and show how various indicators of complexity relate to innovation. Some important indicators of product complexity were discussed above. These include the quantity of tailored components and subsystems, the hierarchical manner in which they are integrated and the degree of technological novelty of the product or system in question.

Figure 2.4 extends the range of critical product dimensions to include, for example, the variety of knowledge bases included in each product. The listing, compiled from discussions with senior engineers and project managers, shows which product features directly relate to difficulties of managing projects, controlling innovation processes and coping with uncertainty and risk. Some important product dimensions seem to be neutral with respect to risk and uncertainty (e.g. whether the product is stand-alone, as in the case of an aircraft, or networked, as in the case of a business information system). The amount of embedded software and IT is an important feature of product complexity, especially if new vintages of technology are used in production (e.g. new IT design tools, or bidding or project management systems).

Figure 2.4 emphasises the point that complexity, hierarchy and other critical product features are a matter of degree. We should also recognise that some more complex products may be easier to produce because of the experience of those engaged in the project. A relatively straightforward complex product or system may pose incredible difficulties to firms which lack experience (e.g. as in the case of Asian would-be entrants). By contrast even the most complex goods can be produced with relative ease by those firms with long experience.

Most CoPS, by definition, embody a fair degree of complexity and risk in at least some respects. Taken together, the critical dimensions provide an approximation of the relative degree and nature of the complexity of a particular product and suggest the difficulties of coordinating projects, especially when many firms are involved.

It is probably unhelpful to make too sharp a distinction between product and project in assessing product complexity. These two features are inextricably entwined, with the product shaping the nature of the project and *vice versa*. Equally, it is helpful to view the product in relation to the market in which it is embedded, as the quality of its attributes can be understood only in the light of the demands of the marketplace. As discussed below market structure (often a duopoly in major capital goods) and the exigencies of regulation shape many of the parameters and choices within a particular project.

Turning to key product dimensions, Henderson and Clark (1990) in their work on architecture at the single product level show the importance of the interconnections between components and subsystems in the evolution of product design. The quantity and complexity of alternative system architectures can pose significant management problems for system suppliers, especially when system integrators, users and regulators have to agree on the system architecture and the path of innovation before a design can be signed off (Miller et al., 1995). Certain 'normal' architectures can be stabilised within standardised designs for periods of time, influencing the capabilities and strategies of suppliers. However, the larger the number of tailored components and subsystems, the more difficult the architectural choices will be. With many organisations involved in making architectural decisions, elaborate meso-level organisational structures may need to be put in place (Arena, 1983; Dosi, 1988; Richardson, 1972). For very large systems, the required capabilities may be beyond the managerial span of control of any single firm (Penrose, 1959).

Within the architecture of a complex product many alternative design routes for particular components may exist (Iansiti and Khanna, 1995) and what appears to be incremental evolution at the system performance level can mask substantial discontinuities at the component level. As Metcalfe and de Liso (1995: 21) point out, in such cases focusing devices are needed to cope with the danger of 'combinatorial explosion'. This means that the firm is faced with impossibly large numbers of alternative design paths so that it cannot make any realistic, rational estimates of how to proceed. In complex products the problem of narrowing design choice can be daunting, especially under conditions of rapid technological change, unclear user requirements and multiple, customised components.

To make project management even more difficult, there may be substantial feedback loops from later to earlier project stages as alterations to overall system architectures or to the design of specific components are required. Such feedback loops are commonly found in military systems where elaborate procedures are imposed by purchasers (such as the Department of Defense (DoD) in the US and the Ministry of Defence (MoD) in the UK) in order to monitor and control changes to specifications, as these occur regularly during product development (Chambers, 1986; Lake, 1992). Systems engineers in such sectors acknowledge the need to proceed through stages of product development with incomplete information, changing user requirements and emerging (unpredictable) system properties (Boardman, 1990). Indeed, the capability to master these project processes and their risks can confer considerable competitive advantage on particular suppliers. Nevertheless, even with a clear view of user needs and design options, collaborative projects often fail in one respect or another (Pinto and Prescott, 1988; Shenhar et al., 1994).

Other related dimensions of product complexity include the variety of distinct knowledge bases which need to be integrated into the final product or system. In modern aircraft, for example, a wide variety of knowledge bases embracing new materials, software technologies, fluid mechanics and communication systems need to be mastered (Vincenti, 1990). The need for systems integration knowledge can expand the variety of skills required far beyond the competencies of even the largest individual producers which then have to work closely with specialist engineering and software/IT producers to produce the final system. Often the route to project completion depends critically on the tacit knowledge embodied in individuals and groups, in contrast to the codified forms of knowledge required to mass produce simpler goods.

Another factor to test the ingenuity of complex product suppliers is the intensity of user involvement and the user's understanding of final requirements. Sometimes, the user is unclear precisely what needs to be (or indeed can be) supplied. Or the user may make changes to requirements as the project unfolds, as their own needs change. The intensity of other supplier involvement can further complicate management difficulties. Other things being equal, the larger the number of firms involved in product definition, design and manufacture, the more complex the management task. The degree to which the project is outside the prime contractor's span of control directly influences the challenges of project management.

Management challenges also derive from the changing regulatory environment. In some CoPS the intensity of regulatory involvement can significantly influence the path of innovation. Regulation may be needed for safety reasons (e.g. as in aircraft and buildings), for interfacing standards (e.g. as in telecommunications) or for security reasons (as in military and information systems). In some industries, regulators take an intense interest in new products, approving design innovations, verifying production methods and adding new criteria to system validation and accreditation.

Figure 2.4 indicates that the extent of embedded software and IT in the product is important. This is because of the way that software has transformed many CoPS. The use of sophisticated software within products, spurred on by low-cost computer power, has improved the control and performance of many systems (e.g. large computer-controlled machine tools). Software engineering has become a core task in flight simulators, military systems, telecommunications exchanges, air traffic control systems, aircraft engines, avionics and many other complex products.

Developing software has proved to be a problematic, risk-intensive activity (Humphrey, 1989a and 1989b; Paulk, 1993; Buxton and Malcolm, 1991). Most observers acknowledge the extreme difficulties of ensuring software-intensive projects are completed within budget and on time (Charette, 1989; Lyytinen et al., 1995; Boehm, 1991). Indeed, there is now sufficient evidence to argue that embedded software is a major stumbling block in the execution of many large systems, leading to delays, cancellations and cost overruns (Gibbs, 1994; Peltu, 1992; Littlewood and Strigini, 1992).

Figure 2.4 can be used to develop a product complexity profile of a particular system, as in the case of examples A (an air traffic control system) and B (a flight simulator). This method helps to show overall product complexity and identifies in which specific areas products and systems are complex as defined.

A heavy bias towards the left-hand side of Figure 2.4 indicates very high management risk (e.g. a new space project, involving the development of new materials and information systems). Conversely, a scoring towards the right-hand side indicates relatively little technological novelty and low risk, such as a repeat-order civil flight simulator. However, even the latter is likely to pose more management difficulties than, say, a bicycle, which is based on standard components and fewer knowledge inputs.

Although most simple goods exhibit fewer design and architectural options, some may score fairly highly on particular dimensions (e.g. design complexity), especially at the early stages of the product life cycle (e.g. a microcomputer or a car). However, with simple products there are generally fewer problems resulting from intrinsic design difficulties, regulatory constraints and variety of knowledge and skill inputs involved. Simpler goods tend to benefit from a greater degree of learning from prior generations of product, made possible by the codification of process knowhow due to volume production. In complex products, process learning within and between product generations is more haphazard due to the difficulties of transferring knowledge from one project to another, changing user needs and the customisation of component inputs.

Most mass-produced goods will tend to exhibit low scores against most of the critical dimensions above and tend to fall off the right of

Figure 2.4. Generally the challenges facing simpler goods are centred on process control, product–process interfacing, design for manufacture and mass production efficiency.

Complex products vs mass-production models of innovation

Two ideal-type innovation models

In order to explore the implications of the differences between complex and simple products it is helpful to counterpoise two simple ideal-type[4] innovation models: a mass-production 'conventional' model and a complex product/project model (see Table 2.2). The term conventional is used because the model has informed evolutionary theories of technical change and strongly influenced management approaches. The simple model has also influenced views on how the West should respond to the East Asian challenge in cars and other areas (Womack et al., 1991). As with mainstream management theory from Chandler to Drucker to Porter, competition analysis occurs primarily at the single-firm or industry level and multi-firm projects are seldom treated.

For our purposes, the conventional model is a useful approximation of innovation processes in mass-produced, simple goods and the contrast between the two models helps illustrate the broader implications of the complex product vs mass production/simple product contrast, and especially the difficulties confronting project managers.

The conventional model of innovation

An extreme version of the conventional model is summarised in the right-hand side of Table 2.2. Its authors stress similarities in the innovation process, arguing that product and process technologies tend to follow life-cycle patterns from birth to maturity (Utterback and Abernathy, 1975; Abernathy and Clark, 1985; Clark, 1985; Utterback and Suarez, 1993; Klepper, 1996). Firms are assumed to

---

[4] Although ideal types are not intended to be accurate descriptions of the real world, they are useful for helping to compare real-world observations (Cawson, 1986: 31–32; Doty and Glick, 1994: 230–251). The two innovation types below correspond to end points on a scale, standing in logical contrast to each other. Actual cases will tend to fall between the two.

Table 2.2: Complex vs mass-production industries (two ideal types)

	Complex product/system project organisation	Simple products/mass production*
Product characteristics	Complex component interfaces	Simple interfaces
	Multi-functional	Single function
	High unit cost	Low unit cost
	Product cycles last decades	Short product life cycles
	Many skill/knowledge inputs	Fewer skill/knowledge inputs
	(Many) tailored components	Standardised components
	Upstream, capital goods	Downstream consumption goods
	Hierarchical/systemic	Simple architectures
Production characteristics	Project/small batch	High volume, large batch
	Systems integration	Design for manufacture
	Scale-intensive, mass production not relevant	Incremental process, cost control central
Innovation processes	User-producer driven	Supplier driven
	Business to business	Business to consumer
	Highly flexible, craft based	Formalised, codified
	Innovation and diffusion collapsed	Innovation and diffusion separate
	Innovation paths agreed ex ante among suppliers, users etc.	Innovation path mediated by market selection
	People-embodied knowledge	Machinery-embodied knowhow
Competitive strategies and innovation coordination	Focus on product design and development	Focus on economies of scale/cost minimisation
	Organic	Mechanistic
	Systems integration competences	Volume production competences
	Management of multi-firm alliances in temporary projects	Focus on single firm (e.g. lean production, TQM, MRP 11)

	Complex product/system project organisation	Simple products/mass production*
Industrial coordination and evolution	Elaborate networks	Large firm/supply chain structure
	Project-based multi-firm alliances	Single firm as mass producer
	Temporary multi-firm alliances for innovation and production	Alliances usually for R&D or asset exchange
	Long-term stability at integrator level	Dominant design signals industry shakeout
Market characteristics	Duopolistic structure	Many buyers and sellers
	Few large transactions	Large numbers of transactions
	Administered markets	Regular market mechanisms
	Institutionalised/politicised	Traded
	Heavily regulated/ controlled	Minimal regulation
	Negotiated prices	Market prices
	Partially contested	Highly competitive

* Note that flexible specialisation (Piore and Sabel, 1984) is a subset of simple-product/mass-production industries in this formulation. Here, flexible specialisation is an advanced form of mass production.

compete in a technology race while consumers decide which products will be successful through arm's-length market transactions.

Many would not agree with the conventional view. Other innovation analysts point to the heterogeneous nature of innovation and long-lasting inter-industry differences between origins and processes of innovation (e.g. Pavitt and Rothwell, 1976; Freeman, 1994). Pavitt (1990), for example, argues that distinct modes of innovation can be observed across four groups of sectors: (i) science based; (ii) scale intensive; (iii) information intensive; (iv) specialised supplier dominated. Nelson and Rosenberg (1993) point to differences between large-scale, engineering-intensive products, fine chemicals and bulk commodities such as steel. Woodward (1958), Hayes and Wheelwright (1984) and Hill (1993) distinguish five or

so major groups of product for production purposes, showing how process innovation depends on the unit volume of throughput.

Although seldom noted, the conventional model is intimately linked
to the production paradigm of mass-market commodity goods. Firms
and markets tend to be clearly defined entities. Large and small firms
compete to create markets and redefine industries by exploiting technical opportunities (Schumpeter, 1947). The creation and diffusion of
new technologies are usually viewed as separate if not sequential
activities: the R&D lab develops and the market selects (Utterback
and Abernathy, 1975). Similarly, innovation is usually treated as separate from diffusion: innovation occurs and diffusion follows.

In the conventional model, the single firm is a chief unit of analysis
for competitive purposes rather than the project as in complex products
and services. The outcomes of competitive contests are traceable to the
competences, skills and complementary assets that rival firms bring to
the marketplace (Barney, 1991; Teece, 1986). Product markets and
technologies undergo life cycles from fluid immaturity states to maturity (Abernathy and Utterback, 1978; Kotler, 1976). Cycles can cover
long periods of gradual evolution, punctuated by short periods of
disruptive change (Tushman and Anderson, 1986).

According to Utterback and Abernathy (1975), a central event in the
innovation process occurs when a dominant design emerges to galvanise an entire market and to give direction to subsequent technological
trajectories. At the early stage, the rate of product innovation is high,
stimulated by market needs and a wave of new competing entrants.
Product markets are ill-defined, products are unstandardised, processes
are uncoordinated and user–supplier interactions shape the pattern of
innovation. Eventually a dominant design is selected by the market,
signalling an industrial shakeout. Small uncompetitive firms exit or are
acquired by large companies. Eventually, a small number of firms come
to dominate the industry by exploiting scale-intensive, incremental process improvements. As Utterback and Suarez (1993: 2–3) put it:
'Eventually, we believe that the market reaches a point of stability in
which there are only a few large firms having standardised or slightly
differentiated products and relatively stable sales and market shares,
until a major technological discontinuity occurs and starts a new cycle
again.' The latter study is based on seven industries: manual type-
writers, cars, transistors, integrated circuits, electronic calculators, television sets and picture tubes, and parallel supercomputers. Apart from

supercomputers, these are all mass-produced goods (both consumer and industrial) where incremental process improvements eventually play a large part in competitive performance.

According to the conventional view, entry barriers vary according to the stage of the innovation cycle. Typically, at the early stages, the main barriers are knowledge based, whereas the barriers at the later stages are scale based (Mueller and Tilton, 1976). Over time, there is a high turnover of firms in the industry. Entry precedes the dominant design and exit usually follows. Pioneers often fail to survive the harsh selection process of the competitive contest. Furthermore, with the emergence of radical new technologies, old competences can be destroyed, leading to industrial disruption and extinction for laggards in line with Schumpeter's notion of creative destruction (Tushman and Anderson, 1986). Box 2.1 provides a summary of the conventional product life cycle (PLC) view and contrasts this with the life cycle of CoPS.

Box 2.1: The life cycle of complex product systems vs mass-produced goods

The dynamics of innovation and industrial evolution in CoPS cannot be easily understood using the product life cycle framework of analysis, originally based on Vernon's (1966) article on industrial location, trade and competitiveness. The PLC model of innovation developed by William Abernathy and James Utterback (Utterback and Abernathy, 1975; Utterback, 1994) claims that products tend to follow a life cycle from birth to maturity. Drawing upon cases from large batch and mass production, the Abernathy-Utterback model describes three main phases of innovation:

1. A 'fluid phase' dominated by product innovation and characterised by competition between many small firms offering competing product designs.
2. A 'transitional phase' initiated by the emergence of a 'dominant design' which signals a shakeout as an industry becomes dominated by a few large firms and characterised by an emphasis on process innovation and the production of standardised products in high volumes.
3. A 'specific phase' when the rate of product and process innovation declines.

This typical pattern of evolution is intermittently disrupted by discontinuous waves of radical or disruptive innovation, which force firms with capabilities tied to the existing technologies to adopt the innovations or risk being relegated to a minor role in the industry.

The PLC model continues to provide a powerful explanation of the evolution of mass-produced commodity goods such as cars, mobile handsets, cameras and PCs. However, several authors have pointed out that it is less useful in understanding the life cycle of CoPS, such as flight simulators (Miller et al., 1995), high-speed trains (Potter and Roy, 1996) and mobile communications systems (Davies, 1997b). CoPS tend to remain in the early fluid phase of product innovation (Miller et al., 1995). Although CoPS do mature, a phase with stand-ardised products in high volumes for mass markets is seldom reached. In other words, progress in the way CoPS are designed and produced cannot be easily measured in terms of a movement from small-batch customised products organised on a project basis to high-volume standardised production based on assembly, lean, agile or mass-customisation techniques. Therefore, the conventional product and process dichotomy is unhelpful in explaining the nature and determin-ants of innovation in CoPS, where the rate of product innovation is consistently high (Davies, 1997: 234).

What is required are more precise studies of the closely coupled relationship between product and process innovation in CoPS. In particular, the large development costs associated with the develop-ment of each new product generation of a CoPS make it important to maximise the production of a given product design (Mowery and Rosenberg, 1982a: 165) and system architecture or standard. In the commercial aircraft industry, for example, the family concept has been developed so that the design of each product generation – such as the Boeing 727, 737 and 747 aircraft – can be stretched over many years to produce a series of modified designs (Gardiner and Rothwell, 1985). In addition to standalone products such as aircraft and high-speed trains, the concept of a family or generation has been applied to entire systems of technology, each based on a different standard and architecture.

In contrast to the pattern of industry shakeout predicted in the conventional PLC model, Miller et al. (1995) use evidence from the flight simulator industry to develop the hypothesis that CoPS industries are characterised by considerable stability at the systems integrator level across generations of technology and/or products. Bonaccorsi and Giuri (2000) provide further evidence from the history of the turboprop engine industry (1948–97) of a 'non shake-out' pattern and a continuing dominance of the industry by a few leading firms, whose competitive advantage stems from product innovation and strong customer relationships rather than economies of scale and scope.

The comparison with complex products and systems

The left-hand side of Table 2.2 puts forward an ideal-type version of innovation in complex capital goods, contrasting product life cycles, processes of manufacture, industrial coordination, corporate strategies and market features. In many cases CoPS are customised systems which can never be mass produced. Because they are large investment items whose operational life cycles extend over decades, decisions to invest may take months or even years and, in some cases, innovation can occur long after the delivery of the product. Often industrial coordination requires the orchestrated contribution of many suppliers during the innovation process.

CoPS embody at least four closely related characteristics which set them apart from mass-produced goods and deeply influence innovation patterns (these differences are captured in Figure 2.5):

- First, they are high-cost hierarchical systems, made up of many customised, interconnected elements (including control units, sub-systems and components).
- Second, they are produced in projects or small batches often involving more than one firm and frequently many collaborating organisations.
- Third, they exhibit emerging, unexpected properties (discussed below).
- Fourth, there is a high degree of continuing user involvement through which business needs feed directly into the innovation process (rather than through the market as in the standard model).

By contrast, a simple (i.e. mass-produced) product can be defined as one which has:

- first, relatively few, mostly standardised components;
- second, final assembly within a single large firm;
- third, relatively stable, codifiable and predictable properties;

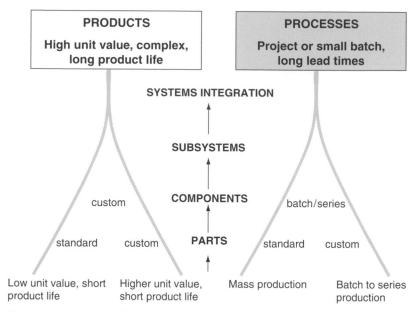

Figure 2.5. Distinguishing features of complex products and systems
Source: adapted from Walker et al., 1988.

- fourth, user involvement mediated through arm's-length, market transactions.

One critical difference between simple and complex products is the standardisation of components or subsystems. While a car is made up of many parts and components, these are mostly highly standardised, enabling them to be mass produced in large volumes at low unit cost.[5] By contrast, a flight simulator consists of highly customised components. Because CoPS tend to be made up of many subsystems and components,

---

[5] The contrast between a car and a passenger jet aircraft is quite startling. As the popular writer Michael Crichton (1997: 27) puts it: 'Compared to these aircraft, cars are a joke...A Pontiac has five thousand parts, and you can build one in two shifts...[Aircraft] are a completely different animal. The widebody has one million parts and a span time of seventy-five days. No other manufactured product in the world has the complexity of a commercial aircraft. Nothing even comes close. And nothing is built to be as durable. You take a Pontiac and run it all day every day and see what happens. It'll fall apart in a few months. But we design our jets to fly for twenty years of trouble-free service, and we build them to twice the service life.' What Crichton does not realise is that there are many

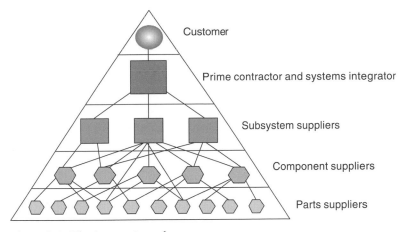

Figure 2.6. The integration of systems

the degree of system hierarchy is greater than in most simple products and systems integration is the chief responsibility of a dedicated prime contractor or systems integrator company, as shown in Figure 2.6. Often, the user sits at the top of the hierarchy, relaying its requirements down the chain and becoming intimately involved in the project.

With CoPS, component parts are usually organised in a hierarchical manner, tailored for specific customers and/or markets. Often subsystems (e.g. the avionic systems for aircraft) are themselves complex, customised and high cost (Mowery and Rosenberg, 1982a). Not all components or subsystems are customised, but many are (e.g. aircraft, intelligent buildings and flight simulators).

Hierarchy is an intrinsic feature of a complex product architecture. For example, military systems can be understood in terms of their hierarchy, extending from materials and components, whose unit costs can be measured in cents or less, to very large systems costing billions of dollars. Within the hierarchy of systems such as Tornado, Trident and the European Fighter Aircraft, the outputs of each stage are the inputs of the next:

'As the hierarchical chain is climbed products become more complex, few in number, large in scale, and systemic in character. In parallel, design and

products with great complexity. Military systems, engineering constructs, intelligent buildings, semiconductor wafer fabrication plants, all exhibit extreme elements of complexity, including large numbers of components. Many are as complex as a passenger aircraft.

production techniques tend to move from those associated with mass-production through series- and batch-production to unit production. Towards the top of the hierarchy, production involves the integration of disparate technologies, usually entailing large-scale project management and extensive national and international cooperation between enterprises. Thus the pyramid is also one of increasing organisational and managerial complexity.' (Walker et al., 1988: 19–20)

System complexity often increases from one generation to another, resulting from ever-rising demands on performance, capacity and reliability. Although simplifying factors often emerge (e.g. the modularisation of previously customised components), many complex products have become ever larger, more elaborate, more costly and more technically demanding through time. For instance, the original turbojet engine designed in the 1930s by Frank Whittle was very simple, having only one moving part (the compressor-turbine combination). But, as Arthur (1993) points out, in order to overcome extreme stress, velocity, altitude and temperature demands, jet designers added more and more subsystems. Yet more subassemblies were added to monitor and control the new subsystems. A complex product evolved as new functions were added to overcome limitations, to deal with exceptional circumstances and to adapt to an ever more demanding environment. Today's jet engines can embody more than 22,000 parts, many of which are customised. Similarly, modern telecommunications exchanges evolved to cope with ever growing telephone traffic requirements, spurring on new forms of modular software and semiconductor componentry.

In contrast with simple goods, complex products exhibit emergent and unpredictable properties. For example, in design and development, the extent of feedback and interdependencies between one stage and the next means that small changes in one part of the system can lead to larger changes in other parts (Sahal, 1985).[6] Equally, from generation to generation, small changes in one part of a system's design can require the addition of sophisticated control systems and, sometimes, new materials, as in the case of jet engines (Arthur, 1993).

Emergent, non-linear properties also refer to a change in the form and structure of a system as it grows. Sahal (1985: 62–63) argues that

---

[6] With simple products, the impact of small design changes is likely to be relatively predictable, due to constraints dictated by the standardisation of components, less complex interfaces and the need to design with mass production in mind.

large systems cannot remain unchanged geometrically, functionally and materially as they grow. Some parts of a system may depend on volume (e.g. capacity for heat generation) whereas others may depend on area (e.g. capacity for heat dissipation). As a system grows, designers may have to offset the excess of volume by selectively increasing the dimensions of certain parts and constraining the growth of others. Equally, a change in the size of a system often requires changes in the material required for its construction. To produce the blades of large turbines for the jet engine, new nickel chromium super heat-resistant alloys had to be developed. Sahal concludes that the growth of a complex product is accompanied by changes in its form and structure and the materials used.

As a result of these properties, product life cycles do not follow those predicted in the conventional model. In complex products, the mass production stage is not reached and the suppliers' chief task is one of design, development and systems integration. New product development requires a deep understanding of the limits and possibilities of system architecture, the capabilities of partner suppliers and the needs of highly demanding professional users. Once installed, a capital good may continue on its path of innovation over many years, with changes being made to control features, subsystems and performance characteristics. The processes of innovation and diffusion are often collapsed together and sometimes indistinguishable. A more in-depth consideration of the limitations of the product life cycle in CoPS sectors is provided in Box 2.1.

As Table 2.2 notes, throughout the product's life cycle the users' involvement in R&D, design, production and subsequent innovations distinguishes complex from simple goods. In the latter, direct buyer involvement in innovation occurs (if at all) only at the early stages. In complex goods, users are often responsible for maintenance, upgrading, performance modifications and generating information feedback for future innovations (Rothwell and Gardiner, 1989). Users may also be obliged to develop de-commissioning techniques, as in the case of nuclear power, chemical and semiconductor plant. When under construction, complex products adapt to feedback from users, as in the case of intelligent buildings (Gann, 2000). Thus, innovation and diffusion overlap considerably and cannot be neatly separated, as in mass manufactures (Leonard-Barton, 1988; Fleck, 1988).

Complex product features are entwined with production characteristics. CoPS tend to be individually developed, tailored and produced in projects (or made in small batches) for particular customers. Transactions are infrequent, large in value and long in duration. For instance, the design and implementation of a power network control system can last ten years (Hughes, 1983). The delivery of high-quality services during the operational life of a product requires continuous feedback from users. Systems engineering and design involves long-lasting, close interactions between buyers and sellers of CoPS (Geyer and Davies, 2000: 998).

Because each CoPS is highly customised, product development and design activities are more important than manufacturing as a source of competitive advantage. Although some mass-produced goods exhibit intense user–producer design interaction at the early stage of the innovation cycle, this eventually stabilises as tacit knowledge is formalised, markets expand and components are standardised. After this, user–producer interaction is mediated through the market, as in the case of cars (Langlois and Robertson, 1989), microcomputers (Langlois, 1992) and electronic consumer goods. By contrast, CoPS do not reach the latter stages of volume production of the conventional model where competitive advantage and the rewards from innovation are centred (Teece, 1986).

Implications for industrial organisation

Theories of industrial coordination

We have seen that the degree of product complexity profoundly affects production and innovation processes. Product complexity is also closely associated with organisational form and coordination. In his seminal article, Richardson (1972: 896) argues that 'theories of industrial organisation should not try and do too much'. Arguments designed to prove the inevitability or superiority of particular forms of organisation are bound to confront contradictory arrangements within sectors, across industries and between countries. In particular, Richardson argues that 'some *ex-ante* matching of plans is to be found in all markets in which firms place orders in advance' (Richardson, 1972: 896). Nevertheless, some tendencies are to be found in complex products which contrast with standard simpler products, at the level of the project, the project-based firm, the wider industrial network and industrial structure.

Often the issue of coordination is posed as a dichotomy between market allocation mechanisms and hierarchy, where the boundary between the firm and market is determined by relative costs (Coase, 1937; Williamson, 1971). Richardson (1972: 887) observes that beyond conscious planning within firms and the spontaneous operation of price mechanisms, there exists a wide continuum ranging from commodity-type market transactions, to an intermediate area of linkages based on goodwill, through to complex interlocking clusters, groups and alliances where cooperation is fully and often formally developed. Vernon (1960) made a similar point, arguing that firms cluster together to change inputs rapidly, to overcome uncertainty, to communicate closely and thereby generate external economies.

Networks of coordination

Typically, CoPS projects are embedded within dense networks which shape the structure and coordination of innovation. Markets tend to be duopolistic and highly institutionalised, involving elaborate price formulas, often negotiated for each single transaction. Transactions tend to be few in number, politicised and regulated. Governments and regulators become involved in the coordination of many complex products for a number of reasons. These include safety (as in large-scale human transportation systems and nuclear power plants), the need for international standards (as in telecommunications systems), the need to prevent monopolistic abuse, and other strategic and military reasons.

Sometimes there appears to be considerable long-term stability in these networks, especially at the systems integrator level (e.g. in tele communications and military systems), despite radical technological change and contrary to the predictions of the conventional model (Tushman and Anderson, 1986). In some cases, this apparent stability masks considerable industrial turbulence among the specialist component makers in the supply network, as illustrated in flight simulators and mainframe computers (Miller et al., 1995; Iansiti and Khanna, 1995).

Often the degree of market contestability is low in CoPS, as purchasers depend on the policies of governments or nationally owned purchasers (e.g. utilities) towards locally owned and foreign suppliers. In the UK, for example, prior to the mid-1980s, the public telecommunications switching market was reserved for a small number of locally owned suppliers (mostly GEC and Plessey), rather like the defence market. Since then, attempts at liberalisation have enabled some foreign suppliers (e.g. Ericsson of Sweden) to capture market share. In many other countries, governments own, control or closely oversee complex product markets, involving themselves in production and operation in sectors such as nuclear power, telecommunications and aircraft.

Higher-cost CoPS markets are often politicised and regulated and are either not contested or only partially contested, as in the case of many large American military systems. Even in less complex, lower-cost products, non-market mechanisms are often evident. This contrasts with the typical commodity mass-market model where many buyers and sellers compete and adjust via entry and exit, signalled by the emergence of dominant designs. The more complex and higher-cost the product, the more coordination is likely to be based on fewer, more irregular market transactions, non-market pricing, biased purchasing policies and administered, regulated competition.

The project as a coordination mechanism

Within the networks for CoPS, the project is the chief form of coordination. The project, a temporary organisational form, is a focusing device which enables different types of supplier firms, users, regulators and professional bodies to agree the fine detail of product development, production and sometimes use. The project is responsible for realising the market, for coordinating decisions across firms, for enabling buyer involvement and for allocating technical and financial resources. The project exists to communicate design and architectural knowledge and to combine the distinctive resources, knowhow and skills of many suppliers. The resources of the participants need to be combined through time in a controlled manner using their project-management skills and systems-integration experience to ensure efficiency.

In the case of very large engineering constructs entire project-based industrial structures are sometimes built by diverse groups of financiers, systems integrators, government bodies and subcontractors for the sole purpose of creating and implementing a single complex product. For example, the Channel Tunnel, which cost more than £11 billion (well over twice the original estimate), entailed a massive task of financial, managerial and technological coordination involving hundreds of contractors, at least 208 lending banks coordinated by 18 instructing banks and around 14,500 employees at its peak (*The Economist*, 1 October 1994: 42; Lemley, 1992: 14).

The project-based organisation

Within supply networks for high-technology capital goods, firms organise their structures and strategies around the needs of projects. Larger projects embody the traditional functional or departmental activities which go on within firms, such as technical support, human resource and financial management covering areas such as project bidding, management, systems engineering and so on. As Chapter 5 shows, firms which organise themselves around major projects are project-based organisations, to be contrasted with the usual functional and matrix organisations commonly found in volume-production, consumer goods industries.

There are many different categories of project-based organisations, ranging from large prime contractors which specialise in project management and systems integration, to tiny specialised subcontractors which supply tailored components, software or services. Any one project may combine these groups in a variety of roles, with the same firm acting as prime contractor in some projects and subcontractor in others.

Individual firm structures and business processes are shaped by the changing profile of projects, especially their size, complexity and duration. Some project-based firms (e.g. in construction) derive most of their income from large projects over which they exercise little span of control (Gann and Salter, 2000). In other cases, firms may direct and control particular projects, largely from within the firm. Some firms may engage in a mix of projects and batch or mass production, combining project-based and functional organisational forms. Although the possible permutations of organisational form are many, each complex product supplier is deeply influenced by the exigencies of project management, systems integration and multi-firm collaboration.

Because production is of a one-off kind oriented to meet the needs of individual customers, the project management task is quite different from the mass-production task. As Woodward (1958: 23) put it in her research into UK companies in the early 1950s: 'Those responsible for marketing had to sell, not a product, but the idea that their firm was able to produce what the customer required. The product was developed after the order had been secured, the design being, in many cases, modified to suit the requirements of the customer.' In mass-production firms, the sequence is quite different: 'Product development came first, then production, and finally marketing.'

Through its influence on projects, the degree of product complexity strongly influences the character of coordination within firms. Prime contractors, themselves usually systems integrators, require distinctive managerial competences capable of bidding for, defining and engineering large-scale systems. In aircraft, according to Mowery and Rosenberg (1982a: 103–135) much of the US\$4–6 billion devoted to R&D for commercial jets in the early 1980s was spent on integrating prototype machines, avionics, propulsion and other aerodynamic components. In addition to their internal tasks, systems integrators have to coordinate the innovation activities of the supply network made up of small firms, major users, large partner companies, regulators, standards bodies and government departments.

Production coordination is very much affected by the breadth of technologies required. The more complex a system, the wider the range of skills and capabilities needed for bidding, design, development and manufacture. Flight simulator producers, for instance, require skills in mechanical, electromechanical and precision engineering, as well as software engineering, systems integration, materials, electromechanical interfacing, automated data exchange, human–computer interaction and pilot training. Much of the required knowledge is embodied in people and cannot easily be formalised or codified.

The central role of the user

In contrast to commodity goods, the user is often directly involved in CoPS production. The user tends to be a large organisation with a considerable interest in the outcome of each project. The user is the primary organisation through which the needs of the business environment feed directly into the innovation process rather than through the arm's-length market transactions of the conventional mass market model. Users, sometimes owners and operators, frequently collaborate with suppliers in R&D, design and production as well as maintenance, upgrading and re-design, as in the case of aircraft, hovercraft, chemical process plants and electricity network control systems (Gardiner and Rothwell, 1985; Rothwell and Gardiner, 1989; Grieve and Ball, 1991; Hughes, 1983). Because these are business-to-business, capital goods, users depend upon them for their business growth, profitability and sometimes survival.

Unlike mass-market buyers, users of complex products and systems often need to maintain deep systems design and architectural capabilities in order to be effective in their own business. Intimate user–producer links allow buyers to feed their needs directly into the specification, design, development and manufacture of capital goods. In telecommunications, for example, large user organisations (e.g. AT&T) heavily influence the innovation trajectory of exchange systems. Successful users can be demanding and intelligent buyers, endowed with high levels of technological competence. The depth of user involvement at various stages of the innovation process is one of the critical dimensions of complex products (see Figure 2.4). In some cases, user involvement may tail off at the point of production (e.g. in flight simulators) whereas in others it may carry on through to de-commissioning (e.g. nuclear power equipment).

Implications for management theory

Generally, the chief unit of analysis for strategy and competition is the single firm.[7] However, with CoPS, companies create markets and compete within multi-firm projects. In fact, as we argue in Chapter 3, collaboration in bidding and executing projects is a core capability for many CoPS producers. Purposive strategies for inter-firm collaboration are demanded by the nature of the task. Indeed, one of the chief functions of the prime contractor is to coordinate the human and physical resources across firms and other organisations to good effect. The capability to manage across the web of producers, users and regulators is an important feature of successful project-based firms. Typically, the supplier of a CoPS will adopt particular competitive strategies and deploy management skills centred around effectiveness in bidding, design and development rather than production economies of scale as with simple goods. The management of projects

---

[7] Most of the renowned writers on strategy and management focus on the single firm (e.g. Chandler 1962, 1990; Cyert and March, 1963; Drucker, 1977; Porter, 1980, 1985; Mintzberg, 1989; Rumelt, 1974; MacCrimmon, 1993; Simon, 1993; Peters, 1987; Teece and Pisano, 1994; Hamel and Prahalad, 1994; Hammer and Champy, 1994). Although there is now a large body of literature on networks, this has yet to address itself to the issue of product complexity (see Hobday, 1994, for a summary of the network literature).

has to cope with uncertainty over emerging properties and changes in user specifications. As a result, the capability to deal with feedback in a variety of ways and at different stages of project execution is the prime asset of project-based firms (Morris and Hough, 1987; Morris, 1994).

In contrast with consumer goods with long production runs, the disbanding of product teams at project completion has direct and negative implications for production learning and organisational efficiency. In the functional or departmental organisation, firms are able to learn by gathering data on routines and improving group practices (Garvin, 1993; Stata, 1989). However, because complex projects are temporary and often highly customised there is far less scope for routinised learning and efficiency gains. But as we show in Chapter 7, these difficulties in capturing and sharing knowledge from one project to another can be overcome by systematic attempts to promote project- and business-led learning.

Many of the standard production management tools, including manufacturing resource planning, statistical process control and lean production, were developed to enhance production efficiency. However, these tools have in mind the single firm rather than the multi-firm project and either are inappropriate or require substantial modification for use in complex products.

In large multi-firm projects, because the chief unit of competition is the project rather than the single firm, isolated improvements at the individual firm level have only limited impact on project performance. To be most effective, improvements in production require the optimisation of the total project network rather than any one supplier. Such problems stretch much conventional management wisdom to its limit.

Project management has to take into account differences in the objectives, cultures, styles and management structures of participating firms, many of which may well be competitors in other projects. In order to achieve the common project objective, suppliers need at least temporarily to reconcile any differences in aims or culture with other firms in the project. Preferred partners emerge as firms learn who best they can cooperate with and trust in major collaborative projects so that innovation paths can be agreed before and during projects. The shaping and reshaping of supplier–user networks depends on previous company performance in specific projects.

One key practical question for managers is the extent to which projects can be managed in the rational style advocated by Porter (1980) or whether the alternative, craft-based approach offered by Mintzberg (1989) is more appropriate. On the one hand, responsive crafted management is needed to deal with uncertainty and feedback loops. On the other hand, without effective control over costs and resource inputs, projects might easily fail. Firms must identify which elements of projects are conducive to detailed planning and which must remain fluid to respond to change in order to execute projects efficiently.

For innovation management purposes, the organic approach proposed by Burns and Stalker (1961) is more suited to complex projects and project-based organisations than the mechanistic, hierarchical management they describe. By reducing hierarchy and bureaucracy, project managers stand a better chance of keeping options open, coping with uncertainty and dealing with feedback loops from customers and regulators. Certainly, the organic approach is more suited to foreseeing and reacting to risks and, when necessary, embracing new technological developments during the execution of longer-term projects.

Conclusions

This chapter shows why the nature of the product (especially its complexity and cost) shapes innovation processes, organisational form and style of management. In the case of high-cost, complex products and systems, the project and the project-based firm are natural forms of organisation. This also applies to major projects which go on within large firms in other sectors, such as pharmaceuticals or cars. Although these firms may not require 'full-blown' project-based structures, they too can learn from the experience of managing projects in CoPS industries.

In contrast with the routine manufacturing processes which go on within functionally based organisations, CoPS are produced in projects or small batches and tailored for individual users. Under these conditions, the chief unit of analysis for competition purposes is the project rather than the individual firm. Therefore, the standard management theories and best practices which focus on the single firm serve as a poor and sometimes misleading guide to the project business which is essentially multi-firm in character and project driven.

Increasingly, firms in other types of industries need to approach projects from a strategic perspective. For example, in the case of the introduction of a new semiconductor product line, the task of designing and implementing the systems and processes across national boundaries is today likely to be carried out by a heavyweight project manager or director responsible directly to the board rather than being left to a functional department. Similarly, in the case of a radical new drug, a pharmaceutical producer is likely to turn to an experienced project leader to plan and execute the new business, at least in the crucial initial stages.

With CoPS, competition tends to occur among rival coalitions of firms at the bidding stage of projects. Competition often takes place in bureaucratically administered and politicised markets rather than in the arm's-length market transactions of the conventional innovation model. Indeed, one of the key distinctive features of CoPS is that many organisations need to work together to realise new markets, carry out production and agree innovation decisions in advance of production.

The stark comparison between complex products and simple mass-produced goods should not be pushed too far and there are many differences between different kinds of complex products. Indeed, there exists a continuum of product complexity from the relatively simple, through various intermediate levels, to extremely high-cost and exceedingly complex artifacts, systems and service packages. Some of the constituent dimensions of product complexity, including technological novelty, cost, customisation, product architecture and hierarchy, apply to high-technology consumer goods, although to a lesser extent. In the case of a new personal computer or car, here too modern firms need to collaborate to produce new designs and to manage enormously complex projects which embody risk and uncertainty. In these kinds of new product development projects, consumer goods producers also need to decide among alternative design paths using a wide variety of knowledge and skill bases.

Clearly, where firms operate in stable business environments and undertake largely routine manufacturing processes as their core activity, the lessons from complex product makers will be few and far between. However, where firms are consistently involved in high-technology projects, then the experiences, lessons, failures and best practices from CoPS represent a useful source of knowledge. In cases where major projects are essential to business success, where firms use projects to enact new business strategies, where firms need to work closely with clients, suppliers and others in design and production, then the lessons from complex products can be brought to bear. This applies not only to traditional manufacturing and process industries but increasingly to high-technology services, such as information technology and mobile telecommunications, where projects are the mainstay of business development.

3 | Business strategy and project capability

THE previous chapter provides the broad context in which project-based activities are undertaken within a wide range of CoPS industries. This chapter shows more specifically how projects are used to improve a firm's operational effectiveness, achieve its strategic business objectives and enhance its competitive position. Drawing upon resource-based theories of the firm (Penrose, 1959; Richardson, 1972; Nelson and Winter, 1982; Wernerfelt, 1984; Teece and Pisano, 1994; Teece et al., 1997), the framework we introduce includes the definitions and concepts required to understand how a firm's project resources and capabilities form the basis of its growth and competitive advantage in project business. Following Penrose's (1959) original contribution, it is now well understood that organisational capabilities are critical to a firm's ability to mobilise and use its resources to grow and compete successfully in rapidly changing technologies and markets (Chandler, 1990; Grant, 2002). However, with a few exceptions (Amsden and Hikino, 1994; Cusumano and Nobeoka, 1998) the resource-based view of the firm has largely ignored the project as an organisational capability and source of competitive advantage.

In addition to the well-known strategic and functional capabilities of the firm described by Chandler (1990), we show how the concept of project capability explains how firms deploy projects to innovate and compete in dynamic markets. Effective bid and project management is necessary to improve a firm's operational performance in an existing technology or customer base. Projects are also used to implement corporate strategies to enter new fields of technology and create new markets. There are three basic innovation strategies, all centred on base-moving projects: (1) expand into a new business base using new technology to meet the requirements of new sets of customers, (2) diversify into a new market base using existing technology, or (3) expand into a new technology base to supply new products to existing customers. Strategic decisions

56

to innovate by moving along one of these three paths is about taking risks and deploying scarce resources in projects that may or may not succeed.

The chapter outlines the basic concepts of firm resources and organisational capabilities which provide the foundation of the modern analysis of business strategy and competitive advantage (Grant, 2002). It augments the traditional model by showing how project capability is also central to the competitive advantage of firms in all types of industries, emphasising the different roles that projects play in high-volume and CoPS industries. We explain how firms exploit project capabilities to improve their operational performance and achieve strategic objectives by moving into new technologies and markets. In Chapter 7 we build on our framework by using recent case study research to show how successful firms manage the project-based learning processes to build the capabilities needed to move into new strategic positions.

Business strategy and organisational capabilities

Penrose (1959) laid the foundations for the modern resource-based analysis of business strategy.[1] She recognised that the profitable expansion of the firm within its existing technology and market base is underpinned by improvements in productivity driven by the increasing specialised – or product-specific – use of resources. But she emphasised that a firm's innovative capacity to mobilise and redeploy its resources to diversify into new technology and/or market bases is more important to its long-run competitive survival and growth.[2] The *technology base* of the firm refers to the knowledge and skills required to perform research, development and productive activities related to a specific field of

---

[1] Penrose's analysis depends on the distinction between resources and services (Penrose, 1959: 25). The firm is defined as a collection of resources within an organisational structure. Firms use two types of resources to produce and sell products and services: physical resources (tangible assets such as raw materials, plant and equipment) and human resources (including intangible assets such as financial, managerial or technical knowledge and skills). Resources consist of a bundle of potential services that can be used in a variety of ways.

[2] Penrose (1959 and 1960) made two main points about how firms deploy resources: (1) the internal resources of a firm are rarely fully utilised in the process of production, and (2) the products and services produced by a firm are at any given time merely one among several ways in which a firm can use its resources. The existence of a pool of underutilised resources and the ability to switch resources to other productive uses provides a powerful incentive to innovate and an opportunity to branch out in new directions (Penrose, 1959: 85).

technology, such as electronics, avionics or packet-switching systems. A *market base* refers to the competence necessary to respond
to the demands of different types of customers, such as understanding
new client needs, cultivating customer relationships, sales and
order taking and organising the installation and maintenance of
equipment.

A firm's path of growth is shaped by the dynamic interaction
between its technology and market bases. By developing a strong
technology and market base a firm can 'adapt and extend its operations
in an uncertain, changing and competitive world' (Penrose, 1959: 137).
As an example, Penrose (1959: 120–124) showed how General Motors
used its technology base in engineering for mass production to diversify
into the growing markets for trains, aircraft engines, refrigerators and
other consumer goods. When a firm diversifies in this way, it must
mobilise its resources and develop or acquire the new combinations of
knowledge and skills necessary to perform activities in the new
technology and/or market base. Building on Penrose's original contribution, this chapter shows how projects are used as a highly flexible
and efficient way of using a firm's resources and capabilities to exploit
current technology and market bases and move dynamically into
new ones.

Capabilities in a changing environment

In the resource-based literature, Richardson (1972: 888) was among
the first to emphasise that organisations can gain a competitive
advantage by developing the 'appropriate capabilities' – or knowledge, experience and skills – to perform specific industrial activities
in a particular technology and/or market base. An organisation's
capability is distinctive or core when it provides a unique source of
competitive advantage which is not widely available to other firms in
an industry (Kay, 1993; Prahalad, 1993; Hamel and Prahalad, 1994;
Iansiti and Clark, 1994; Leonard-Barton, 1992; Leonard, 1995).
A core capability is difficult to imitate and uses scarce resources that
cannot simultaneously be implemented by large numbers of firms
(Barney, 1991).

In Penrose's original study, the influence of the environment was 'put
on one side in order to permit concentration on the internal resources of
the firm' (Penrose, 1995: xiii). Subsequent research has focused

explicitly on the dynamic interplay between the firm's internal capabilities and changing external conditions, recognising that learning is the main way in which organisations interact with, and are changed by, their environment (Nelson, 1991). Assumptions about this relationship between a firm's internal capabilities and the environment continue to influence the progress of research in this field. The greater the rate of change in a firm's external environment, the more important its internal resources and breadth of capabilities are to the long-term success of a firm (Grant, 2002: 135).

Nelson and Winter (1982) argued that a firm's knowledge and experience reside in its memory, which is located in its organisational routines. These repetitive and predictable patterns of productive activities form the basis of a firm's organisational capability (Grant, 2002: 148). A reliance on routines is a strength for companies operating under stable conditions. As we discuss in Chapter 7, however, difficulties occur when organisations continue to follow established routines in a changing environment. Such routines and capabilities which are effective for existing technologies and market bases may be experienced as core rigidities as a firm attempts to meet new opportunities (Leonard-Barton, 1992).

The ability of a firm to adapt to a changing environment depends in part on a capability called absorptive capacity. Largely a function of a firm's prior knowledge and experience, absorptive capacity refers to the ability to recognise the value of new, external knowledge and information, assimilate it and apply it to meet new market objectives (Cohen and Levinthal, 1990). Hamel and Prahalad (1994) emphasise the need for managers to identify, sustain and build core capabilities so that a firm is able to adapt to and shape its environment. The concept is used to refer to a firm's primary technology or market base and to show how a firm may have overstretched itself in terms of efficient and profitable management and should re-focus on its core. Radical changes in the environment can force a firm into totally renewing its capabilities. Teece and Pisano (1994) and Teece et al. (1997) argue that new forms of competitive advantage in fast-changing environments stem from dynamic capabilities. The term dynamic refers to the firm's ability to adapt, reconfigure and renew its capabilities and to create innovative responses to a changing technology or market environment. Firms grow into new technology or market positions along distinctive paths shaped by their traditional resources and capabilities.

Organisational capabilities and competitive advantage

As Penrose (1959) emphasised, resources alone do not create competitive advantage. A firm must develop the organisational capabilities required to use its pool of resources and perform activities that improve its competitive position. For example, a firm's designers, engineers, research labs and manufacturing plant are of little use on their own. It is how they are organised (e.g. in research departments or cross-functional projects) to provide the capability required to develop new products that creates added value. Chandler (1990) identified some of the organisational capabilities that provide the internal dynamic for the continuing growth and competitiveness of firms in all types of industries and environments. He defined organisational capabilities as the collective physical facilities and human skills located in all the main strategic and functional levels of the firm.

According to what is now conventional wisdom in resource-based theory, strategic capabilities refer to a firm's ability to move dynamically into new technologies or markets more quickly, and out of declining ones more rapidly and effectively, than its competitors. Strategic management is responsible for allocating resources and implementing long-term plans to maintain, renew and expand a firm's organisational capabilities (Chandler, 1990: 594). The task of top management is to create flexibility for action by effectively monitoring internal operations and adjusting strategies to a changing environment.

By contrast, functional capabilities are required to improve a firm's R&D, product design, production, marketing, distribution, purchasing, finance and general management. Middle managers develop and apply functional- and product-specific managerial skills, and coordinate, integrate and evaluate the work of the functional departments. Functional departments represent silos of knowledge which are essential for the preservation and perpetuation of a firm's functional skills and expertise.

In developing the capability view of the firm, Chandler (1990) shows that the growth, profitability and survival of the firm depend on its ability to both (a) diversify successfully into new technology and market positions and (b) produce a variety of products in increasingly large volumes and at lower costs. His framework explains how companies grow by (1) obtaining economies of scale and scope in the production of a variety of products; (2) creating a marketing and distribution network so that the volume of sales matches the volume of production; and

(3) establishing a management structure to coordinate functional activities and to strategically plan and allocate resources for future technologies and markets. Firms that produce new or improved products and use new or improved processes gain first-mover competitive advantages. First movers are leaders in exploiting cost advantages of scale and scope economies and have a head start in developing functional capabilities. First movers are able to move down the learning curve in each of the functional activities before the challengers go into operation.

In recent resource-based studies, capabilities are treated as strategically vital assets that are supposed to permeate all levels and all functions in an organisation. Unlike Chandler, however, the concept is often defined at the strategic level only.[3] From this top-down perspective, it is difficult to identify the growth, adaptation and learning that take place at lower levels in organisations. Leonard-Barton (1992) and Carlsson and Eliasson (1994) point out that if a capability is defined as one that provides competitive advantage, then such capabilities may reside at all levels in the corporate hierarchy, such as the technical functions at the bottom of the pyramid.

Although largely ignored in the resource-based literature, several studies in the 1990s began to recognise the importance of an additional set of organisational capabilities located at the project level within the firm, including project management competencies to improve operational performance (Morris, 1994), project execution capabilities in late industrialising countries (Amsden and Hikino, 1994) and multi-project management capabilities in new product development (Cusumano and Nobeoka, 1998). A project is a temporary organisation established apart from the main permanent or semi-permanent organisation in order to achieve specific objectives. Cross-functional capabilities can be harnessed in product development by taking people with different skills located in a firm's functional organisations (e.g. departments, units and divisions) and putting them together in temporary projects (Prahalad, 1993; Hammer and Champy, 1994; Leonard, 1995).

---

[3] For example, while recognising that competence is embedded at all levels and in all functions in an organisation, Prahalad (1993) stresses that it is the top-down responsibility of strategic management to build shared values at all levels in an organisation, to manage linkages across business units and to develop strategies for acquiring capabilities.

In contrast to the importance of functional excellence in high-volume industries, Davies and Brady (2000) argue that competitive advantage in the the provision of CoPS depends centrally and routinely on project capability. Cost advantages based on large throughputs of standardised products and services are difficult to realise in CoPS because the design, production and installation of products (e.g. high-speed trains, flight simulators or mobile communications systems) is confined to low volumes: unit or small batch production. Every CoPS is different and each order for a CoPS constitutes a new project. An ability to win bids, learn from previous project experiences and manage consecutive projects efficiently and effectively is therefore more important to operational effectiveness in low-volume project-based activities than traditional scale and scope advantages. In addition, firms are increasingly using projects as the vehicle to explore strategic opportunities to diversify into new technology or market positions.

Compared with high-volume producers, suppliers of CoPS also depend on different types of strategic and functional capabilities. Functional capabilities in CoPS are built around the core technical disciplines of software and systems engineering needed to design complex systems rather than operations management, mass marketing and other volume-based skills. Because buyers of CoPS are large business customers (e.g.Vodafone and British Airways) rather than final consumers, the ability to maintain strong customer relationships and broker deals at the highest levels of management (e.g. CEO to CEO) are essential areas of strategic capability in CoPS.

Project capability

Until now, the nature, origins and scope of project capabilities have not been addressed within the resource-based literature. However, as we show below and throughout this book, various kinds of project capabilities form one of the core sets of organisational capabilities that firms need to acquire to compete in any changing business environment (see Figure 3.1).

Project activities

By project capabilities we mean the appropriate knowledge, experience and skills necessary to perform pre-bid, bid, project and post-project

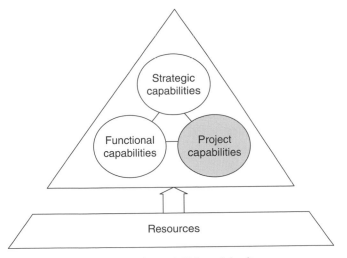

Figure 3.1. Organisational capabilities of the firm

activities (see Table 3.1). A firm can undertake a project to serve itself or its customers' needs. Members of bid and project organisations are responsible for:

1. engaging with external customers in deal structuring during a pre-bid phase;
2. preparing proposals, winning competitive bids and developing offers for strategic partners;
3. setting up a project organisation to achieve specific goals and managing the life cycle of activities involved in project execution and hand-over of a working system for the customer;
4. arranging the provision of operational, maintenance and on-going support services.

These four components of project capabilities are central to firm survival and prosperity. For example, bid managers are responsible for running the bid team and preparing a successful proposal. Productivity improvements in the bid phase can be obtained by shorter bid-preparation times and an improved quality of submitted bids, which help to increase a firm's market share. However, if the customer is a strategic partner, the proposal team makes an offer rather than a bid, thus avoiding the necessity of engaging in costly and time-consuming competitive bids (Cova et al., 2002).

Table 3.1: Project capabilities

Pre-bid, bid and offer activities	Project and post-project activities
• Engaging with the customer (understanding customer needs and problems; offering solutions) • Setting up and managing a bid team or programme of bids • Requirements gathering (extracted from customer documents) after receiving an invitation to tender from a customer • Conceptual design specifying components in the proposed system • Estimation of costs, taking into account many factors (e.g. the quality, reliability and cost of components sourced internally and externally) • Defining levels of service • Risk management • Scheduling of project activities • Selection of subcontractors • Preparing the bid or offer document (including contractual agreements) by integrating information determined in the previous steps	• Setting up and managing a project or programme of projects • Integrating functional and project resources • Purchasing resources inside and outside the firm • Managing and reallocating resources through the project life cycle using milestones and deadlines • Working on a team basis • Using a number of project management tools, computerised techniques and concepts – e.g. concurrent engineering, milestone scheduling and PERT (Program Evaluation and Review Technique) • Providing technical support and operational services • De-commissioning

Project managers are responsible for satisfying the triple constraints of completing projects within budget, on time and to specification. However, these traditional measures of project management success and failure pay too little attention to an increasingly important fourth constraint, namely customer satisfaction (Frame, 1994: 5; Pinto and Kharbanda, 1995: 43). As we show in Chapter 8, many firms today are developing the capabilities to satisfy their customer needs by acquiring the new skills required to understand the customer's business and to design products and services that solve each customer's specific problems.

As distinct from departmental units staffed with people from similar functional disciplines, such as finance and marketing, most projects are composed of cross-functional teams of people assembled from each of the relevant functions. One of the core challenges facing bid and project managers is to create and manage a cohesive team out of a group of individuals with a variety of functional backgrounds, experiences and attitudes (Sapsed and Salter, 2004; Sapsed et al., 2005).

Bid and project managers perform activities through the different phases of the project life cycle from bidding to project execution and delivery to the customer. In an increasingly competitive environment, however, this narrow conception of the project life cycle may encourage bid and project managers to ignore important pre-bid and post-project delivery phases. To meet a customer's needs, senior commercial and bid managers have to enter into high-level pre-bid negotiations with the customer to discuss business problems, often before an invitation to tender has been issued. As Morris (1994) has shown, effective management of the front end of a project leads to better overall designs and improved productivity during later phases. To ensure customer satisfaction, the life cycle can extend into a phase of operations if members of a project team are responsible for ensuring that the system they have designed works well after it is delivered.

Project management skills in scheduling, budgeting, allocating resources and using tools – such as PERT (Program Evaluation and Review Technique), Gantt charts and WBS (Work Breakdown Structure) – are employed to manage bids and projects efficiently. However, an increasingly commercial focus on meeting customer needs for business solutions means that project managers have to develop new sets of 'hard skills' such as contracting, business finance, measuring performance, life-cycle costing and risk management. They also have to develop 'soft skills' such as negotiating, managing change, working in teams and listening to customers. The successful management of projects extends beyond individual projects to the management of an organisation's complete project portfolio. Senior managers use programme management techniques to run several projects in parallel, all of which compete for organisational resources.

The concept of project capabilities also draws attention to temporary forms of organisation that make use of resources that are external to the firm (Packendorff, 1995; Lundin and Söderholm, 1995; Gann and Salter, 2000; Grabher, 2002; Sahlin-Andersson and Söderholm,

2002; Turner and Müller, 2003; Sydow et al., 2004). Many firms participate in multi-firm project alliances, joint ventures or consortia and form new coalitions with different partners when a project disbands. For example, Rail Link Engineering is a joint venture company (the consortium includes Arup, Bechtel, Halcrow and Systra) responsible for the design and project management of the UK's high-speed Channel Tunnel Rail Link. In a loosely connected web of business relationships, a firm can find itself competing with its rivals to win a major bid whilst cooperating with them on another as coalition partners. It can interchangeably assume the role of subcontractor on one project coalition led by a competitor and prime contractor and on another employ its main rivals as subcontractors.

A great deal of project knowledge and experience is, therefore, embodied in project team members who operate in multi-firm project alliances that extend beyond the traditional boundaries of the firm. Managers working in such multi-firm project environments have to exercise control and influence through informal methods and the use of contractual agreements rather than rely on vertical lines of communication and interactions that typically occur in a functional hierarchy.

Origins of project capability – overcoming functional weaknesses

Some of the most important innovations in project management and project organisation were developed by firms in the US aerospace and military sectors to overcome some of the weaknesses of traditional functional management (Gaddis, 1960; Middleton, 1967). Functional organisations were originally established in large-batch, mass-production and continuous-process industries to carry out the routine tasks involved in maintaining a high volume of throughput of standardised products and services (Woodward, 1965). However, faced with the challenge of developing advanced aerospace and military systems during and after the Second World War, several US manufacturers, such as Lockheed and General Dynamics, soon recognised the limitations of using functional organisations to accomplish complex and novel tasks (Johnson, 1997; Hughes, 1998). These firms were among the first to establish project management organisations to handle special assignments to meet definable goals, such as new product development, producing one-off or highly customised products for internal or external customers and investigating moves away from their traditional base business.

As Chapter 5 shows in more depth, several types of project-based organisations can be distinguished from functional units, ranging from a pure project to a matrix organisation (Marquis, 1969: 29). Whereas functional organisations group people together on a more or less permanent basis in a specialised unit to perform recurring and repetitive activities, in temporary project organisations people stay together for as long as it takes to complete a particular episodic activity. A pure project-based organisation is one in which all functions and personnel required to accomplish the project work in a dedicated team and report directly to the project manager rather than the line manager in a functional department.[4]

The matrix form was pioneered by US aerospace manufacturers in the late 1950s to provide a more efficient way of integrating the project and functional resources involved in delivering many complex projects.[5] Project and matrix organisations were created to overcome functional weaknesses that could impair the successful completion of a project. The three main types of project organisation can be located on a modified version of Galbraith's (1973) continuum of organisational forms (see Figure 3.2).[6] Increases in product complexity, task novelty and customisation exert pressures to move a firm towards a pure project organisation. Increases in product standardisation, functional specialisation and economies of scale or scope exert pressures to move a firm towards a functional organisation. A functional organisation is designed

---

[4] In the traditional functional organisation, by contrast, specialists are located in one department (e.g. R&D, design, engineering, procurement, manufacturing and sales) and report to a functional manager. Functional departments are integrated into the organisation in different ways: some have 'staff' and others have 'line' authority.

[5] See Lawrence and Lorsch (1967), Middleton (1967), Galbraith (1973), Knight (1976) and Davis and Lawrence (1977) for classic early studies in this area. Note that the matrix replaces the traditional single chain of command of functional or total project organisations with two-dimensional reporting structures. Each member of the matrix organisation reports to two bosses (the functional specialist and the project manager) and is associated with two groups: the functional unit composed of fellow specialists and the team of co-workers in the diverse specialities required for a single project.

[6] While Galbraith's diagram refers to the product vs function choice along a continuum, he explicitly states as well that 'it could be project–function' (Galbraith, 1973: 113).

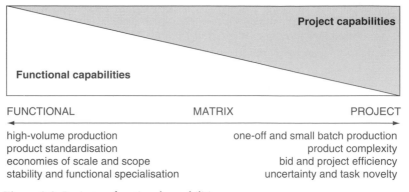

Figure 3.2. Project vs functional capabilities
Source: adapted from Galbraith 1973: 114.

to perfect standardised tasks rather than invent new ones. A project organisation is a problem-solving, not a performance-based, structure designed to encourage innovation (Mintzberg, 1983: 254). A matrix organisation is required if these opposing needs are equally strong. Firms often create different types of organisation for various phases in the project life cycle by establishing a project organisation during the proposal stage, a matrix organisation during project implementation, and upon delivery of the product shift to a functional organisation to provide operational support and maintenance.

In a stable environment of incremental technological change and growing mass markets, functional organisations have traditionally provided an effective way of ensuring that a firm's internal resources are fully utilised to achieve high volumes of throughputs. However, the trend for firms across all types of industries to organise a growing proportion of their internal activities in projects has been given impetus since the 1990s by efforts to leverage cross-functional capabilities (Hamel and Prahalad, 1994) and promote business process re-engineering (Hammer and Champy, 1994). In an increasingly competitive global business environment, many firms are finding that the project form is a more adaptive and responsive structure which can easily be configured, dismantled and re-configured to respond quickly and flexibly to fast-changing technologies, market segmentation and shifts in customer demands. Members of projects working in horizontal team-based organisations with flatter management styles concentrate on achieving tasks and making decisions in response to a customer's needs rather than performing roles in a functional hierarchy.

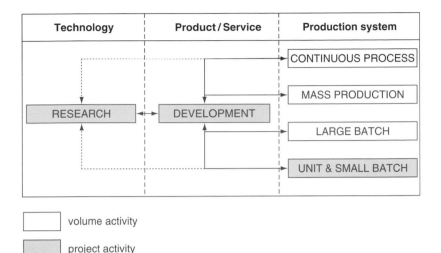

Technology	Product / Service	Production system

CONTINUOUS PROCESS

MASS PRODUCTION

RESEARCH ◄──► DEVELOPMENT

LARGE BATCH

UNIT & SMALL BATCH

☐ volume activity

▨ project activity

Figure 3.3. Projects and the innovation process

Project capability and industry differences

Projects are becoming a key management tool used by all types of businesses and industries. In particular projects are used to achieve organisational renewal, change programmes and quality initiatives. But project capability also differs in important ways across industries. We can show this in Figure 3.3 by examining the various ways firms and industries use projects to perform the three interrelated phases of the innovation process – research, development and production. All firms use projects to perform research and development activities. In most industries, the output of R&D, such as a product prototype or service application, is the input to a production process undertaken in high volumes (large batch, mass production or continuous process) for the market. Unit and small batch production (including CoPS) is the only industrial category in Woodward's (1965) classification of production systems to carry out its primary productive activities as well as R&D on a project basis.

Research and development projects

In the past, firms have partitioned the innovation process into the two distinct linear phases of research and development (e.g. Freeman, 1974; Allen, 1977). Research projects explore the possibilities of existing or new fields of technology. Development projects adapt a stable technology (the output of research) to the requirements of the market by creating products and services that can be produced profitably (e.g. Iansiti, 1995 and 1998; Kusunoki et al., 1998; Lindkvist et al., 1998). Development activities concentrate on achieving design freeze prior to market introduction. However, this overly simplified linear relationship suggests that technology flows downstream from research through product development to the market. In practice, development is often tightly coupled to research by a process of mutual adaptation, involving feedback loops and interactions between upstream technology builders and downstream product and market developers (Chesbrough, 2003a). For example, Nokia's R&D centres (employing 20,000 people in 14 countries in 2002) are responsible for ensuring that research is closely connected to product development and market needs. They conduct research projects to meet the market requirements of Nokia's business groups as well as longer-term projects beyond the current product horizon. The centres also act as incubators for technology-based ventures in existing and new markets.

In the 1970s, R&D organisations used a variety of functional, project and matrix structures to accomplish multi-disciplinary projects (Allen, 1977). But recent improvements in the performance of development projects have been linked to the use of project organisations to coordinate interdependent tasks and to promote cross-functional interactions (Clark and Fujimoto, 1991; Iansiti, 1998: 14). In a shift away from the development of isolated products, multi-project management capabilities enable firms to harness core common components and design knowledge across a coordinated stream of new products, permitting reductions in development and production costs (Cusumano and Nobeoka, 1998). Nokia's new product design process, for example, requires people with different skills (e.g. handset design, wireless engineering, multimedia applications, manufacturing and finance) to work together on each new mobile handset design project. When a new handset model is designed and goes into production, the project is finished and the team is disbanded, its members moving on to participate in other development projects. This circulation of people from project to project fosters cross-functional learning and knowledge transfer between different parts of the firm.

CoPS projects

As explained in Chapter 2, by CoPS projects we mean the implementation of large, high-value complex products to meet the specific requirements of large business, institutional or government customers. In many cases the innovation process in CoPS is partitioned into three consecutive phases of project activities flowing from (1) upstream technology research, through (2) product development to (3) downstream implementation.[7] Take Ericsson for example. In our case study research we have found that Ericsson typically operates three distinct types of projects, corresponding to each phase in the innovation process. First, it conducts research projects to develop each new generation of mobile communications technology, based on a variety of technical standards, such as GSM and Wideband CDMA. Second, it carries out product development projects to adapt each generation of technology for different market applications. Third, it performs numerous implementation projects to design and install mature product lines (based on existing mobile network technology), which are configured to meet each mobile operator's specific needs.

As we discussed in Chapter 2, the innovation process in CoPS is distinctive because the customer often plays a leading and active role in all phases of the innovation process (Gardiner and Rothwell, 1985; von Hippel, 1988). In consumer goods (e.g. PCs, cars and cameras), the customer largely appears only at the downstream end of the process: the marketing department is responsible for articulating the needs of target customers during research and new product development, and the design is frozen prior to high-volume manufacturing and market introduction. In CoPS, by contrast, the product is developed after a customer's order is obtained and the design is modified to meet a customer's changing requirements even during late stages of a project. Suppliers have to remain in close contact with the adaptation processes taking place in innovative lead customer organisations and incorporate user-initiated modifications in the design and development process (Gardiner and Rothwell, 1985: 7).

Ericsson, for example, participates in large development projects called First Office Application (FOA) with lead customers to create new products based on each generation of mobile technology. In 1996, Ericsson completed a large development project conducted over three

---

[7] Implementation projects cover several activities: obtaining a customer's order, system design, the physical production of components and their assembly or integration in the finished product. Although the finished product or system is uniquely tailored to each customer's needs, the components and subsystems integrated in the product or system can be manufactured in high volumes (see Chapter 2).

and a half years to create a new mobile base station product for 2G networks based on the GSM standard (Davies, 1997a). In this collaborative FOA project with lead customers – Telia, Vodafone and Mannesmann (now owned by Vodafone) – Ericsson developed a new generation of base stations, which were subsequently offered as part of the company's mature product line for GSM technology and used in the roll-out of hundreds of implementation projects for mobile operators.

The partitioning of innovation into distinct phases is, however, difficult to apply in CoPS projects that involve the creation or first use of new technology (see Chapter 2 on high-tech and super-high-tech projects), such as military weapons systems or new generations of high-speed trains. To meet a customer's requirements for such technologically advanced and complex products, research, development and implementation project activities often overlap and feed back upon one another. In other words, innovative efforts to research, develop and incorporate new technology in a product, which is configured to a customer's operational needs, are undertaken concurrently within the scope of a single CoPS project. For example, the UK's National Air Traffic Services (NATS) project to design and build the Swanwick air traffic control centre involved the first use of technology for a customer, which according to NATS 'was more advanced than anything that is being tried anywhere in the world' (House of Commons, 1998: viii).

High-volume producers – such as large banks, carmakers and pharmaceutical manufacturers – are also involved in the CoPS as producers as well as buyers and users. Many of these large firms meet their internal requirements for CoPS by undertaking one-off or consecutive projects to design and install large items of fixed capital such as IT, telecoms, scientific instruments and factory automation systems. For example, Morgan Stanley, the global investment bank, has developed the capabilities to manage the numerous projects it undertakes to meet in-house needs for complex IT systems. It has also established systematic post-project review procedures so that the learning gained from previous projects is used to improve project performance and address potential risks encountered in subsequent projects.[8]

---

[8] Together with R&D, such project-based CoPS activities may represent a growing proportion of the total activities undertaken by high-volume producers due to the increasingly widespread practice of outsourcing standardised production activities to low-cost manufacturers (see Chapter 4).

Project capability and competitive advantage

In this final part of the chapter, we show that project capability is essential to the operational effectiveness and strategic positioning of the firm.[9] Focusing on suppliers of CoPS, we explain how firms use project capability to create competitive advantage by (1) managing projects more efficiently in an existing technology and market base, and (2) utilising projects to envisage and implement strategies for diversification.

The project capability base: operational effectiveness

To maintain its competitive position in an existing technology or market base, a firm can use projects for improving the efficiency and effectiveness of its operations. The traditional discipline of project management provides systematic tools and techniques for conducting project scheduling, budgeting and resource allocation within and between projects. By developing its capabilities in project and programme management – bidding, proposal writing, project set-up and execution, and on-going support – a firm can gain a competitive advantage by performing these activities better than its rivals. Such project capabilities are embodied in company-specific organisational routines and procedures such as bid documentation and project management manuals, which contain detailed instructions about how to win bids, execute and close down projects.

Unique and repetitive projects

A project is often described as unique, one-off or novel to differentiate it from volume-based routine operations.[10] In volume production, instant feedback and systematic learning about operational performance on a daily basis can be used to modify and improve repetitive and routine processes. It is often assumed that project activities provide fewer opportunities for cumulative learning because the tasks performed are

---

[9] Porter (1996) distinguishes between (a) operational effectiveness which 'means performing similar activities *better* than rivals perform them' and (b) strategic positioning which 'means performing *different* activities from rivals or performing similar activities in *different ways*' (Porter, 1996: 62).

[10] Project management is used to manage non-routine processes to produce unique or novel products and functional management is used to manage routine operations to produce repetitive or standardised products (Turner, 1999: 19).

Table 3.2: Unique and repetitive project tasks

	Repetitive projects/tasks	Unique projects/tasks
Goals	Immediate, specified	Visionary, abstract
Experience	Own or codified by professions	Others' or none
Competence	In codes and tacit knowledge	Diverse or unknown, requires flexibility and creativity
Leadership/owner of temporary organisation	Low or middle managers	Top management
Development process	Reversible	Irreversible
Evaluation	Result oriented	Utility oriented
Learning	Refinement and exploitation	Renewal and exploration

Source: adapted from Lundin and Söderholm, 1995: 441.

non-routine and customised to a particular customer's needs. However, it is important to emphasise that many projects and project tasks are also based on systematic bid and project management routines. Although the result of every project is a unique or one-off configuration of products and/or services, the tasks and processes by which the result is achieved range from (a) unique and one-off to (b) highly standardised and routine. A project can therefore be located on a spectrum of tasks ranging from unique to repetitive (Lundin and Söderholm, 1995; Packendorff, 1995). By focusing on the tasks performed it is possible to distinguish between unique and repetitive projects.

A unique project performs novel and complex tasks to achieve a one-off objective which is unlikely to occur again, such as the Channel Tunnel Rail Link, Millennium Dome and Heathrow's Terminal 5 project. A repetitive project performs standardised and routine tasks that will be repeated in future, such as a large portfolio of implementation projects based on mature product lines. Whereas a unique task is characterised by uncertainty and less predictable behaviour, a repetitive task involves recurring project roles and institutionalised routines. The key differences between unique and repetitive tasks are summarised in Table 3.2. At any particular time, a firm may carry out a variety of unique and repetitive projects, including hybrid projects that combine unique and repetitive tasks.

The ability to use a firm's existing base of project knowledge, experience and skills to improve operational performance varies depending on the type of project task performed. When an organisation performs a unique task, members of the project and the wider organisation have little or no immediate knowledge or experience of how to win the bid and manage the project. The tasks performed have to be defined and the new type of organisation required to undertake them has to be created. Because of the high risks of failure in unique projects, managers with entrepreneurial skills and strong leadership qualities are needed. To cope with task uncertainty and novelty, they must be willing to revise or abandon traditional approaches and be creative in their search for experiences from previous projects that will help develop new routines.

When a project performs a repetitive task, members of the project use existing project routines and institutionalised procedures to guide their actions. Although the end result (the complex product or system) of a repetitive project is often unique or highly customised, project tasks are standardised and codified in company project management handbooks. However, project tasks become routinised and predictable only if they have been repeated over many projects. When a new project is established around a repetitive task, roles and responsibilities are clearly defined. Members of a repetitive project 'know what to do, and why and by whom it should be done' (Lundin and Söderholm, 1995: 441). They share similar experiences and a common perception of the situation because they have performed similar projects in the past.

Economies of repetition and recombination

Improvements in operational performance are not as easily realised in unique projects because of the difficulties of systematically transferring learning from projects which are not repeated in future. Some learning is possible, however, because the roles performed by individual members of project teams may be similar and some of the particular problems encountered may reappear in other projects. In repetitive projects, by contrast, there are opportunities for cumulative learning and efficiency gains because the learning accrued on previous projects can be applied repeatedly in concurrent and consecutive projects.

However, efficiency gains in low-volume project-based production are not based on the traditional scale advantages and learning curves attributed to high-volume functional organisations. Although the concept of the learning curve helps to show how the production of capital goods in large batches (e.g. aircraft and electronic equipment) diminishes by a fixed percentage (Adler and Clark, 1991), the emphasis is on cumulative learning in manufacturing and cost reductions per product. By contrast, productivity improvements in lower-volume project activities are measured in terms of the reduction in costs per bid submitted and project executed (within cost, on time and to customer specifications). Despite the difficulties entailed in learning from one project experience to another (see Chapter 7), there are opportunities for systematic learning and efficiency gains because firms carry out similar categories of projects (e.g. new product development (NPD) projects or implementation projects using known or proven technologies) which involve repeatable cycles of activity and replicable components. Bids and projects are referred to as similar when the same sets of capabilities, routines and components are required for their repeated execution.

A firm can obtain economies of repetition by performing a growing volume of similar types of projects more efficiently and effectively (Davies and Brady, 2000: 941). When bids and projects are repeated, recognisable patterns of organisational behaviour tend to occur. Certain outcomes can be predicted based on previous experiences and the learning gained can be used to foresee and avoid any conceivable hurdles to project success. New organisational structures and capabilities can be developed to routinise and perfect bid and project tasks and improve performance by standardising processes (e.g. programme management, project management guide books and IT-enabled processes). As Amsden and Hikino (1994: 130) emphasise, a firm can increase its capability to perform an expanding volume of projects with in-house resources, knowledge and skills because the 'greater the number or frequency of projects the firm undertakes itself, the greater the knowledge acquired about project execution'.

A firm can obtain the cost advantages attributed to economies of recombination (Grabher, 2002b: 1916) by converting the knowledge gained from previous projects into standardised product or service modules, such as replicable components of hardware, software and services. Each project can be tailored to a customer's unique requirements using increasingly standardised, reusable and easy-to-deploy modules based on product platforms and service portfolios. Firms can increase their flexibility and speed of responsiveness by combining the modules into novel configurations of products and services for each customer and rapidly recombining them in many future projects. By sharing common components across a platform of products and portfolio of services, firms can provide the different combinations of components necessary to meet each customer's unique needs more efficiently and effectively.[11]

As we show in Chapter 7, the move into a new technology or market base usually starts with the establishment of a unique or first-of-its-kind project and the initiation of a dynamic process of organisational learning and project capability building. As an increasing number of projects of the new type are undertaken, a firm can realise economies of repetition and recombination by establishing the project capabilities, structures (e.g. new project organisations, units or divisions) and common modules required to deliver a growing volume of repeatable projects. The customer benefits because the project business can design and build reliable and high-quality products at lower cost than others by reusing proposals, project plans, hardware and software modules that have been fine-tuned and proven successful.

Base-moving project capability: strategic positioning

Projects are becoming the basic unit for achieving a firm's strategic objectives for innovation and diversification. A project becomes strategic when a firm attempts to 'manipulate its future' (Obeng, 1995: 185). The survival and growth of a firm depend on its ability to adapt projects to a fast-moving business environment and to change it. However, the capabilities required to move into a new technology and/or market base are very different from those required to conduct operational projects in an existing base.[12] To move into new technology or market positions, a firm

---

[11] High-volume manufacturers (e.g. Kodak) develop standardised product components and common processes that can be shared at lower cost across a platform of standardised products (Robertson and Ulrich, 1998). In our research, we have found product platforms are also important in low-volume CoPS production. In addition, service portfolios are being developed to standardise, simplify and reduce the costs of service-based activities undertaken throughout the project life cycle (see Chapter 8).

[12] Diversification within a firm's traditional base refers to 'the production of more products based in the same technology *and* sold in the firm's existing markets' (Penrose, 1959: 110).

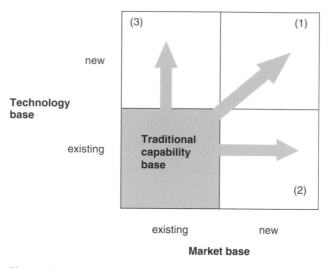

Figure 3.4. Base-moving project paths

can establish strategic projects to pursue one of three paths of diversification (Penrose, 1959: 110).[13] The paths refer to (1) the expansion into *new markets* with new products based in a *new technology* base, (2) the move into a *new market* base with new products using an *existing technology* base, and (3) the expansion in an *existing market* with new products based in a *new technology* base. The initial step along one of these base-moving paths shown in Figure 3.4 often begins with a project assigned to the unique task of exploring the new business opportunity.

Strategies for diversification can be offensive or defensive.[14] Offensive strategies are implemented to take the lead in the development of new technology or to create first-mover advantages in new product, customer or geographical markets. Defensive strategies are implemented to adjust to a changing environment, such as rapid technological obsolescence or changes in customer demands.[15] For

---

[13] Ansoff (1957) distinguished between the various product-market diversification strategies rather than technology-market alternatives.

[14] Freeman (1974) identifies six types of innovation strategies: offensive, defensive, imitative, dependent, traditional and opportunist. However, his focus is on innovative projects in upstream R&D rather than productive and market-facing projects.

[15] External changes of this kind can be so important that they encourage a firm to implement defensive strategies to keep pace with the frontiers of research.

example, Boeing maintained a dominant position in the world commercial airplane industry by pursuing an offensive strategy of creating successive generations of commercial airplanes, such as the 737, 747 and 767, incorporating major technological advances. By the mid-1980s, however, Airbus, the European consortium, had gained a significant share of the commercial airplane market. To regain the competitive lead from Airbus, one of Boeing's largest and riskiest projects was launched in 1990 to develop the 777, an entirely new twin-engine commercial airplane, which entered service in mid-1995. The new airplane cost billions of dollars to develop, thus risking 'the very life of the company on the venture' (Petroski, 1996: 124). Boeing subsequently followed a new defensive strategy by redirecting its resources away from risky investments in commercial markets towards projects for the US military involving less financial risk. To consolidate its lead over Boeing, Airbus initiated a radical offensive strategy to challenge the monopoly that Boeing's 747 had in the very large, long-haul aircraft market. Launched in December 2000, the £9.5 billion Airbus A380 project developed the world's largest commercial jet, a twin-decked airliner with 555 seats, due to enter service in 2006. Boeing engaged in a new offensive strategy to reverse its loss of market share to Airbus. The 787 Dreamliner project was launched in April 2004 to create a mid-sized long-range airliner, due to enter service in 2008.

Building on Penrose's analysis, we can identify project-led strategies to implement offensive or defensive moves. These base-moving project initiatives can result from top-down strategies beginning with the establishment of a major project or from bottom-up unplanned and small-scale project initiatives led by various business units within the firm. The different base-moving project-led paths that a firm may follow are shown in Figure 3.5.

In many cases, base-moving efforts are top-down initiatives led by a firm's main strategy, R&D and corporate divisions. Initial moves begin with a strategic decision to create a major pioneering project which is able to mobilise the large-scale resources needed to expand into new activities. The senior management team is responsible for deciding whether to expand a firm's existing activities or implement a strategy for diversification into new technology and market positions. The strategic project director or programme leader requires a broader range of skills than are necessary in the management of operational projects. Whereas in operational projects the focus of managerial

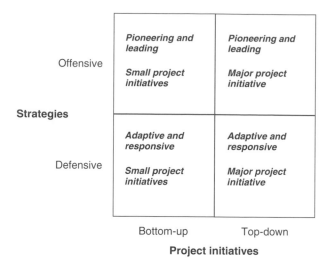

Figure 3.5. Base-moving project-led strategies

attention is on achieving the practical goals of meeting time, cost and quality specifications, in strategic projects the focus is on achieving a firm's overall business objectives. Managers must be prepared to bring their projects to an abrupt end if they are no longer required to meet an organisation's overall business objectives (Obeng, 1995: 189).

A decision to diversify requires the identification of a range of possible projects necessary for diversification, evaluation of those projects and selection of one or more projects on the basis of the evaluation.[16] In deciding whether to embark on an innovative R&D project, for example, managers must employ project-selection procedures to estimate the costs of developing, producing and marketing the innovation, the future revenue stream arising from the sale of the innovation and the probability of its success (Freeman and Soete, 1997: 242–264). Under stable conditions, managers will often show a preference for projects with predictable outcomes rather than ones whose outcomes are uncertain. In a turbulent environment, a larger proportion of the projects selected will be outside the traditional

---

[16] Using a resource-based analysis, Moss (1981: 53) explains that the main 'difference between the expansion of existing activities and diversification is that the investment required for expansion is well-defined from the outset, while the investment project required for diversification must first be defined'.

project capability base. By maintaining a balanced portfolio of projects, it is possible to offset a few high-risk and uncertain projects against a large number of relatively safe and routine projects so that radical and long-term innovative opportunities are not ignored.

Base-moving initiatives of this kind often begin with the creation of a high-profile, strategically important project, such as a cross-functional product development team, technology incubator or skunk works operation. For example, Lockheed Martin established a separate skunk works organisation to carry out super-high-tech projects, such as the U-2 spy plane (Rich and Janos, 1994). Operating at a distance from the firm's traditional organisation provides the project with the autonomy to develop new cross-functional and project capabilities required to master the new technological or market opportunities whilst minimising the risks of such moves.

Base-moving efforts can also be bottom-up initiatives, because as Penrose recognised, 'projects are constantly being created and executed, some of which are never considered in the higher reaches of management' (Penrose, 1959: 50). Such bottom-up initiatives to move into new technology/market bases can start out as numerous smaller projects and seed-bed initiatives scattered throughout an organisation, each requiring only limited resources (Baden-Fuller and Stopford, 1999: 17). The rate at which bottom-up projects are started autonomously depends on the amount of slack or underutilised resources available at the operational level which can be redeployed for other purposes. It also depends on the culture of the company. Some firms are keen to promote new experimental market and technology initiatives. Others may be more focused internally on organisational change and efficiency issues. Still others may find themselves threatened by new projects which might destabilise existing operations in the future. Over time, bottom-up project initiatives may become supplemented by larger base-moving projects that cross functional divides and make more systematic use of corporate-wide resources. The larger projects supplement the numerous smaller initiatives and collectively enable the firm to consolidate its position in a new technology or market base.

Many large established firms, such as DuPont, General Electric and IBM, have used internal corporate venturing (ICV) projects for years as important bottom-up vehicles to initiate organic growth and diversification (Burgelman, 1984; Kanter, 1985; Tidd et al., 1997). In a process of organisational development, an individual ICV project can grow into a sizeable and separate new business. ICV projects constitute an important source of strategic renewal for established firms. Burgelman's study of a high-volume producer looked at how ICV projects grew into new businesses based on new technology. The projects were responsible for linking technological possibilities to new or poorly served market needs (Burgelman, 1984: 36). However, project initiators often encountered top management resistance to proposals which went against conventional corporate wisdom. They also found it difficult to obtain the resources they needed to move into uncharted and fast-moving technology or market areas.

The phenomenon of bootlegging, which became widespread in the 1980s and 1990s, is an extreme example of a bottom-up project initiative undertaken without the knowledge of top management (Augsdorfer, 1996). It refers to under-the-table, unofficial projects conducted covertly within corporate R&D or other innovative organisations (Freeman and Soete, 1997: 245). Often tacitly accepted by senior management, bootlegging can lead to highly innovative projects, such as new product developments, being initiated by individual researchers or managers. If successful, bootlegging projects can later become official projects.

As Mintzberg (1983) emphasised, however, strategy formulation in project organisations cannot be easily placed at the top-down or bottom-up operational levels. Strategy is constantly evolving as projects change, depending on what projects come along and how well a firm is performing in its current projects. Projects are also constantly changing, with some moving in unexpected and exciting new directions. In other words, each 'project leaves its imprint on strategy' (Mintzberg, 1983: 264). This means that strategy formulation is controlled by those responsible for engaging with the customer, developing proposals and deciding what projects are carried out and how. In a project business, this includes managers at multiple levels in the organisation, from the bid or commercial manager to the project manager, project director and CEO.

A firm's core project capabilities shape its approach to strategy formulation, which can be deliberate or emergent (Mintzberg, 1996). If the firm already has some project learning and experience which it needs to perform the new activity, it can develop a deliberate strategy to reduce the false starts and inefficiencies resulting from its unfamiliarity with the new type of project. The firm has a good understanding of the problem it is tackling and how to implement the strategy. An emergent strategy, by contrast, is developed to cope with unfamiliar situations or events that are changing more quickly than a firm's ability to learn from past experiences. In such cases, the required capabilities are unrelated to its core project capabilities and strategy formulation falls outside the firm's current thinking because the project has never been undertaken in the past. A successfully managed base-moving project can provide an opportunity to innovate by breaking away from carefully evolved past routines and experimenting with new ones that will form the basis of its future project capabilities.

The strategic role played by such base-moving projects can be illustrated by historical evidence and some examples of our case study research with Ericsson. Over the past three decades, Ericsson has diversified beyond its traditional base as a manufacturer of fixed telecommunications equipment for public telecommunications operators to become the world's leading supplier of mobile communications systems for a new set of customers – mobile phone operators (see Box 3.1).

Box 3.1: Ericsson's base-moving projects

Path 1: Business-moving projects

The most radical base-moving path a firm can follow is to create projects which depart from its traditional business by successfully expanding into a new technology *and* new market base. In the 1970s, Ericsson combined its improved digital switching technology based on the AXE exchange with radio transmission technologies. By developing this new technology base, Ericsson was able to expand beyond its traditional fixed telephony markets into mobile communications in the early 1980s (Granstrand and Sjölander, 1990: 44; Granstrand et al., 1997: 14).

Ericsson's successful move into mobile telephony was not the result of a planned top-down or offensive strategy (Mölleryd, 1997). Instead it was made possible by two pioneering base-moving projects initiated in response to customer demands. First, Ericsson was selected in 1978 as one of the equipment manufacturers responsible for developing mobile switching and base station technology and delivering equipment for the Nordic Mobile Telephone (NMT) system in a project consortium managed by the participating Scandinavian telephone operators. Ericsson's AXE exchange technology had to be adapted to the requirements of mobile telephony.

Second, Ericsson won another project in 1979 to build a mobile phone network using NMT technology in Saudi Arabia. The world's first commercial mobile network opened for service in Saudi Arabia on 1 September 1981, followed closely by the Nordic NMT network which was inaugurated on 1 October the same year.

These pioneering projects used existing resources from two previously unrelated parts of Ericsson: the Public Systems Division responsible for AXE technology and the radio communications subsidiary. During 1981, these two organisations worked closely together to create the bidding capability within Ericsson to meet the growing number of customer requests for project proposals to design and build mobile networks throughout Europe (Meurling and Jeans, 1994: 57–58).

Path 2: Market-moving projects

The second base-moving path refers to the use of an existing technology to offer new customers an existing range of products and services or to provide existing customers with new combinations of products and services. In 1995, Ericsson's base-moving efforts focused on expanding into new markets for existing customers: providing mobile phone operators with a new type of turnkey project to meet customer demands for major outsourcing contracts (Davies, 1997b).

As we will see in Chapter 7 when the case is examined in detail, Ericsson's first move into the new market for turnkey projects began in the UK in 1995 when it signed a contract to perform all the activities required to design and build a mobile network for One2One, the UK operator now owned by T-Mobile. This was a defensive strategy because the demand for the new type of project was initiated by the customer. But it was a high-profile, strategically important project initiative for Ericsson, bringing together resources from within Sweden, the UK and other parts of the corporate group as well as externally to form a separate project organisation. The project was soon supplemented by numerous other turnkey projects launched autonomously within Ericsson's various product divisions in response to growing demand from mobile phone operators.

Path 3: Technology-moving projects

The third path of diversification is to provide existing customers with new products based on new technology. To move into a new technological base, a firm has to undertake basic research to create a stable technology and product development to adapt the technology to the application context prior to market introduction. For example, the market introduction of Ericsson's 3G mobile communications, which incorporate advances in internet protocol (IP) technologies to provide high-speed packet switching of data traffic, was preceded by around ten years of pre-market collaborative R&D (Gessler, 2002).

Ericsson's efforts to commercialise 3G technology have focused on two high-level First Office Application projects in collaboration with Vodafone – one of Ericsson's lead customers – to start 3G mobile services in the UK and Japanese markets (Davies and Tang, 2003). In these two projects, Ericsson and Vodafone have worked closely to prepare 3G technology for market introduction, to develop, test and conduct commercial trials of 3G products and service applications, and to ensure backwards compatibility with existing 2G networks.

Base-moving project paths across industries

There are important differences between the base-moving project paths followed by firms in CoPS compared with those in high-volume industries. In CoPS, initial attempts to move base begin with the establishment of a unique project to explore the new business opportunity. In a growing market, a firm can realise economics of repetition and recombination by moving from the first-of-its-kind project to the execution of a large volume of standardised portfolios of repetitive projects. In consumer goods and services, the establishment of a base-moving project – such as an NPD, skunk work or ICV project – can also lead to repeat business. However, once a prototype is taken into production the capabilities required to manufacture and distribute the new product in high volumes are more important than those required for the management of repetitive projects.

Conclusions

This chapter shows that many firms today rely on project capabilities to improve their operational performance and create new sources of competitive advantage through innovative project-led strategies. Project businesses face what Mintzberg (1983: 279) calls the dual pressures of producing routinely and being innovative. In other words, firms must obtain efficiency gains in their existing technology and/or market bases while exploring the possibilities to move base.

By developing its capabilities in bid and project management, a firm can create and maintain a competitive position through improving its ability to engage with customers, developing successful proposals and delivering projects that address new customer needs. At the operational level, project management capabilities, tools and techniques are required to deliver different types of projects ranging from the unique to the repetitive. Important efficiency gains can be obtained in the delivery of repetitive projects by exploiting economies of repetition and recombination (see Chapter 7). Such operational improvements are difficult to achieve in unique projects, but are by no means impossible. Ultimately, projects can help leading firms to diversify into more defendable positions in industry value streams and create entirely new markets, as we show in Chapter 8.

Although firms in all types of industries use projects for a variety of tasks, such as change programmes or quality initiatives, we showed how project capability differs across industries and according to distinct phases of the innovation process. Consumer goods suppliers use project capabilities for R&D, new product development and a whole host of internal activities, but depend on extensive functional capabilities to perform volume manufacturing and marketing activities. CoPS suppliers, meanwhile, use projects to organise almost all of their production and marketing activities as well as new product development and R&D.

The framework introduced in this chapter shows how firms deploy projects to diversify into new technology and market positions. The knowledge and experience gained during a base-moving project are vital for senior management to understand the viability of moving further into a new technology or market position and the costs and benefits of doing so. In other words, projects shape strategy as much as strategy shapes projects.

The framework can be applied to suppliers of CoPS and high-volume producers that undertake major projects on a continuous basis to meet their internal requirements for CoPS. In pharmaceuticals, for example, firms like GlaxoSmithKline (GSK) and AstraZeneca have conducted internal projects to develop complex genetic databases and networks that are exploited by scientists to improve the discovery of high-quality drugs and lower the risk of failure in development (Nightingale, 2000). GSK has moved into this field by implementing projects as part of an integral top-down strategic move – based on a vision of how genetics would transform drug discovery. AstraZeneca followed a different path to the same goal. It established small projects to conduct proof of concept studies. The results of the studies were used to bid for internal funds for larger studies that eventually led to the creation of major new research projects to develop and exploit genetic technologies.

Over the past decade, more firms in all types of industries have been using projects to improve the efficiency and effectiveness of their existing operations and to achieve strategies to diversify into new technologies or expanding markets. Indeed, some authors argue that in the twenty-first century project management may even replace traditional functional management as the key to creating and maintaining competitive advantage (Pinto and Kharbanda, 1995: 48–49). As we show in Chapter 7, decisions to establish base-moving projects and embark on new and uncharted project paths can represent the beginning of far-reaching transformations in the overall strategic direction of the firm.

4 | *Systems integration and competitive advantage*

T HIS chapter examines one of the core capabilities of producers of CoPS and other high-technology goods and services, namely systems integration.[1] Systems integration is defined as the core technical and strategic capabilities which enable a project business to combine all the various production inputs, including components, subsystems, software, skills and knowledge, to produce a product, system, construct, network or service.[2] The aim of the chapter is to assess the nature and importance of systems integration by examining historical and recent research. It shows how systems integration evolved from its original application in the 1940s and 1950s in the military arena to other CoPS sectors and more recently to high-volume, technology-driven industries.

As a capability, systems integration has become increasingly important for organising production both within and across firms.[3] As the chapter shows, while systems integration began as a technical, operations task (part of the wider functional discipline of systems engineering),

---

[1] This chapter draws from Hobday et al. (2004).

[2] This definition focuses on the provider of high-technology products of various kinds rather than the downstream user or support organisations or upstream raw material suppliers and component manufacturers. It includes some aspects of outsourcing (e.g. the capabilities needed to specify, design and integrate key components) but excludes others (e.g. support services such as payroll or personnel recruitment). As we show in Chapter 8, it includes many new capabilities needed to integrate services with physical products as bundled solutions and to undertake collaborations for jointly producing components and subsystems. It excludes (a) simple low-technology products (e.g. newspapers), (b) craft-based activities (e.g. basic construction), (c) routine manufacturing activities (e.g. assembly tasks) and (d) downstream services (e.g. distribution and finance).

[3] For a collection of recent papers by the authors and others see Prencipe et al. (2003). Following Chapter 3, this chapter adopts a capability view of the firm based on Penrose (1959), Richardson (1972), Chandler (1990) and subsequent work by authors such as Teece and Pisano (1994), Teece et al. (1994) and related work on competencies by Barney (1991) and Hamel and Prahalad (1994).

today it is a strategic business capability, central to the management of many high-technology projects. The more complex, high-technology and high-cost the product, the more significant systems integration is to the capability and strategy of the firm. The chapter shows how systems integration underpins the competitive strategy of the CoPS firm as well as the particular position the firm takes within the value stream of an industry.[4]

With the increase in outsourcing over the past decade or so, systems integration capability has become vital to the operations, strategy and competitive advantage of industry leaders in sectors as diverse as software, computing, automotive, telecommunications, military systems, hard disk drives and aerospace. In one sense systems integration is the 'other side of the coin' of outsourcing and the capability which underpins successful outsourcing. However, as the chapter argues, systems integration is not simply the counterpart to outsourcing, but a method of managing particular kinds of outsourcing (as well as 'joint sourcing' and 'insourcing') activities, which permit the lead integrator firm (potentially at least) to gain the advantages of both outsourcing and vertical integration through different phases of the product life cycle.

Traditionally, as an engineering task, systems integration has had 'two faces', similar to the two faces of research and development identified by Cohen and Levinthal (1989). The first face concerns the internal activities of firms as they develop and integrate the inputs they need to produce new products. The second face, which has become more important in recent years, refers to the external activities of firms as they integrate components, skills and knowledge from other firms to produce ever more complex products and services. Other firms include input suppliers, users, partners and, sometimes, competitors as firms work together and compete in projects, usually led by systems integrator firms.

However, we show that both faces of systems integration are strategic in character, going beyond the traditional domains of systems engineering and project management to become a capability central to the competitive advantages of prime contractors such as General Electric, ABB, Dell, Ford, IBM, Hewlett-Packard, BAE Systems,

---

[4] As discussed in Chapter 8, the term value stream refers to the industry-wide chain of activities rather than the intra-firm value chain. Porter (1990: 42) refers to the former as a 'value system'.

Cable & Wireless, Siemens, Nokia, Rolls-Royce, Boeing and Thales. As industry leaders, one of their main tasks is to integrate various kinds of technology, knowledge and hardware supplied by other organisations involved in projects. The chapter provides evidence of the benefits of strong systems integration capabilities and shows how systems integration differs from industry to industry and how it adapts through different stages of the product life cycle.

To show the evolution of systems integration, this chapter examines its American military origins, identifying the factors and organisations which drove its initial development as a technical discipline within, and then beyond, the defence sector. It then examines non-military capital goods, arguing that here too systems integration appears to be a widespread strategic activity rather than merely an operational or engineering task. Recent evidence from two high-volume industries, namely cars and hard disk drives, is presented in more depth to show how some firms deploy systems integration capability to upgrade technologically from one product to another. Finally, we consider recent trends in high-value CoPS industries, showing how major firms have begun to use systems integration capabilities to bundle services together with hardware and software in order to gain competitive advantage. Although most of the chapter concerns CoPS, the traditional domain of systems integration, as in other chapters, it also compares CoPS with high-volume consumer and component industries to identify similarities and differences in the scope and direction of systems integration.

The military origins of systems integration

Sapolsky (2003) describes the military and Cold War origins of systems integration in the United States, the first country to develop and institutionalise formal systems integration processes. As Sapolsky shows, the American government believed it needed more than financial investment and determination to wage the Cold War against the Soviet Union. America needed to create the institutions that could build and coordinate, over the long term, the complex new technologies and industries needed for military purposes.

During the Second World War, many of the basic weapons technologies needed to wage the Cold War were under development, but not the organisational systems required for the development, deployment and renewal of these technologies in the prolonged Cold War period.[5] American military structures could command coordination when most in society were ready to accept military discipline and priorities because of war. However, these structures began to be severely tested in partial mobilisation of the Cold War.

Military systems were themselves becoming more complex and ambitious and the traditional single-discipline, linear approach to systems development which involved making one part of the system, then the next, and so on was coming under increasing pressure. There was a need for multi-disciplinary project teams involving different kinds of scientists and engineers to work together on systems in a way which optimised design, engineering development, production and operations. In response, a variety of special organisations and skills were developed which allowed the military to manage more effectively the design and development of complex weapons systems. Key among them were the systems integration skills and processes needed for building and operating complex weapons, as well as the new project-based organisational structures which were then developing.

Today, most major military systems producers refer to themselves as prime contractors. They see their primary task as one of systems integration and have developed sophisticated processes and structures for this task. Figure 4.1, for example, presents the case of the UK aerospace and military producer, BAE Systems. Similar diagrams can be found in the annual reports of many large aerospace and military systems makers, both civil and military. BAE Systems and competitor firms such as Thales and McDonald Douglas see their main business task as occupying the prime contractor space in the production pyramid. They then outsource production, design and other activities to a wide range of other suppliers. In Figure 4.1, the prime contractor can be separated from the systems integrator which means that, in some cases, the systems integration task itself is outsourced to a supplier firm.

In fact, the pyramid in Figure 4.1 is slightly misleading. In most cases, the customer (e.g. the Ministry of Defence or the Air Force) occupies

---

[5] Also see the classic work of Hughes (1998) on major projects. Hughes describes major US projects in the 1950s such as The Atlas (the first intercontinental ballistic missile system), led by General Bernard Schriever of the Air Force and Simon Ramo of manufacturing and services company TRW. Atlas was the first major project to formally deploy systems engineering to coordinate the activities of large numbers of private companies and thousands of scientists and engineers working across a diverse set of technologies.

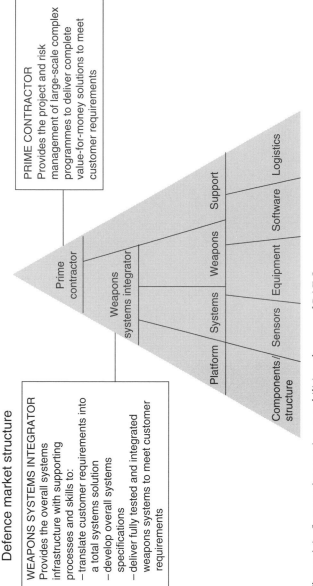

Figure 4.1. Systems integration capabilities: the case of BAE Systems
Source: British Aerospace (now BAE Systems) Annual Report 1998: 2.

the tip of the pyramid, providing instructions, guidance on customer requirements and overall systems specifications. The customer will often specify which firms are below the prime contractor in the pyramid and lay down fairly tight guidelines on project processes, risk management arrangements and scheduling. Beneath the top two sections of the pyramid, there is a layer of subsystem suppliers. As we discussed in Chapter 2, these are usually very large firms themselves which act as systems integrators and prime contractors in other projects. Beneath this subsystem layer is another tier of firms made up of component suppliers, some of which are large producers of civil technology (e.g. semiconductors, software and computer suppliers) as well as military products. Their inputs can also be extremely complex, specialised and high-technology based (e.g. microprocessor components or supercomputers). Like the subsystem suppliers, these firms drive the base technology forwards. Beneath this tier lies another tier of basic parts and material suppliers who form the base of the pyramid or food chain of production.

Figure 4.1 shows that systems integration is no longer solely or even mainly a technical task. Instead, it is also concerned with the apportioning of production and innovation tasks across the industry value stream, the organisation of major projects, the choice of business partners and decisions over what to source internally and externally.

However, during the Second World War and the Cold War, these systems integration ideas and structures had not yet been formulated and emerging notions of systems integration were primarily technical. During the late 1940s and early 1950s, in order to develop and deploy systems such as the atomic and hydrogen bombs, jet fighters, ballistic missiles, satellites and strategic defence command-and-control systems, the military created two related, now commonplace, approaches. On the one hand, engineers devised the technical discipline of systems engineering (including systems integration) for designing and developing systems with the emphasis on meeting technical specifications. On the other hand, managers and business leaders created project management tools, techniques and organisations to manage system development. Here the emphasis was on meeting cost and schedule targets and customer needs. A well-known, highly successful project was the Polaris missile system which invented management tools such as PERT which rapidly spread to other military projects and civil production (Sapolsky, 1972).

At the time, weapons systems were becoming much larger in scale and were incorporating new technologies and components (e.g. radar, nuclear weapons, rocket propulsion and electronic controls), making them more complex and difficult to design, produce and operate. As one indicator, the number of aircraft gas turbine engine parts increased from 9,000 in 1946 to 20,000 in 1957 while the cost of weapons increased tenfold during the period 1945–55. These systems demanded the integration of a wide range of engineering and scientific knowledge and skills. No individual engineer or single engineering discipline could cope with the design and development of such complex systems.

In response, engineers, physicists and rocket scientists joined together in multi-disciplinary teams to create an alternative to the traditional sequential approach (Johnson, 1997). Before and during the Second World War, customer organisations such as the US Army Air Forces procured aircraft from prime contractors. Afterwards, the customer added its own components and modifications (e.g. engines and armaments). By the late 1940s, formal systems engineering had begun to take hold. Under this approach, all weapons systems components had to be designed and developed together from the start (including airframe, electronics and armaments), prior to integration. A very early example was the mobile ground radar units used in the Second World War. Ivan Getting, the engineer on the project, realised that radar and fire control components behaved differently when working together than they did individually. To account for the differences, he ordered that specifications on each unit be written with full consideration of the features and capabilities of other units. His early innovation was to allocate a systems integrator to each project. Close coordination between radar and gun subsystems was achieved by assigning MIT's Radiation Laboratory as the formal systems integrator. The Laboratory had access to all information and the authority to test models and to provide feedback on design through all stages of development.

By the late 1940s, systems engineering began to set new standards for military projects. As a discipline, systems engineering was concerned with the whole system rather than any single subsystem or technology. The idea was that an integrated system was a whole greater than the sums of its parts and that entire weapons systems and their components had to be designed together concurrently so that the system could be integrated successfully. By the late 1950s, however, some authors were beginning to question the central assumption of systems engineering that the final configuration of a system can be fully known or predicted at the outset, because customer requirements, strategic priorities and technologies can all change dramatically, even within the life of a single project (Klein and Meckling, 1958). As Hirshman and Lindblom (1962: 361) clarified: 'Once it is understood that a system is never complete or will never stay complete, the case against spending considerable effort on early integration and simultaneous development of subsystems is further strengthened.' These authors emphasised the need to keep the system design as flexible as possible from the outset to cope with emergent events and new technological possibilities and to exploit knowledge gained from learning during system development.

The advantages of the systems integration approach began to be widely appreciated and systems engineering and integration techniques quickly spread beyond the military to other complex systems. For example, in 1950 Bell Labs deployed a version of systems engineering to maintain its telephone network. In 1952, MIT began to put on the first weapons systems engineering courses. The first textbook on systems engineering (Goode and Machol, 1957) was soon followed by others in aerospace and telecommunications.

A landmark was the use of systems engineering in intercontinental ballistic missile (ICBM) projects. Bernard Schriever famously promoted its use when he became head of ICBM programmes in 1953. The complex requirements of ICBMs necessitated across-the-board competences in a range of physical sciences. The multi-disciplinary systems engineering approach enabled the project team to push the technological frontier of ICBM development much further than had been possible previously. For Simon Ramo, of Ramo-Wooldridge (and the 'R' in TRW), the systems engineering-integration approach was a 'cure for chaos' (Ramo, 1969).

Regarding the specific functions of systems engineering, as Figure 4.1 indicates, at the technical level the primary task is to draw up a set of overall specifications which map the performance of each subsystem and its interactions with every other. Other tasks include the evaluation of subsystems during development, the planning of their integration, the controlling and testing of subsystems and the assessment of the operational environment in which systems (e.g. weapons) are to be put to work.

Systems engineering allows engineers to partition systems into smaller, manageable subsystems, assemblies and subassemblies and at the same time to develop interface specifications for each component before they are actually constructed. The purpose is to enable engineers to minimise the interactions among subsystems and so reduce emergent properties which adversely affect the design and final functioning of the system. The approach allows engineers to freeze the systems design at the most appropriate point in order to reduce the ripple effects of many design changes.

In short, systems engineering-integration was an attempt to provide a systematic, multi-disciplinary approach to systems development which was concurrent not sequential. In retrospect, the approach looks quite obvious and logical.[6] However, in the 1950s it was a major breakthrough both in the way engineering was taught and in the way systems were produced. Using concurrent engineering, components were designed, produced and tested simultaneously, reducing delays and later technical difficulties. The advantages were quickly seen in superior performance (Sapolsky, 1972) as more systems were developed on time and to specification. The approach also allowed engineers to understand the dynamic interaction between the system and its environment and to predict design changes which might be needed through the operational life cycle of the system.

As Sapolsky (2003) points out, the American military forced the pace of technological change in a number of large complex weapon projects. Spurred on by its own internally competitive organisational structures, the military learned and helped others to learn the skills of systems integration. The art of conceiving, designing and managing the development and deployment of large systems involving multiple disciplines and many participating organisations became commonplace among military suppliers, aerospace firms and government agencies.

The organisations involved in systems integration

Today, as systems integration has become increasingly sophisticated to cope with the complexity of weapons systems, no single organisation can claim to have a monopoly on systems integration capabilities in any one project. Each major subsector has its own profile of supplier and user organisations, all involved in systems integration. For example, in modern American defence systems, as Gholz (2003) points out, various organisations share the overall task of systems integration. They include the prime contractors and major subcontractors that

---

[6] Similar techniques are widely used today in the car and electronics industries and terms such as concurrent engineering are commonplace.

build the weapons systems, non-profit technical advisors (including university groups), specialist government laboratories, and organisations that manage weapons acquisition (e.g. the DoD), as well as the military users of the weapons (e.g. the army or navy).

However, each of these groups has a slightly different perspective on the meaning of the term, reflecting its own particular interest in the system under development. For the major private-sector firms that manufacture weapons (e.g. BAE Systems or Lockheed Martin), systems integration is mainly the ability to generate the conceptual design, control the supplier network and produce to specification. For acquisition planners that award contracts (e.g. the MoD or DoD), systems integration is the expertise to set the initial technical requirements of the system and evaluate competing bids from prime contractors. For military organisations (e.g. the army or navy), systems integration is the skill to understand the capabilities and limitations of the weapons platforms and their suppliers and to predict the use of the system in an operational environment.

In the defence sector Gholz (2003) points to the different levels and types of systems integration capability, dividing them into three major types: component systems integration, platform systems integration and architecture systems integration. As Table 4.1 shows, different organisations maintain and develop these capabilities in each area. In components, firms such as Northrop Grumman Electronic Systems and Raytheon Missile Systems have developed the capabilities to design and integrate major components in relation to others in any particular system. Systems integration at the weapons platform level is carried out by prime contractors such as Lockheed Martin Aeronautics and General Dynamics Bath Ironworks. In terms of overall concept or architecture technical advisors such as MITRE and SAIC, as well as the DoD or in the UK the MoD, are engaged. The skills of the organisations listed in the table are not exclusive to them. For example, platform systems integration involves many technical capabilities which overlap with those of subcontractors, while component systems integration often involves some assembly tasks as well as subcontractor management skills.

Gholz also describes the network of organisations involved in systems integration in US naval defence (Table 4.2). Each specific product or system will involve different combinations of these organisations and a different profile of systems integration capabilities. Many organisations have some expertise that contributes to systems integration for the American military. The US Navy employs various technical organisations

Table 4.1: Levels of systems integration capability in the defence industry

	Component systems integration	Platform systems integration	Architecture systems integration
Distinguishing skills	Technical capabilities in specific core areas	Project/ subcontractor management	System definition
Key implementing tasks	Engineering development, component production	Production, system assembly	Trade-off studies, customer interface
Example organisations	Subcontractors like Northrop Grumman Electronic Systems and Raytheon Missile Systems	Prime contractors like Lockheed Martin Aeronautics and General Dynamics Bath Ironworks	Technical advisors like MITRE and SAIC

Source: Gholz (2003: 282).

such as the SPAWAR Systems Center and the Naval Air Warfare Center and the Naval Surface Warfare Center to conduct these activities on its behalf. Some of these organisations have small-scale activities that over-lap with the capabilities of other firms in the matrix in Table 4.2. For example, the SPAWAR Systems Center in San Diego is not only con-cerned with policy but also manufactures Link 16 antennas for surface combatants.

Systems integration in non-military sectors

Suppliers of CoPS

In many industries over the past decade or so, systems integrators have taken a stronger role in leading the innovation process and coordinating networks of internal and external suppliers (Rothwell, 1992). In the area of high-cost, complex civilian systems, supplier firms need a deep

Table 4.2: The organisations involved in systems integration in US naval defence

	Government	Private, non-profit	Private, for-profit
Policy analysis	System commands (SPAWAR, NAVSEA, NAVAIR)	Center for Naval Analysis, Institute for Defense Analysis, Rand	ANSER, TASC, Booz-Allen
Scientific research	Naval Research Laboratory, SPAWAR Systems Center – San Diego	APL, Lincoln Laboratory, Software Engineering Institute	
Technical support	SPAWAR Systems Center – San Diego	APL, MITRE, Aerospace Corporation	SAIC, SYNTEK
Production			Lockheed Martin – Naval Electronics and Surveillance Systems, Raytheon Command Control Communications and Information Systems
Testing and fleet support	SPAWAR Systems Center – San Diego		

Source: Gholz (2003).

systems integration capability to compete (e.g. aircraft engines, flight simulators, air traffic control networks, railway engines, civil engineering, telecommunications systems and internet equipment). As in the military, the major users of these systems, and associated regulatory and government bodies, also need an understanding of systems integration and, sometimes, specific capabilities. In some cases, users as well as suppliers may need to establish a formal system integration function or body where it does not already exist (e.g. in the case of European air traffic control where at the time of writing no formal systems integration function operates). Here, one of the roles of the systems integrator is to define and plan the evolution of the system and resolve any conflicting priorities and pressures which may exist (e.g. over the environment vs capacity growth in the case of air traffic control). In order to make these plans, the systems integrators at the platform, component and architectures levels need an understanding of the changing supply and demand structure of the systems environment as it evolves.

In infrastructural networks supported by high-technology systems (e.g. railways, air transport, information and communications systems, electricity and gas networks) the drivers for more elaborate systems integration capability at the various levels are similar to those witnessed in military systems: the increasing complexity of networks and system components, the rapid pace of technological change, and the increasing range of knowledge and skill required to produce the capital goods and systems in question. As in the case of military systems, producers of high-technology civilian capital goods are extensively outsourcing to lower-tier suppliers as they themselves move downstream to service their final customers, the users of complex products and systems. Users are demanding more functions and higher performance of the systems as liberalisation, increased competition and the de-regulation of markets proceeds (e.g. in the utilities and telecommunications), forcing users to move out of systems development and into the supply of differentiated, higher-quality services to final customers.

Firms as systems integrators – an historical perspective

Taking an historical perspective, Pavitt (2003) points to the growing role of individual firms specialising in systems integration and the powerful underlying logic of systems integration as a form of industrial specialisation across many sectors. He argues that systems integration, as a business function, is simply an unfolding of industrial specialisation, another example of Adam Smith's division of labour. Firms specialising in systems integration, Pavitt contends, are the result of two intensifying features of technical change that have shaped recent forms of industrial organisation. First is the continuous increase in specialisation in the production of both artefacts and knowledge.

Second is the advance of information and communications technology (ICT). These two forces have, he argues, increased the opportunities for disintegration, both within product development activities themselves and between product development and manufacturing. Disintegration is another term for the outsourcing of production activities while outsourcing can be viewed as the other side of the coin of systems integration as mentioned earlier. Firms can outsource only if they acquire the capability to integrate the components, knowledge or software produced by their specialist suppliers.

As Pavitt (2003) argues, some firms specialising in systems design and integration have grown to challenge large-scale manufacturing firms, although in many areas there are limits to complete outsourcing (or division of labour) because arm's-length relationships can be an inefficient means for exchanging and integrating fast-changing fields of knowledge. However, even in those firms which have made heavy investments in product development, we see some vertical disintegration in manufacturing processes and design. This process has been happening since the nineteenth century, for example in machine tool manufacture, as pointed out by Rosenberg (1963). Specialised machine tool makers emerged in the nineteenth century as a result of advances in metal-cutting and metal-forming technologies. This led to technological convergence in operations that were common to a number of manufacturing processes. For example, boring accurate circular holes in metal was common to the making of both small arms and sewing machines. Although the skills associated with such machining operations were craft-based, their output could be codified and standardised. Once the market for these common operations became large enough, small specialised firms designing and making the machines emerged. The larger manufacturing customers could therefore benefit by purchasing these machines as they incorporated the latest improvements fed back from many users in many different industries. These machines were superior to those which could be produced internally by manufacturers. In other words, designing and making such machines in-house no longer gave large manufacturing firms a distinctive competitive advantage.

The machine tool user firms described by Rosenberg became the systems integrators of other producers' goods. As Pavitt (2003) shows, these historical processes based on technological convergence and outsourcing have been occurring constantly in many sectors (see Table 4.3). New opportunities for convergence have emerged from

Table 4.3: Modern examples of increasing outsourcing and systems integration

Underlying technological breakthrough	Technological convergence	Vertical disintegration
Metal cutting and forming	Production operations	Machine tools makers
Chemistry and metallurgy	Materials analysis and testing	Contract research
Chemical engineering	Process control	Instruments makers
		Plant contractors
Computing	Design repeat operations	CAD makers
		Robots makers
New materials	Building prototypes	Rapid prototyping firms
ICT (information and communications technology)	Application software Production systems	KIBS* contract manufacture

*   Knowledge-intensive business services.
Source: Pavitt (2003: 83).

technological breakthroughs which have enabled common production applications across product groups. These breakthroughs have occurred in material shaping and forming, the properties of materials, continuous chemical processes, and the storage and manipulation of information for controlling various business functions, including manufacturing operations and design. These breakthroughs have led, for example, to the emergence of contract research firms which specialise in materials analysis and testing (Mowery and Rosenberg, 1989) and firms which produce measurement and control instruments for continuous processes. Computer-aided design and manufacturing systems, originally developed in the transport sectors, are now widely used, as are robots, originally developed in metal manufacturing.

Specialised applications software and rapid prototyping are deployed in a wide range of industries. In the heavy chemical industry, outsourcing in production has also progressed. Specialised chemical engineering firms which began designing and building complete large-scale continuous production facilities for a number of products owed their emergence to technological convergence based on an improved understanding of chemical processes (Arora and Gambardella, 1999; Landau and Rosenberg, 1992).

The impact of ICT on outsourcing

More recently, as Pavitt (2003) argues, there is evidence of intensification in the outsourcing of product design by manufacturers. Unlike most of the cases in Table 4.3, this form of technological convergence does not occur between similar elements of manufacturing operations in different industries but between the total manufacture of different product designs in the same industry. Sturgeon (2002), for example, has pointed to the rise of outsourcing (called contract electronics manufacturing) in electronics. In this sector, specialised suppliers not only take over product designs from electronics manufacturers but also carry out the detailed engineering and manufacture. Although this trend is well known in East Asia (Hobday, 1995), Sturgeon argues that outsourced, contract manufacturing is also growing in other industries, including apparel, footwear, toys, data processing, offshore oil drilling, home furnishings and lighting, semiconductor fabrication, food processing, automotive parts, brewing, enterprise networking and pharmaceuticals. In addition, Prencipe (1997) has documented increases in the outsourcing of production of aircraft engine components.

As Pavitt points out also, other scholars (e.g. Balconi, 2002; D'Adderio, 2001; Zuboff, 1988) have analysed the effects of recent advances in ICT on the links between product design and manufacture. These studies suggest that ICT has increased technological convergence, and outsourcing, for at least two reasons. First, it has reduced the costs of searching for standard components and subsystems to undertake a specified function within a product architecture. Second, it has increased the standardisation of production through automation and the adoption of standard software tools (e.g. integrated enterprise software systems such as product data management (PDM) and enterprise resource planning (ERP) (D'Adderio, 2002)).

Furthermore, advances in ICT may have reduced the costs of outsourcing to product-designing/systems-integrating firms in three ways. First, simulation technology and modelling have both increased the scope of learning before making (Pisano, 1997), thereby reducing the risks of 'bugs' and technical difficulties in subsequent production

(D'Adderio, 2001). Second, ICT can increase the ease with which digitised information about new products can be transferred from product designer to producer. This can reduce ambiguity and provide a common basis for debates and agreements among the groups involved in product development and manufacture. Third, in some cases, ICT enables product designers to monitor subsequent production instantaneously and gain valuable feedback, helping to resolve manufacturing difficulties and improving design for production.

However, in spite of advances (often hyped up by supplier firms and consultants)[7], Pavitt (2003) goes on to argue that ICT has yet to fully achieve the conditions for a modular production system with complete outsourcing. Linkages between product design and manufacture are not the same as activating the <print> instruction on a personal computer after writing a paper. They are not, and cannot, be based entirely on codified information. Indeed, complex products and systems are probably even more difficult to formalise than language.

As detailed research by D'Adderio (2001) shows, product characteristics can be digitised to create simplified models which must subsequently be 're-actualised' by the human teams responsible for production. Therefore, despite ICT codification, the production process still requires close personal contacts, involving the transfer of tacit knowledge, especially in highly complex products and systems. Also, as Brusoni et al. (2001) and Dosi et al. (2003) point out, the division of labour in knowledge and technology is not necessarily mirrored by a division of labour in production. Firms which outsource design often have to retain substantial knowledge about production and product design in-house, especially in complex capital goods.

Therefore, although systems integration may have intensified and broadened its scope as a method of coordinating production, producers and designers remain involved in relational transactions rather than purely arm's-length market transactions. This is not surprising and follows the earlier patterns identified by Pavitt (2003), of outsourcing by product

---

[7] For example in the automotives sector: 'Our global vision is that by 2005, every production factory will be planned, built, launched and operated first using full simulation before going to bricks and mortar. Every digital vehicle must pass the digital factory quality gate – meeting cost, quality and timing targets – before approval will be given for the actual factory' – Sue Unger, Chief Technology Officer, DaimlerChrysler AG (*Manufacturing Daily*, 28 August 2002), cited in Pavitt, 2003: 89.

design and manufacturing firms and producers of specialised capital goods. In short, the complete outsourcing of production and manufacture has not yet been achieved by most prime contractors or systems integrators, despite advances in ICT and systems integration as a formal activity.

Systems integration as a strategic business activity

It is clear from the evidence that systems integration is much more than an operational or technical task. At the strategic level, systems integration capability and performance can confer competitive advantage for at least two sets of reasons. First, at the technological level, systems integration is the capability which underpins new product development and market introduction. As Prencipe (1997) shows for the case of aircraft engines, systems integration embodies the static (intra-generation) technological capabilities a firm requires to establish a product concept design, decompose it and coordinate the network of suppliers needed to produce a new product *within a given technological family*. However, perhaps even more important to long-run competitive advantage, systems integration also refers to the *dynamic* (inter-generation) capabilities required to envisage and produce new product architectures and novel product families. Because the evolution of new products derives from the interaction of a variety of technological fields and key components, one of the most important difficulties facing firms is how to establish dominion over these fields which cross organisational boundaries.

Second, at the level of the value stream, as noted earlier, systems integration is the capability for deciding where a firm can and should situate itself, directly influencing how a firm competes, who it collaborates with and who it competes with. These, arguably, are among the most important boardroom decisions because they decide the market positioning of the firm and how this changes through time. Best (2003) argues that one of the key roles of the systems integrator firm is to exploit the specialised skills and technological capabilities that reside in networks of other firms, sometimes located in regional clusters. He cites the cases of Silicon Valley, Boston's Route 128 and the UK Cambridge Science Park to illustrate the importance of the external face of systems integration. Sometimes product design is decentralised among networked enterprises. In these cases, small teams, individual entrepreneurs and large high-technology firms draw upon the pools of knowledge and skill which exist above and beyond any individual firm.

Insights from cars and hard disk drives

Cars – limits to modularity

As noted earlier, systems integration is undertaken not only in military sectors but in cars, hard disk drives, building and construction, health-care, bio-technology information systems and many other industries. The car example is especially interesting because it shows that despite the rhetoric of outsourcing, the lead systems integrator companies (i.e. the major car manufacturers) retain a great deal of control over the design and production of components. As Sako (2003) shows, in cars, systems integrators have turned to strategies of modularity to cope with the demands of technological complexity and operational efficiency. Essentially, modularity is a method of outsourcing major subsystems and components to first- and second-tier suppliers, allowing the systems integrator firm to move downstream to service the final customer more directly (e.g. in styling, distribution, after-sales service and finance).[8]

Pressures on car producers have led them to adopt a variety of modularity strategies, following different decision paths towards out-sourcing modules. This, in turn, has led to greater outsourcing and new power balances between final carmakers (or OEM, original equipment manufacturer) and supply chain manufacturers. As Sako (2003) shows, outsourcing represents the reallocation of tasks from within one organisational unit to another unit, normally separated by ownership. Some OEMs have moved towards the outsourcing of the entire design and development of fairly high-cost, complex modules. Others outsource only some basic production and assembly, while still others outsource both sets of activities. Regarding design and development, a module supplier may assume full responsibility for the module. Alternatively, the OEM may co-develop the module with the contractor in a co-located design team and perform the systems integration task with the supplier.[9] In such cases, as Sako (2003) argues, cultural and geographical proximity are both important for

---

[8] Modularity can therefore be seen as a particular form of systems integration strategy, to be compared, for example, with integrated strategies where product architectures are designed with interfaces and components tailored for each product (e.g. in complex software packages and ICT networks).
[9] These types of arrangements are also very common in high-volume consumer electronics and semiconductors (Hobday, 1995).

success. In production and assembly, the outsourcing of modules tends also to occur in an 'integral' organisation so that geographic proximity can enable the close interaction and communication needed for production, especially in the systems integration phase.

Figure 4.2 provides a typical example of the sequence of an outsourcing strategy. In this case, the OEM has decided first to outsource the logistics and assembly of modules, second, quality assurance and purchasing and third, the development and sourcing of major components, giving the contractor greater control over second-tier suppliers. Eventually, the contractor is given full engineering and development responsibility.

In each phase, the systems integration capability of the OEM is transformed as the lead firm moves away from detailed involvement in component design and manufacture to the systems integration knowledge and skills needed to integrate the modules produced by others in the supply chain. In this kind of example, gradual outsourcing by the OEM in theory allows a step-by-step increase in the buyer–supplier confidence which, in turn, is supposed to prevent the OEM being captured by the contractors. In principle, the development of large intermediate markets allows contractors to gain economies of scale and specialisation leading to an improved technological focus and greater efficiency. Contractors, it is argued, can capture more value-added by learning to design modules and through systems-integration activities at the module level (as in the case of military systems described above).

This step-by-step sequence provides an incentive for contract suppliers to engage in the initial low-margin, assembly-only business. In some cases (e.g. in developing country locations such as Brazil) the OEM may never intend to allow locally based suppliers to progress much beyond the assembly of modules designed by the OEM or other first-tier suppliers. By contrast, some large module suppliers, such as Intier (which produces the car wing of the Magna), have invested heavily in systems knowledge about the whole car so that they compete by designing and developing whole modules from the outset.

However, in reality, as Sako (2003) shows, despite much rhetoric there is less modularity in the car industry than might be imagined. Figure 4.3 provides detailed evidence of which particular firm – the OEM or the module supplier – has control over selecting the second-tier suppliers of the components which form cockpit modules produced in Europe. As the figure shows, in most cases the OEM still nominates component suppliers despite the view that OEMs should relinquish

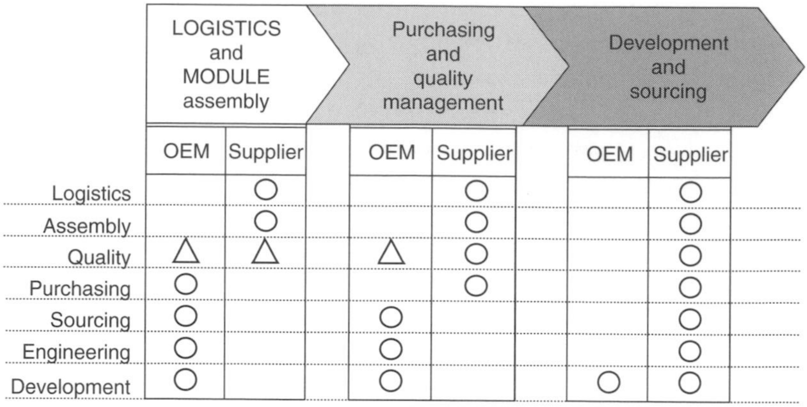

	LOGISTICS and MODULE assembly		Purchasing and quality management		Development and sourcing	
	OEM	Supplier	OEM	Supplier	OEM	Supplier
Logistics		O		O		O
Assembly		O		O		O
Quality	△	△	△	O		O
Purchasing	O			O		O
Sourcing	O		O			O
Engineering	O		O			O
Development	O		O		O	O

Figure 4.2. Sequencing of tasks for outsourcing to module suppliers in cars
Source: Sako (2003: 238).

	A	F	G	H	I	J	K	L	M
IP / dashboard	△	X	X	X△	X△	X△	X	△	X
Cross car beam	△	X	X	O	X△	O	O		△
Instrument cluster	△			△	△	△	△	△	X
Central displays / dials				△					X
Switches	△			O	△	△	△	△	△
Centre console	△			X	△				X
Radio / I.C.E.					△		△	△	X
Sat. navigation etc.					△	△			
Glovebox	△	X	X	X△	△	X	X	△	O
Airducts	△	△		XO	△	X	X	△	O
Bezels / vent control	△	△	△	O	△	O	X	△	O
HVAC system	△			△	△	△	△		X
Steering column	△			△	△	△	△		X
Steering wheel	△			△					
Driver airbag	△			△					
Passenger airbag	△	△		△	△	△	△	△	X
Pedal box					△	△			△
Wiring harness	△			X	△	△	X	X	X
Other wiring				X					
Firewall					△				△
Keyless entry				△					
Steering column shroud				X△	△				
Sound insulation					△				

X = produced in-house by module supplier
O = bought from suppliers selected by module supplier
△ = bought from suppliers nominated by OEM

Figure 4.3. Control over components for car cockpits in Europe
Source: Sako (2003: 238) (original data from IMVP European Module Supplier Survey).

control over such components. Indeed, when interviewed, many contractors complained about the OEMs' 'reluctance to let go' and the practice of 'shadow engineering' by the OEM.

As Sako (2003) goes on to show, this seemingly wasteful duplication of design and supplier selection tasks is, in fact, an attempt by OEMs to retain, sustain and increase their systems integration capabilities in order to maintain their control over not only current but also future vehicle designs, as occurs in the case of aircraft engines (Prencipe, 2003). The publicly expressed strategies of OEMs (e.g. that they wish to focus purely on styling, financing and marketing and withdraw from manufacturing and assembly) are in fact not the actual practice. Few OEMs risk delegating systems integration responsibilities to powerful first-tier suppliers that could take over the design of the whole car.

Hard disk drives – the dynamics of systems integration

Research into the hard disk drive (HDD) industry throws interesting light on the dynamics of systems integration which may have relevance to cars and other high-volume products. As shown earlier by Prencipe (2003), systems integration is not simply a static capability concerned with current product generations, it is also a dynamic capability essential for moving successfully from one product generation to another. This dynamic feature of systems integration capability is borne out in the case of HDDs, where research by Chesbrough (2003b) vividly illustrates what happens to this capability when firms move from one generation to another.

Chesbrough argues that systems integration is not an end stage in the evolution of a technology or a product. At regular, recurring points existing product architectures must be transcended if performance limits are to be overcome and technological progress is to continue. The case of HDD components shows that new product designs can oscillate between modular and integrative states as progress from one design to another occurs. In the modular state there is far more scope for outsourcing backed up by arm's-length systems integration. However, in the integrative state, there is far less scope for component standardisation, the basis of modularity, and a greater proportion of component design and production occurs in (the systems integrator's) house, compared with the relatively steady state where component interfaces are predictable or known. In these new design phases, the systems integrator plays an intense part in defining key components and their interfaces.

Chesbrough (2003) shows that a failure to sustain and nurture different kinds of systems integration capabilities in *all phases* of the product life cycle can result in a modularity trap where lead manufacturers no longer possess the ability to incorporate novel components and new technologies into the product or system. In other sectors, firms such as Microsoft and Intel, aware of this fact, have made substantial investments in systems integration (including product design and architecture, testing equipment, design tools and so on) to avoid these difficulties. In fact, this is probably also the case in cars as Sako's research suggests (Sako, 2003).

In sectors such as disk drives, PCs, TVs, microwave ovens and so on, core product architectures are unlikely to remain in a steady stage indefinitely and this constrains the scope for component standardisation and modularity in production. Choices and strategies differ from firm to firm and affect the nature and degree of vertical integration pursued by major corporations.

In HDDs, Chesbrough (2003) shows that the depth of integrative knowledge in components such as thin-film heads and magnito-resistive (MR) heads[10] evolves over time. In the 1980–86 period, there was a performance advantage to using the thin-film head and especially the components produced in-house. However, by the 1994–95 period, when thin-film heads became widely available and MR heads began to be used, thin-film heads were negatively associated with competitive performance. By contrast, the MR head was becoming crucial to superior performance, with leading firms gaining advantages by supplying MR heads (compared with businesses which outsourced these components). What Chesbrough shows was that during times where modular conditions became feasible and a competent supply chain emerged, competitive advantages were gained from outsourcing in the marketplace. By contrast, when new technology led to new types of components (e.g. MRs), internal integration was a superior strategy.

After a period (in this case circa 1995), the performance of firms producing MR drives internally fell when the detailed knowledge associated with MR became better understood. In the late 1990s MR technology became widely available, independent head makers could then offer products in large volumes at low prices and the intermediate market for MR heads began to expand and mature. Still later,

---

[10] MR heads offered a tenfold improvement over the performance of earlier thin-film technology (Chesbrough, 2003: 183).

a new head technology (GMR, giant magneto-resistive) entered the market, based on IBM's research, and advantages were again seized by the integrated drive manufacturers which had internal capabilities not only in R&D but also in materials and associated electronics. In each phase drive manufacturers with deep systems integration capabilities were better positioned to incorporate new head technology into their HDD product designs.

This particular research shows not only that internal and external systems integration knowledge is a key factor in competitive advantage but also that, in fast-growing, mass-produced goods, an understanding of the integration-modular cycle is an essential part of forward-looking competitive strategy. Even during the modular-outsourcing phase, the HDD example shows that major manufacturers needed to retain an in-house systems integration capability covering a wide range of technologies and disciplines. Some firms' failure to sustain and upgrade these integration technologies resulted in a poorer competitive performance as new product designs entered the marketplace.

Systems integration as a core strategic capability

The evidence above emphasises the role and importance of systems integration as a core strategic capability of the high-technology firm. For example, although a large amount of production does not rely directly on systems integration, much of it depends on infrastructures and capital goods which do depend on the systems integration skills of integrator firms. Probably all of the large technical systems described by Hughes (1998), Bijker et al. (1987) and others depend on the CoPS and services provided by systems integrator firms. Systems integration is therefore a key dimension of modern industrial and infrastructural development and how it differs across industries and infrastructures matters for our understanding of industrial modernisation in both developed and developing countries. Even manufacturers of high-volume products moving into new product generations and new markets will usually enlist systems integrators in the development of the new production processes and equipment they need (e.g. in semiconductor or car production).

Systems integration capability is also important to the productivity of the modern firm. On the one hand, the traditional literature informs us that increasing specialisation and the division of labour improves productivity (Pavitt, 2003). Vertical disintegration can lead to the growth of intermediary markets and the growth of specialist firms which are able to produce inputs more creatively and efficiently than large manufacturers. On the other hand, increasing and more effective integration can also, potentially, improve productivity.[11] Rather than pose the productivity question in this stark fashion, the evidence suggests there are benefits and disadvantages to both specialisation and integration through time, in different kinds of industrial products, and through the life cycle of new generations of the same product.

Systems integration is the primary capability by which lead firms simultaneously manage (and gain the benefits from) the *twin* processes of vertical integration and disintegration, as these change through time for each product and system in question. How these processes are managed technically and organisationally for both current and future generations of technology is very important, as indicated by studies of aircraft engines (Prencipe, 1997) and HDDs (Chesbrough, 2003). Rather than assuming one is always better than the other (i.e. specialisation vs integration), the evidence suggests that system integration capabilities allow firms to decide whether to move up or down stream, integrating some activities and disintegrating others, and which particular systems integration skills are needed to do this. System integrator skills and experience are among the key factors which enable firms to choose where and when to move up and down stream.

Systems integration is also important for theories of industrial organisation. As Dosi et al. (2003) argue, systems integrators and their capabilities provide a means for combining the benefits of vertical integration and specialisation. According to this view, systems integrator firms represent the visible hand of the marketplace deploying purposeful strategies to create supply chains or networks of production, using both market competition and vertical integration to deliver products and systems.

Recent trends in high-value complex products and systems

Research not only shows how firms deploy systems integration capabilities to achieve competitive advantage but also points to major contrasts

---

[11] As Nightingale et al. (2003) argue, the benefits from integration at the firm level include capacity utilisation which can lead to falling costs and prices. Improved capacity utilisation itself can flow from the controlled allocation of resources to specialised services (Nightingale and Poll, 2000).

between CoPS and high-volume goods and components. The cases of cars and HDDs show that as volume products become more complex and technologically sophisticated, systems integration allows various kinds of modular strategies to be undertaken. However, in the case of CoPS , the scope for final product standardisation and modularisation is typically less than in mass-produced goods, whether consumer products (e.g. cars or camcorders) or mass-produced components (such as HDDs or semiconductors).[12] In capital goods, because each product (or batch) is tailor-made for a particular client and because volumes are far lower, the scope for volume production, standardisation and the development of high-volume intermediary markets is more limited.

As we explained in Chapter 2, CoPS tend to remain in the fluid design stage and never reach the mass-production stage. Consequently, for each unit of production the scope for modularity and outsourcing is less than in high-volume consumer goods. However, the importance of systems integration per unit of production in manufacturing is greater than in the case of high-volume goods. In CoPS, systems integration is always a major challenge in production, whereas in mass-produced goods it becomes a routine part of manufacturing during the high-volume stage of the product life cycle.

As a consequence of such generic differences between low-volume, high-cost capital goods and high-volume products, the dynamics of systems integration follows a different path and integrator firms follow different strategies. In the case of CoPS, the scope for integrating high-value services into each product is greater than in the case of most volume-produced goods. As we show in Chapter 8, CoPS suppliers are adopting so-called 'integrated solutions' strategies which deploy systems integration skills across a wide range of services designed to produce a package which meets the specific needs of individual business user organisations and thereby gain competitive advantage in the marketplace.

This trend implies a broadening of the scope of systems integration capability, and core competencies in general, as firms move out from their traditional technology or market base to provide a range of services in partnership with other suppliers or based on new in-house

---

[12] However, while the final product or system is usually tailored for specific customers, there is some scope for modularisation at the components and sub-system level depending on the type of product and the volume of production. Using 'off-the-shelf' components wherever possible is an important feature of competition in areas such as military systems and software packages.

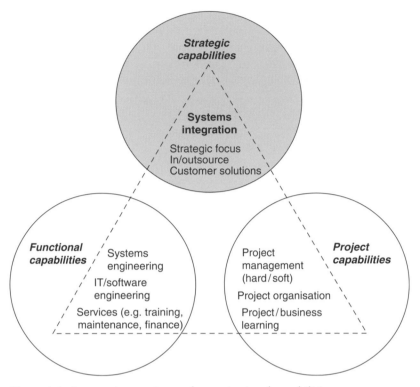

Figure 4.4. Systems integration and organisational capabilities

divisions. This strategy goes against conventional notions of core competence which imply 'sticking to your knitting'.[13] In fact, as firms transform themselves into integrated solutions providers, the ability to integrate non-core services, support and sometimes externally produced hardware becomes critical.

The nature and scope of systems integration continue to evolve in response to changes in the business innovation environment. From its origins as a narrow technical application of the discipline of systems engineering, modern systems integration has grown to embrace new areas of functional expertise including software engineering and various services, such as operations, maintenance, finance and other business functions, that have to be integrated as part of the customer solution. There is a wider appreciation that system requirements cannot be fully

---

[13] See, for example, Hamel and Prahalad (1994).

understood or predicted at the start of a project in an environment driven by changing customer needs, new strategic priorities and evolving technological possibilities. But by developing strong project capabilities, systems integrators can manage some of these risks and uncertainties and take advantage of what has been learned during the life of a project. In effect, systems integration is made up of specific functional and project capabilities discussed in the previous chapter, based primarily on converging systems engineering and project management techniques, as shown in Figure 4.4. This combination of technical and business knowledge, experience and skills feeds into the core strategic systems integration capability of the high-technology project business.

Conclusions

This chapter shows how systems integration has become a core capability of the modern high-technology firm, including all the prime contractors and final integrators of high-technology products, systems, networks and constructs as well as the suppliers of major components, control units and subsystems. For each major project, successful firms need to deploy advanced systems integration skills. Systems integration is no longer solely an engineering or operations task and perhaps never was. Today, it is a strategic business capability with technical, managerial and organisational dimensions. As a capability it permits a supply chain leader to develop and supply new products, coordinate supply networks and continually change its position within the value stream of an industry. The historical path, depth and trajectory of a system integrator's capability help determine a firm's distinctive position in the marketplace and shape its decisions over who to partner with and whether to buy, make or collaborate in design and production. The distinctive strength and dimensions of this capability enable a particular firm to choose whether or not to outsource specific elements of design and production of key components and subsystems to other firms, including other high-technology competitors and specialised small and medium-sized firms. As system scale and complexity increase, systems integration capability becomes more important to both the strategies and operations of a diverse range of high-technology firms.

The chapter shows how the concept of systems integration has evolved and taken on new meanings. Recent evidence (see Chapter 8) suggests that systems integrators of CoPS develop long-term service-intensive partnerships with downstream customers (the users of the systems) in response to new customer demands and, in some cases, privatisation and de-regulation.

Viewed in this way, systems integration is a capability at the heart of the strategic management of the modern high-technology corporation, particularly as firms increasingly becoming the integrators of other firms' outputs.

Recent evidence reveals major differences in the strategies of systems integrators depending on the product in question. In high-volume products such as cars and hard disk drives, firms use their systems integration capabilities to achieve competitive advantage by exploiting upstream component supplier relationships in different ways according to the particular phase of each product life cycle. By contrast, in CoPS, firms are seeking greater profits by focusing on exploiting downstream relationships with system users by integrating services such as maintenance, finance, consultancy and operations within their product offerings. Whether in high-volume products or in low-volume capital goods, systems integration capability underpins the ability of these leading firms to move selectively, and simultaneously, up- and downstream to gain advantages in the marketplace.

The evidence shows that systems integration capabilities underpin the success with which firms optimise the twin, concurrent processes of vertical integration and disintegration. In CoPS those firms which fail to build up the capabilities to integrate services to provide customer-centric solutions are likely to fall behind competitively (see Chapter 8). However, the system user must manage the potential risks and disadvantages of lock-in, as prime contractors offer bundled solutions on a long-term contractual basis. Despite the lack of attention to systems integration in much of the management literature, there can be little doubt that systems integration is today a core capability of the firm and a fascinating perspective for helping to understand the changing landscape of CoPS and other high-technology industries.

5 | *The project-based organisation*

T HIS chapter examines the organisational dimension of project capabilities, focusing on how leading firms structure their productive activities.[1] It asks: What is the most efficient and appropriate organisational structure for firms engaged in project business? In contrast to traditional functional and matrix organisations, the so-called project-based organisation (PBO) has been put forward as a form ideally suited to managing increasing product complexity, especially when confronted with fast-changing markets, the need for cross-functional business expertise and customer-focused innovation. This applies particularly to the high-value, sophisticated capital goods which underpin the production of consumer goods and services. Some studies suggest that the PBO is a natural organisational form for CoPS producers, especially when several partner suppliers are engaged with the user through the various stages of innovation and production (Hobday, 1998; Gann and Salter, 1998).

Research has explored the potential advantages of PBOs, tensions between project- and corporate-level processes and the suitability of PBOs for producing service-enhanced products (Brusoni et al., 1998; Gann and Salter, 1998). Also, focusing on the project rather than the firm, the new product development field points to the benefits of strong projects in NPD, the leadership requirements for 'heavyweight' project teams (Clark and Wheelwright, 1992) and the need for the greater professionalisation of project management as projects assume increasing importance across various high-technology industries (Pinto and Kharbanda, 1995).

Until recently, however, there has been very little research on the scale or pace of diffusion of the PBO form or how the PBO actually operates in practice in the management of CoPS. We know very little about the PBO or how its processes differ from those of the various matrix and

---

[1] This chapter draws upon Hobday (2000).

functional forms of organisation or how disadvantages of the PBO can be overcome in practice. Nor has there been much discussion of the various types of PBO (e.g. large vs small PBOs, single-project vs multiple-project PBOs).

The aim of this chapter is therefore to identify the key features of the PBO by looking in depth at how one-off or unique CoPS projects are managed in one large PBO, comparing this with CoPS produced in a functional division of the same company. The purpose of taking a bottom-up project perspective is to illustrate the dynamics of project structures, processes and performance in the PBO vs a functional organisation. The case evidence illustrates some of the key advantages of the PBO form. However, it also points to major disadvantages of the PBO form for firms executing major projects. In particular, it points to problems of learning in the PBO and tensions which often arise between projects and company-wide processes in PBOs. The chapter shows how some of the problems intrinsic to the PBO form can be overcome in practice.

We begin by examining the importance of projects in CoPS. We provide a working definition of the PBO and develop a simple model to show how the PBO differs from other forms of organisation identified in previous research. We then present the case of Complex Equipment Inc., a producer of highly complex, particle accelerator systems, to illustrate the advantages and disadvantages of the PBO structure, focusing on project processes, problems and performance. In our interpretation of the case evidence we argue that the PBO provides a concurrent and outward-looking approach to project management, while the functional/matrix form embodies a more linear, inward-looking and less flexible approach. Several strategies can be used (e.g. the deployment of a milder form of PBO, called here the 'project-led organisation') to resolve problems inherent in the PBO, including links between projects and corporate strategy as well as company-wide learning difficulties.

The project form in complex products and systems

CoPS are often produced within projects which incorporate prime contractors, systems integrators, users, buyers, other suppliers, small and medium-sized enterprises (SMEs) and sometimes government agencies and regulators. Often, these actors collaborate, taking innovation (e.g. new design) decisions in advance of and during production.

Sometimes users and suppliers engage in co-engineering throughout the production process. Prime contractors and systems integrators tend to manage CoPS projects in temporary multi-firm/user alliances. The project is a focusing device which enables different types of innovation actors to agree the fine detail of CoPS development and production. The project is responsible for realising the market, for coordinating decisions across firms, for enabling buyer involvement and for matching technical and financial resources through time. The project exists to communicate design and architectural knowledge and to combine the distinctive resources, knowhow and skills of the collaborators.

As we saw in Chapters 2 and 3, because CoPS production is in low volumes and oriented to meet the needs of large business users, the project management task is fundamentally different from the mass-production task. The specific CoPS in question will shape the form and nature of the project. In the case of very large engineering constructs, entire project-based industrial structures can be called into being by various stakeholders for the purpose of creating a single product. For example, whereas the Channel Tunnel was a multi-firm project involving hundreds of contractors and several banks, with smaller CoPS (e.g. flight simulators and telecommunications exchanges) much of the project task is carried out within the managerial span of control of a single firm.

In CoPS, design intensity and product complexity lead to many extremely complicated, non-routine and often unique tasks (Hobday and Rush, 1999). Users frequently change their requirements during production, leading to unclear goals, uncertainty in production and unpredictable, unquantifiable risks. Success and failure are multi-faceted and hard to measure. Managers have to proceed from one stage of the project to the next with incomplete information, relying on inputs from other suppliers who may be competitors in other projects. In some cases these challenges have led firms to re-organise their entire business activities along project-based lines, leading to project-based organisational structures.

The nature of the project-based organisation

Definition and key propositions

In contrast to the matrix, functional and other forms, the PBO is one in which the project is the primary unit for production organisation, innovation and competition.[2] Although the PBO is commonly used in manufacturing enterprise, it is also deployed in other organisations (public and private), including the legal profession, consultancy firms, marketing, the film industry and advertising. While a project can be defined as any activity with a defined set of resources, goals and time limit (e.g. for information technology or new materials), within a PBO the project is the primary business mechanism for coordinating and integrating all the main business functions of the firm (e.g. production, R&D, engineering, NPD, marketing, personnel and finance).

Within a pure PBO (i.e. an organisation in which no other form is present), major projects will embody most, if not all, of the business functions normally carried out by departments of functional and matrix organisations. In some cases the project involves a consortium of companies (e.g. Sematech, Airbus, the Channel Tunnel and the Millennium Dome). In other PBOs, much or all of the project may be carried out within the boundaries of a single company. Because core business processes are organised within projects rather than functional departments, the PBO is an alternative to the matrix, where business functions are carried out both within projects and along functional lines. In the PBO, the knowledge, capabilities and resources of the firm are built up through the execution of major projects.

Project managers within the PBO typically have very high status and direct control over business functions, personnel and other resources. Project managers and directors are senior to resource coordinators (the nearest equivalent to the functional manager in the PBO), whose role is to support the needs of projects and project managers and, sometimes, to coordinate business functions across various projects (e.g. technical, human and financial resources for project bidding, management, systems engineering and so on).

Because the project is a temporary organisational form, the PBO is inherently flexible and reconfigurable. This contrasts with the anti-innovation bias of large integrated, hierarchical organisations described by Williamson (1975) and Teece (1996) and the core rigidities identified by Leonard-Barton (1992).

Within the PBO, a project is often a major business endeavour and the normal mechanism for creating, responding to and executing new

---

[2] We use the term PBO rather than project-based firm as a single firm may deploy both project-based divisions and functional divisions (as in the case example).

business opportunities. Each project is likely to involve a specific well-defined product and one or a few identified customers. In many cases, the customer (often a user or owner-operator) will be closely and directly engaged in primary innovation and production processes, as each project will tend to be critical to the business functioning, performance and profitability of the user. The PBO is widespread in traditional industries (e.g. construction, shipbuilding and major capital projects), industries which have been regenerated through new technologies (e.g. aerospace and telecommunications), newly emerging industries (e.g. information and communication technologies) and many other examples of business-to-business, high-technology, high-value capital goods.

In principle, the PBO is not suited to the mass production of consumer goods, where specialisation along functional lines confers learning, scale and marketing advantages. However, some large multi-product firms embody both PBO and functional divisions (or strategic business units) to deal with different types of products, technologies and markets (e.g. producers of both telecommunications handsets and exchanges, such as Ericsson and Nokia).

PBOs organise their structures, strategies and capabilities around the needs of projects which often cut across conventional industrial and firm boundaries. In CoPS industries, there are many different categories of PBO, ranging from large prime contractors, which specialise in project management and systems integration, to tiny specialised subcontractors which supply tailored components, software or services. Any one project may combine these groups in a variety of roles, with the same firm acting as prime contractor in some projects and subcontractor in others. Not all firms within a project are necessarily PBOs. Also, PBOs can range from firms servicing one single project to firms which execute many hundreds of projects at any one time (e.g. in construction).

The structures and business processes of PBOs are likely to be shaped by the changing profile of projects, especially their size, complexity and duration. Some PBOs (e.g. in construction) are likely to derive most of their income from large projects over which they exercise little direct span of control (Gann, 1993). In other cases, firms may direct and control particular projects, largely from within the firm, as noted earlier. Major new projects become central innovation events in some CoPS industries, giving rise to new business opportunities and novel technological trajectories.

Previous research on the project form

Various bodies of research help inform our understanding of the position, nature and advantages of the PBO. At the project level, research on NPD has long recognised the importance of the project for integrating business functions and responding to complex technical challenges for the purpose of developing new products. Clark and Wheelwright (1992), for example, describe four basic types of organisational structure for NPD: (1) functional; (2) lightweight project structure; (3) heavyweight project structure; and (4) project-based. In conventional functional/lightweight project structures, project managers (PMs) tend to be junior to functional managers and have no direct control over resources. In the heavyweight project approach, functions such as marketing, finance and production tend to be coordinated by managers across project lines, but PMs have high status and direct control over financial resources and people.

In their analysis of the influence of management structure on project success, Larson and Gobeli (1989) show how both project management structure and other variables such as new technology, project complexity, managerial competence, top management support, project size and well-defined objectives impact on project success. Pinto and Prescott (1988) analyse how critical success factors vary over the life cycle of projects, while Pinto and Covin (1989) show how such factors depend on the type of product and activity in question. Shenhar (1993) provides insights into the importance of new knowledge in project risk and uncertainty, comparing low- with high-technology projects. Dvir and Lechler (2004) show why it is vital to change plans effectively during projects to meet changing user needs and not stick to original plans.

Focusing on the benefits of the project form, some management scholars have argued that projects and project management will become increasingly important due to greater technical and product complexity, shortening time-to-market windows and the need for cross-functional integration and fast response to changing client needs (Pinto and Kharbanda, 1995). It is certainly reasonable to assume that as market change, risk and uncertainty increase, the project form will grow in importance in a wide range of industries and tasks.

At the firm level, traditional innovation studies have long recognised the advantages of flexible project-based organisational forms. Burns and Stalker (1961) made the classic distinction between organic and mechanistic organisational forms, arguing that if a stable routine environment prevailed and the market was fairly predictable, firms could reap advantage from mechanistic, functional organisational forms with clearly defined job descriptions, stable operational boundaries and standardised methods of working. However, in the case of rapidly changing technological and market conditions, open and flexible (organic) styles of organisation and management are required which are able to link functions such as R&D and marketing. Building on the work of Burns and Stalker, Mintzberg (1979) points out that appropriate organisational forms are contingent on factors such as market, task and technology. He describes five basic organisational forms: the machine bureaucracy with highly centralised control systems, suited to a stable environment; the divisional form suited to mass-production efficiency; the professional bureaucracy made up of flat organisational structures, useful for delegating complex, professional tasks (e.g. in universities); the simple or entrepreneurial structure, valuable for its informality and flexibility; and the adhocracy, which is a temporary project team structure, suited to complex tasks and turbulent and uncertain markets.[3]

More recent research draws attention to how temporary forms of collaboration are widespread in project-based enterprises such as the film industry, software and new media (DeFillippi and Arthur, 1998; Grabher, 2002b). This work, like this chapter, shows how temporary and flexible project-based organisations provide an important way of integrating resources from inside and outside the firm. Research also shows how projects are situated within both an historical context and an external environment which shapes project path and performance (Engwall, 2003).

---

[3] Similarly, Teece (1996) proposes six categories of firm: (1) stand-alone entrepreneur inventor; (2) multi-product integrated hierarchy; (3) high-flex, Silicon Valley type; (4) virtual corporation; (5) conglomerate; and (6) alliance enterprise. Taking an historical perspective, Miles and Snow (1986) argue that organisations have evolved from the owner-manager of the eighteenth century to the vertical organisation of the mid-nineteenth century, through to the divisionalised and matrix organisational structures suited to the mass production of industrial goods in the mid-twentieth century. They argue that a new form (the dynamic network) has recently emerged in high-technology production. In the network, large and small firms collaborate, responding to fast-changing market needs. Key business functions such as product design, R&D, manufacturing and distribution are performed by independent firms which cooperate and are linked by brokers who provide information to network members and coordinate overall operations. In Miles and Snow's formulation, brokers and partners are similar to Teece's virtual firm and alliance enterprise, respectively.

A simple positioning framework for the PBO

As we saw in Chapter 3, in order to understand the relationship between the PBO and other types of organisation, Galbraith (1971, 1973) describes a range of alternatives from pure functional form through to pure product or project form, where management structures are centred upon each product or project (equivalent to the PBO). Building on Galbraith's work, Larson and Gobeli (1987, 1989) describe three distinct types of matrix. First is the functional matrix, where the PM is confined to coordinating resources, monitoring progress and reporting to one or more functional managers. Second is the balanced matrix, where responsibilities and authority for each project are shared between functional managers and PMs. The third is the product (or project) matrix, where the project manager has authority over personnel, finance and other resources. In addition, as our research shows, the pure product/project-based form is an extreme form where the business is organised solely around product/project lines.

Interpreting the above literature, Figure 5.1 provides a description of six ideal-type organisational forms ranging from the pure functional form (Type A) to the pure project form (Type F). The various functional departments of the organisation (e.g. marketing, finance, human resources, engineering, R&D and manufacturing) are represented by F1 to F5, while notional CoPS projects are represented by P1 to P5. Type B is a functionally oriented matrix, with weak project coordination (FMD, as described in the case study below). Type C is a balanced matrix with stronger project management authority. Type D is a project matrix where PMs are of equal status to functional managers.

Beyond the project matrix lies a form not identified in the literature (Type E) but one which we identify below in our case study. Here we call it a 'project-led organisation', in which the needs of projects outweigh the functional influence on decision making and representation to senior management, but some coordination across project lines occurs. Finally, Type F is the pure PBO, illustrated by PBD in the case study below. Here there is no formal functional coordination across project lines; the entire organisation is dedicated to one or more CoPS projects and business processes are coordinated within the projects.

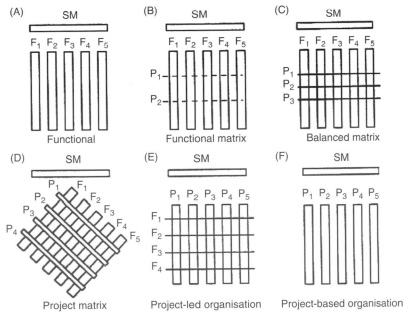

Figure 5.1. Positioning the project-based organisation

Key:
F_1–F_5 = various functional departments of the organisation (e.g. marketing, finance, human resources, engineering, manufacturing, R&D)
P_1–P_5 = major projects within the organisation (e.g. CoPS projects)
SM = senior management
Note: The number of functions and project will vary according to the organisation in question. Various permutations are used here for illustration.

Figure 5.1 helps to contrast the various forms of organisation available and to highlight those most suited for different types of CoPS, accepting that a mixed organisational structure is possible even within a single business unit. Forms A to C are unsuitable for managing CoPS because they are not appropriate for complex projects in an uncertain, risky and changing environment. CoPS projects require super-heavyweight professional project managers (or directors), capable of integrating both commercial and technical business functions within the project and building strong lines of external communication with both the client (often the source of the innovation idea) and other collaborating companies. These external innovation actors typically have different goals, structures and cultures and the task of the CoPS project director is to skilfully negotiate a path towards successful completion.

The pure PBO is probably best suited for large innovative projects and single-project firms, where resources have to be combined and shared with other firms in the project (the multi-firm CoPS project). The PBO is a form suitable for meeting innovative needs, responding to uncertainty, coping with emerging properties, responding to changing client requirements and learning in real time. By contrast, the PBO is weak where the functional matrix is strong: in coordinating resources and capabilities across projects, executing routine production and engineering tasks, achieving economies of scale and meeting the needs of mass markets.

More broadly, the framework implies that in choosing an appropriate organisational form the nature, scale and complexity of the product must be considered. With a balance of small batch, CoPS and mass-production products, organisational choices become messy, complex and dynamic. Mistakes can be costly. As the product mix evolves, organisations need to change in order to respond to product market needs.

Gaps in the literature

Although Galbraith (1971) and others provide useful tools for positioning the PBO in relation to other organisational forms, they fall short of examining the PBO itself and do not analyse its advantages and disadvantages. Much of the above literature tends to assume products are being developed for the marketplace whereas CoPS are usually transacted with the user (and other suppliers) in unique combinations and rarely, if ever, transacted in an arm's-length market setting.

Similarly, although studies of NPD and project performance help disentangle the many facets of project success and failure, they do not explore the PBO, nor do they tend to distinguish between complex capital goods and mass-produced products. Nor does the project success literature tend to examine the changing nature of projects through time. This issue is especially important for CoPS projects which involve several outside innovation partners in different ways through the various stages of the project.

To contribute to an understanding of innovation management in CoPS, the next section illustrates how one PBO deploys its resources to create and deliver single complex products. By comparing the progress of CoPS projects in the PBO and functional matrix forms, the case shows how well suited the PBO is for creating and executing large and risky CoPS projects. However, the case also highlights the difficulties PBOs face in capturing and transferring knowledge and learning from one project to another, which is examined in depth in Chapter 7.

Case study of Complex Equipment Inc.

Research approach
The purpose of the case study is to assess CoPS project performance and processes and to look at the nature, strengths and weaknesses of the PBO in comparison with the functional form through the lens of two major projects, one in a PBO division and one in a functional division. The case also examines how PBO disadvantages can be overcome in practice.

The case study focuses on Complex Equipment Inc., a large German-owned pan-European firm which employs around 4,000 people and produces a wide range of advanced, high-cost scientific, industrial and medical equipment.[4] For some years, the company had experienced serious problems (delays, cost overruns and customer dissatisfaction) in producing CoPS within its functional matrix division (called here FMD) in one of its strategic business units which produced both CoPS and small batch, simpler products. In another strategic business unit, reporting to the same senior management, a pure project-based division (called PBD) had been converted from a matrix organisation to deal solely with large CoPS projects.[5] In our research with the firm (the method is discussed in Appendix C) we examined two similar projects (termed Project P in PBD and Project F in FMD) in order to review and compare project processes, problems and performance and to draw lessons for both organisations. The CoPS in question was an experimental form of synchrotron particle accelerator which is used in submicron

---

[4] The name of the company, as well as project names, have been changed to protect confidentiality.
[5] PBD corresponds to Type F in Figure 5.1, while FMD corresponds to Type B. The firm provides an unusual opportunity to compare a PBO with a functional matrix organisation in a single company, with the same company culture and senior management.

semiconductor R&D and other scientific applications. The price of each unit was in the order of $10 million and the duration of both projects was around 18 months.

Organisational structure

FMD was run as a functional matrix with lightweight PMs. Projects were resourced by the heads of the functional departments. Although PMs were nominally in charge of projects they had no direct staff or control over resources, nor a regular reporting mechanism into senior management. Within the matrix, PMs for CoPS reported to one of the functional managers (usually engineering). Traditionally, FMD was heavily biased towards the needs of the functional departments and standard product lines produced in small batches. However, increasingly CoPS were being produced in FMD, leading to problems, as noted earlier.

In contrast to FMD, PBD had been organised along project-based lines for about two years, with project managers in direct control of project resources, team building and project outcomes. The PBO had been an experimental move and was widely viewed as a success. As noted earlier, the directors of Complex Equipment Inc. wished to learn the lessons for the rest of the company and in particular wanted to assess whether or not to implement a PBO to resolve CoPS problems at FMD.

Project management and leadership

Because of its functional orientation, the PM of Project F (as with other PMs in FMD) had little direct control over project resources, nor a heavyweight representation into senior management. This lightweight PM structure had been introduced some years earlier to run alongside the functional organisation to deal with CoPS projects.

Given the number of functional departments (and bosses) in FMD, each with standard reporting systems and procedures, a wide range of reporting requirements and sometimes conflicting demands were placed on the PM for Project F. There were five main functional departments: engineering, manufacturing, marketing, finance and human resources. Reporting into the five departments absorbed a great deal of time and energy, leading to a reactive rather than a proactive stance towards risk, client management, product design, manufacture and so on. Customer relations were also difficult, with the PM looking to functional managers for answers to technical and schedule questions raised by the client, but with little direct contact between the functional managers and the client. This led to delays in dealing with client problems and also to some confusion. In some instances, the two main sets of client demands (commercial and technical) were in conflict (e.g. new technical specifications were called for alongside demands to maintain costs and keep to schedules). These demands led to difficult negotiations with the functional managers and frequently placed the PM for FMD in a difficult position with the client.

By contrast, in PBD the heavyweight PM had direct control over resources and team personnel, as well as a strong and direct representation into senior management (the company directors). The PBD PM for Project P was more senior to other staff in PBD and on equal terms with functional managers in FMD. The PM for Project P dealt directly with the client, having both control over and responsibility for all technical and commercial issues.

PBD/Project P was particularly strong on the intangible, informal activities essential to project success in uncertain environments (e.g. project management, close customer relations, good communications, open, honest meetings and mutual respect among team members). In PBD/P a good level of communication and trust was built up with subcontractors, both large and small. The PBD/P team was as flexible and responsive to changes in specification, risks and so on as one would hope from a well-managed PBO. However, there were problems not only within the project but also in the wider organisation. These were proving difficult to address within the PBO structure.

Team identity and coherence
The FMD/Project F team felt that the project was under-resourced, given its size, complexity and development nature, and that insufficient numbers of full-time technical staff worked on the project at any given time. Most individuals worked on more than one project (some as many as six) and few, apart from the PM, felt any identity with Project F. Some team members were under great pressure and two resigned from the company, partly due to the demands of Project F. Overall, the project suffered from weak team coherence, poor team spirit and fragmented communications. This was due in part to initial project under-resourcing, itself a reflection

of the weak bargaining position of the PM who was unable to insist upon a dedicated team within the functionally oriented organisational structure. These problems were seen as resulting from the functional structure and had occurred before in CoPS projects in FMD, leading to the decision to consider introducing a PBO structure similar to PBD.

By contrast, in PBD/Project P the team felt they had achieved a highly effective and professional approach to project management and implementation, with strong team coherence and close identity with Project P. Most of the team were dedicated to Project P and all felt allegiance to it. Team members viewed project leadership and management as strong and internal communications proceeded well.

Client and client management

The FMD/Project F team had developed poor and confused relations with their client and felt 'unlucky to have a bad client'. Early on in the project's development, the PM had reacted to new client demands for changes in specification by attempting to please the customer. However, the PM did not have the time or authority to carefully negotiate full costings or rescheduling, or to carry out the detailed internal planning needed. This had resulted in unclear business relations. Conflicts developed as team members felt their customer was unwilling or unable to divulge essential information on detailed requirements or to sign off pieces of work when requested to. They also felt let down by their PM and senior management who did not seem able to sort out the difficulties. To them, seemingly arbitrary changes in specification were called for, causing delays in delivery and severe technical problems.

However, official client procedures and behaviours on FMD/Project F were not dissimilar to those on PBD/Project P, coming from a different division in the same buyer organisation. FMD/Project F team members reacted defensively to client demands, putting problems down to internal customer politics and commercial inexperience on the client's part. Project F members perceived requests for changes as placing unreasonable demands on the project team who were already stretched and under-resourced. In the absence of clear rules of engagement, expectations on both sides of FMD/Project F were difficult to manage and potential risks materialised to the detriment of the project. Team members felt that the responsibility for dealing with these issues rested with the various functional managers (e.g. manufacturing for delivery, finance for costs and engineering for specification changes), while some senior functional managers felt that the PM should have dealt with these problems or highlighted them earlier. All agreed that client relations were difficult and unclear.

By contrast, PBD/Project P members felt they were fortunate to have a 'good client', who was willing to entrust design and development decisions to them. This was partly due to the involvement of PBD engineers in an early design study for the client which specified some of the system. However, the team had also developed a shared business 'negotiation' mentality, now common in PBD. This assumed, for example, that any requests for changes to specification had to be negotiated between the PM and the client, fully costed and, if necessary, reflected in extended delivery schedules.

Although this approach had developed informally in PBD (no explicit systems or detailed contractual arrangements existed over and above those in FMD), the negotiated approach had become standard practice because it helped meet the needs of engineers, especially when confronted with large complex projects where frequent iterations with the client were needed. The rules (e.g. on specification changes) were alluded to in the contract (as in the case of FMD/Project F) but also, and more importantly, communicated through the tone of day-to-day channels of communication at all levels of the project. This, in turn, required team ownership of the project and good internal communications. By establishing project ground rules at the initial bid stage, changes to design, day to day misunderstandings and other uncertainties could be dealt with in a systematic, professional fashion.

In PBD/Project P most of the liaison with the client was carried out or coordinated by the PM who was able to build a good working partnership. As the project progressed, more team members became involved directly with the client as the PM entrusted particular team members, at various stages, to take actions with members of the customer's team. As a result, Project P team members felt that relations with the client were orderly and understood.

Risk management

Three types of risk were identified in both divisions: (a) risks wholly outside the control of the project (external); (b) risks wholly within the ambit of the project (internal); and (c) risks subject to negotiation/internalisation (negotiated risks).

In FMD/Project F the PM was unable to establish a proactive approach to risk, particularly in relation to risks inherent in customer–supply relations (e.g. major changes to specification), common in CoPS. Organisationally, the PM felt he 'was being torn limb from limb' by the various demands of the functional bosses, unhappy team members and the client. As a result, the PM was unable to establish an orderly business framework for managing client relations from the outset. Failing to meet changing needs, the project team had developed defensive relations with the client. The team members were unable to manage internal and external risks well and allowed negotiated risks to emerge. Because of the lack of team coherence and resources, the PM and senior engineers were unable to visit the customer or key suppliers regularly to avoid risks (e.g. delays in the delivery of subsystems). Because management systems (e.g. internal design reviews) were not carried out regularly, as they should have been, problems of risk were intensified by the failure to share information in either formal or informal meetings.

By contrast, partly due to its tightly integrated project structure, PBD/Project P members managed internal and external risks well and increased their control over negotiated risks. The PM and senior engineers paid regular visits to key suppliers and helped to resolve delays in the delivery of components and subsystems. The team avoided risks by sharing information in their formal two-weekly review meetings, informal meetings and conversations, and regular client and customer visits.

The business approach made possible by the super heavyweight project structure allowed PBD/Project P to deal with two major sources of external risk (supplier and client relations), allowing space for dealing with unexpected events and scope for internalising negotiated risks. The Project P team felt pleased with the informal way most problems were handled, the only formal risk management tools being a two-page weekly reporting form and the two-weekly project meetings. In the event, despite some problems, Project P progressed well and was delivered on schedule, although slightly over budget.

On the negative side, senior management at Complex Equipment Inc. felt that they 'did not really know enough about PBD/Project P', given its importance as a new product line for the company as a whole. This had also been the case for other projects carried out in PBD. The lack of regular reporting into senior management created some tensions between project progress and corporate-wide strategies and goals. Company directors felt a degree of project isolation in PBD had created risks in terms of overall marketing strategy and business coordination. Their solution was to set up more regular reporting with PMs along the lines of FMD.

Formal and informal tools and procedures

Both FMD and PBD had fairly typical tools and systems mandated by the company for bid review, cost and risk management, internal design and specification change management. In both organisations there were formal systems for project recording, controlling and reporting. In FMD detailed procedures were laid down by the functional departments, each with their different goals and needs, leading to a heavy administrative load for FMD projects.

In FMD/Project F actual procedures ('what happened in practice') diverged considerably from formal tools and company best-management practices ('what should have happened'), as reflected in senior management views and contained in a company toolbook and quality manual. Procedures for the early bid stage, internal design reviews, reporting to senior management, cost tracking and control, progress monitoring and risk management were officially in place but were not applied. This was put down to the absence of a coherent team, under-resourcing, time pressures, weak incentives for team members (who reported to functional bosses) and the 'firefighting' mode of the PM and team members. Although Project F was a fairly extreme case, the divergences between formal and actual procedures occurred in other CoPS projects in FMD. Tools and reporting were seen as an added bureaucratic burden, unhelpful in the managing of the project.

By contrast, in PBD/Project P the PM was in charge of implementing company tools and procedures. The 'leanness' and flexibility of formal tools and systems within PBD, which involved no functional reporting or negotiating with departmental bosses, meant that tools and procedures were seen as helpful in getting tasks completed, although again there were some differences between official procedures and real practices, particularly in terms of the informality in the use of tools. Some tools were deployed very sparingly indeed and there were differences in the ways PMs within PBD used company tools and followed procedures. PBD managers, over the past two years, had modified and simplified company tools and systems to suit their project needs and successfully resisted the introduction of more elaborate formal management tools and systems.

Organisation-wide learning and coordination

In FMD, organisational learning (involving informal knowledge sharing, training, reviews, personnel development and technical leadership) was centred on the functional departments. In this area FMD as a whole performed well. Younger engineers felt that they had good overall technical leadership from the senior engineers and functional managers. They could see a career ladder within the organisation. Senior engineers had incentives and resources to recruit, train and retain new, younger engineers and technicians for their departments. Much of the knowledge sharing and communications occurred in informal settings, although there were training programmes and official seminars and meetings. Informally, groups of engineers exchanged tacit knowledge and problem-solving tips through narratives in what are sometimes called 'communities of practice' (Brown and Duguid, 1991). In this important area, FMD outperformed PBD.

In PBD, despite good individual project performance, in the previous two years the high-pressured work environment had left little space for formal training or staff development, either in technical or in commercial areas. It was apparent that many of the formal and informal activities associated with organisational learning and improvement (e.g. post-project reviews, technical mentoring and informal communications) were not being performed. Lessons learned from particular projects were not shared formally because there were no structures or incentives for cross-project learning or communications. It had become hard to learn from project to project, leading to worries within PBD over its long-term effectiveness. The learning silos (represented in FMD by functional departments) were absent in PBD's pure PBO.

The post-project review (PPR) was viewed by the company as an important mechanism for learning from project to project. The official procedure called for a PPR involving all major project contributors, from the bid stage onwards. The PPR should have operated in PBD as a mechanism for capturing lessons (good and bad), sorting out problems (e.g. closing the loop between bid-stage decisions and project outcomes) and building up wider company communications (involving project outsiders and senior managers). However, few PPRs had occurred in the past two years due to work pressures and the lack of structure and incentives within PBD.

At least three other problems of learning and coordination were evident in PBD. The first concerned technical leadership. In FMD, this role was played by senior engineers and department managers. Younger and newer recruits in PBD were concerned with career development and professional progress because of the dispersion of technical leadership across projects. Insecurity was highest towards the end of a project when staff were not sure 'where they would go to next'. Related to this was the lack of incentives for human resource development. The PBD structure had reduced the incentive for senior engineers to bring on younger engineers as they had done under the functional matrix. In FMD, by contrast, there were concrete incentives to groom young staff to improve the performance of various departments, but these incentives did not exist in PBD and no senior individuals had responsibility for this task. The functional departments served this role in FMD, allowing space (and time) for the sharing of knowledge and experience.

A second problem was revealed in some of the small projects undertaken in PBD. Although the organisation was suited to large complex projects, it was overly elaborate for dealing with small routine projects – 'using a sledgehammer to crack a nut' as one engineer put it. In particular, there was no real need for a senior project manager and a dedicated team to control smaller, especially more routine projects. Treating smaller projects as if they were major projects had led to heavy overheads and too much bureaucracy in some cases.

A third problem concerned cross-project integration and senior management coordination and control. Some major projects had 'gone their own way' in PBD and it had become difficult for senior company managers at HQ to keep properly informed and maintain some degree of control and consistency across the activities of PBD. Systems had come to vary somewhat from project to project as PMs exercised their discretion over which tools to apply and how to apply them. The basic minimum of formal controls (e.g. for risk management, cost and design review) was not always adequately applied, as happened in the case of PBD/Project P at the bid stage. Overall, senior management felt that control of PBD had become difficult, especially as the organisation had grown.

Project performance

In FMD/Project F the initial underestimation of costs produced a knock-on effect throughout the project, leading to under-resourcing and, in particular, insufficient full-time staff. As a result, there were major technical problems, the project came in substantially over cost and delivery was late. Both the client and FMD's senior management considered Project F a failure.

There were various causes of the poor performance. In FMD, PMs did not report directly and regularly to the senior management team to share problems, responsibilities and so on. In Project F this led to the initial under-resourcing which prevented both team building and the development of a good team spirit. It was also difficult to rectify the problem later, given the PMs' relatively low status in the organisation. FMD lacked the clear processes and procedures needed for controlling large complex projects. The way the project was managed exacerbated problems with the customer and placed unreasonable demands on team members. Because team coherence and commitment were low, risks materialised and problems were difficult to address. All in all, the functionally oriented structure of FMD was not suited for either the setting up or the execution of CoPS projects. The heavy functional bias was appropriate for small projects and more standard product lines. In scaling up from simple to more complex products, the organisation needed a heavier PM structure with direct representation into senior management.

By contrast, PBD/Project P was considered to be a major technical success and delivered ahead of schedule. However, as noted earlier, the project was completed slightly over budgeted costs and with a lower level of profit than expected. The costs of two subsystems had been underestimated. Neither subsystem posed special technical or supply challenges, but one probable cause was the informality of PBD's bid stage/costing process. Team members felt that a slightly more systematic bid process involving more specialists from other projects would have helped avoid bid/costing problems. Also, despite good relations with suppliers, some items were delivered late. The PM and senior engineers dealt with these problems by visiting supplier sites and risks to the project schedule were averted. Again, the team felt that a little more formality in dealing with suppliers could have avoided some of these problems.

Overall, problems on Project P were fairly minor and both the senior management and the customer were pleased with end results. However, there were wider concerns about long-term learning and technical developments, as discussed earlier.

Organisational strategies and solutions

In order to overcome the mismatch between organisational structure and the needs of large projects, FMD's management decided to move to a heavyweight project matrix structure, maintaining a functional matrix for standard lines (a move from B to D in Figure 5.1). The difficult task of allocating resources between functions and projects was to be undertaken at senior management level, with project directors responsible for negotiating for and controlling resources. Deploying a heavyweight project structure for CoPS was viewed as more suitable than either the existing functional matrix or the pure PBO, given the need to cope with large numbers of standard items. For major projects, heavyweight PMs would report directly into senior management on a regular basis at the same level as the functional managers.

Recognising the burden placed on PMs in CoPS, FMD also decided for very large projects to split the PM function into two with a commercial PM and a technical project engineer (PE), a practice followed in some projects in PBD. The rationale was to increase the scope for negotiating with the client ('good guy/bad guy' routines) and to try to overcome the need for PMs 'with a super-human range of talents' as one director put it. The PM would have overall business control of the project, including client relations, progress schedules, tools and procedures, team meetings and so on. The project engineer (PE), of equal status to the PM, would be responsible for all technical issues, including specifications, detailed design, construction, subsystem interfacing and so on. The PE would deal with the client on most technical issues but would avoid commercial decisions, leaving those to the PM.

The dual PM/PE system has both advantages and disadvantages. For the system to work effectively, the PM and PE have to be willing and capable partners, able to share in strategy, decision making and team building. In some organisations the system becomes accepted as the natural way of doing business. Sometimes, but not always, the PM is also an engineer (either practising or by background). Regardless of background, the PM is responsible for mastering all the skills of managing projects effectively and efficiently. In some companies, the PM organises commercial training for other team members (e.g. on negotiation skills, new tools, and risk and time management).

In addition, the PM function was to become more professionalised in FMD, not only through training but through the fostering of a commercial PM ethos which values and rewards PMs. Courses on team building and project management were being arranged and individuals were being encouraged to engage in various PM associations and introduce standard PM tools and procedures (e.g. for scheduling, team building, bidding, cost control, risk management and negotiation methods), along the lines also being followed by PBD. It was decided not to introduce highly elaborate PM tools (e.g. for risk management, design walkthroughs and cost control), following the lessons of PBD. However, as with PBD, minimum formal processes were mandated. For example, risk management was being built into the design review process so that problems could be communicated, discussed and shared among project staff.

Given the composition of FMD, most PMs would be engineers or scientists who had demonstrated the aptitude, skills and desire to be PMs. People with flair in this direction were to be encouraged to undertake commercial PM responsibilities, sometimes alongside their technical careers, and were to be rewarded for doing so. Alongside the new structure, much more attention would be given to developing a systematic, professional approach to managing client relations and needs, including training in how to establish a business framework, manage expectations and negotiate, again along the lines of PBD. Complex and changing client needs are not unusual in CoPS, therefore a pre-emptive, proactive approach is essential to minimising risks.

Turning to the case of PBD, to address the organisational learning problem, PBD's management decided to establish a programme to build space for learning, training, staff development and PPRs, and to make time to reflect on important technical and business issues (e.g. new technical developments, project lessons learned, time management and cross-project design reviews). To promote the long-term productivity and effectiveness of PBD, younger team members would be encouraged to learn from more experienced staff and to share in some of the tacit knowledge (see Chapter 7) locked up in the heads of otherwise busy, more experienced people.

Although learning went on informally at the within-project level, PBD decided to structure and enable learning to occur in more formal, between-project settings (e.g. regular cross-project meetings, project management workshops, off-site training and special technical seminars with outside speakers). To ensure this occurred, PBD put specific people in charge of coordinating particular themes and programmes across projects, forming a weak functional line across the major projects of the unit. Other functional tasks were being considered to help coordinate subcontractor relations and risk management procedures. The aim was to ensure consistency in project approaches, to share best practices more widely and to keep senior management at HQ better informed through improved reporting procedures. This amounted to a step back to a project-led organisation, but fell short of a project matrix (a shift from F to E in Figure 5.1).

To provide incentives for senior people to give up project time (e.g. to bring on new recruits) a formal mentoring programme was set up with incentives for good performance. PBD also re-structured desk layouts and coffee spaces to enable more informal communications. Senior management recognised that moves in this direction depended on more resources being made available and some degree of organisational slack in the system. However, the good performance and profitability of PBD justified this long-term investment in learning.

Managing PBOs – case study interpretation

This section draws analytical lessons from the case study, interpreting the evidence in relation to project coordination, especially for CoPS. The aim is to provide a framework for interpreting the various organisational choices and strategies available to foster innovation in high-technology capital goods, networks, constructs and systems.

Interpreting the organisational strategies of PBD and FMD

As noted above, FMD was initially a Type B organisation (see Figure 5.1), but this led to extreme problems in project management and coordination, both internally and externally with the client and suppliers. In response to the problems, FMD decided to convert to a project matrix (Type D) with a heavyweight PM structure in order to allow CoPS to be managed more effectively within the organisation.

However, it decided not to move to a PBO (Type F) in order to retain the functional departments needed for standard product lines and batch production. The difficult task of allocating resources between functions and CoPS projects could then be resolved by functional and project managers of equal status, with their senior management (in this case company directors). The directors favoured this arrangement because the emerging CoPS were important new business opportunities and needed to be understood and supported at the highest level. Regular, direct feedback on the progress of these projects was vital to the company.

By contrast PBD, organised as a Type F pure PBO, had achieved a very good record at the individual project level, but the overall organisation was concerned for its long-run performance in areas such as technical leadership, organisation-wide learning and communications. PBD's response was to move back from a pure PBO to a project-led organisation (Type E) in which PMs retain the most senior positions but appoint new resource coordinators along functional or generic task lines which cut across project interests and incentives. This strategy was adopted in PBD to stimulate organisational learning and to provide incentives and resources for greater technical leadership. In PBD task force managers could resolve specific problems and help coordinate, monitor and improve performance across the whole organisation.

From linear to concurrent models of project management

To illustrate the management advantages of the PBO for CoPS, Figure 5.2 contrasts the PM task within a functional matrix – with the weak PM structure (Type B) deployed in FMD – with that of a pure PBO (Type F) deployed in PBD. Figure 5.2A shows the position of the weak PM within the functional matrix, involving multiple lines of communication, control and command, and various department managers.

The PM function embodies a linear or sequential model of project management, in which the project passes through various stages and departments in turn. The model also treats the client and suppliers as external to the project. The PM has to perform a highly complex internal task of balancing the various internal interests and meeting the different demands (e.g. in terms of reporting and quality control) of the departments. Similarly, there are many lines of communication with team members on the project who also report (primarily) to

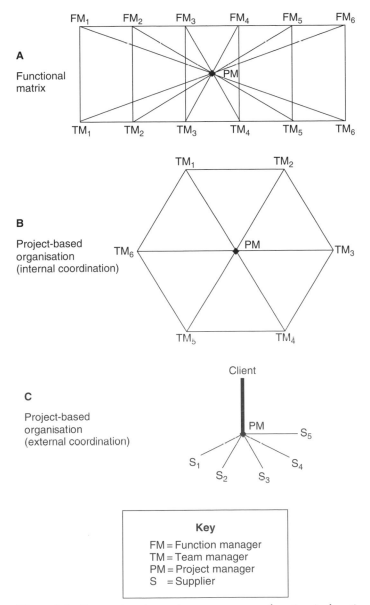

A

Functional matrix

B

Project-based organisation (internal coordination)

C

Project-based organisation (external coordination)

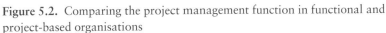

Key

FM = Function manager
TM = Team manager
PM = Project manager
S = Supplier

Figure 5.2. Comparing the project management function in functional and project-based organisations

departmental managers, to whom they owe their career allegiance, and to other project managers (some in FMD worked on four or five projects).

PMs face similar complexities and difficulties in external coordination. To reply to customer requests they often have to gain information and commitments from engineering, purchasing and planning departments. The larger and more complex the project, the more difficult the task of keeping the client informed and responding to requests for changes from the customer.

By contrast, Figure 5.2B shows the position of the PM in a PBO in relation to the specialist functions within the project. The PM is the main line of communication and can exercise control to coordinate and integrate specialists and functions in creative new ways, focusing on the needs of the project. Because there are few internal lines of command and communication to interfere with project objectives, the internal coordination task becomes simpler and clearer.

Similarly, on the external front, clear, strong lines of command and communications can be built up with the client (Figure 5.2C). In principle, the PM is able to quickly assess and react to changes in client needs and learn from feedback from the client and major component suppliers. The PM has both the responsibility and the power to react to unexpected events, negotiate changes with the client and, if necessary, put suppliers of major components together with the customer to resolve difficult problems.

In effect, the PBO embodies a concurrent model of project management. The move to a PBO represents a shift from the linear model of project management, which treats the user and other innovation actors as outside bodies, to a concurrent model of project management which is able to integrate all the business functions within the project and include users and suppliers in the core project processes. For CoPS projects, the concurrent model is potentially very helpful in dealing with uncertainty, risk and emerging properties common in CoPS.

Economic motivations and determinants

Underlying the advantages and disadvantages of the two organisational forms are economic motivations and determinants. In theory it would be possible to mass produce consumer goods such as camcorders or hi-fi equipment in a PBO rather than a functional organisation. Similarly, it would also be possible to produce a large CoPS (e.g. a power station or a flight simulator) in a functional organisation. However, in both cases the costs of production would be far higher than if the more appropriate organisational form was adopted.

As we discussed in Chapter 3, the large functional Chandlerian firm is most effective at achieving the cost advantages of economies, scale and scope, systematically converting lower-value inputs into higher-value outputs. However, efficiency gains in CoPS stem from other sources such as standardised and repeatable bid and project processes, centred on other forms of organisation ranging from matrix to the PBO. The PBO, with its focus and flexibility, can achieve economies of (a) resource allocation – allocating and re-allocating physical and human resources when and where they are needed to each one-off or unique project; (b) knowledge management – applying the knowhow needed to deal with the technology, as well as regulator and client needs; (c) design optimisation – enabling design cycles to be carried out effectively and efficiently by reducing the number of design/re-design cycles (and costs) associated with additional cycles, caused in CoPS by backward feedback loops from later to early design stages; and (d) quality – enabling the organisation to produce a complex good to the exact specification and needs of the buyer. Its inability to achieve such economies indicates that the functional form is economically wasteful as a form of production for CoPS projects.

As shown above, the PBO can also assist in managing risk and uncertainty, especially important in the many CoPS which exhibit emerging properties (unforeseen and unforeseeable features which occur during design, systems integration and production). Given that formal planning is limited in its ability to deal with design and production unknowns, the devolved decision making allowed by the PBO enables a flexible allocation of resources to alleviate these problems when they emerge. Furthermore, the nature of the CoPS project task often changes as clients realise new needs during the design and production phases, especially in very high-value CoPS where production may take two years or more. The PBO, in theory, allows the swift transfer of information to relevant teams and team members who are then in a position to adapt their activities and respond to new contingencies. The PBO, in principle, is an appropriate organisational form for the technological and market environment of CoPS, allowing for efficient project control and resource coordination.

Innovation advantages of the PBO

Beyond the economic advantages of the PBO, there are dynamic innovation advantages over the functional form. Realising a CoPS is often a creative and difficult task, involving feedback and learning as the project develops. CoPS require innovation not only at the product level but also at the process and organisational levels. Design and production in unique projects involve many knowledge-intensive, non-routine tasks and decision taking under conditions of uncertainty and risk. Learning during production is required to assimilate the knowledge required to complete the task of production. These unique tasks cannot easily be reduced to routine project management procedures and planning. However, as we show in Chapter 7, firms that move into a new line of projects in a growing market base can learn systematically from previous projects and improve performance by developing standardised project routines and processes.

Because each CoPS is different, the innovation needs of the product frequently demand experimentation in forms of project management. In short, project-level innovation is required to produce innovative products. Because the PBO creates and re-creates organisational structures and processes around the needs of each product and customer it is, in principle, a highly innovative form. Again, in theory at least, the PBO defies the anti-innovation bias of large functional organisations with their semi-permanent departments and consequent core rigidities.[6] The challenge of managing innovative CoPS projects is one of integrating business functions, ensuring flexibility and responsiveness to the needs of customers, and dealing with the emerging properties which inevitably arise in complex products which embody new knowledge. It is also a challenge of thinking beyond current market and product needs to anticipate future needs and especially to convince buyers of the firm's competence to deliver further new CoPS.

---

[6] In practice, of course, the PBO form may not live up to its innovative potential. Indeed, some project-based sectors are notorious for failing to learn and innovate (e.g. construction). Realising the innovative potential of the project-based organisation is a key challenge for management.

Conclusions

This chapter shows the advantages and disadvantages of the project-based form of production. Using in-depth case material, we compared the efficiency and effectiveness of the functionally oriented, matrix organisation with the PBO, pointing to both the strengths and the weaknesses of the PBO for producing CoPS. On the positive side, the PBO has the potential to foster innovation and promote effective project leadership across the business functions. As resources, technical and other, are formally dedicated to the project, both power and responsibility for project success lie with project managers. The latter, who tend to be super heavyweight, can focus on team building, meeting the client's needs, dealing with technological uncertainties and making a success out of the project. By contrast, the functional matrix is poorly equipped for coping with the needs of one-off or unique CoPS projects.

Regarding project performance, it is extremely important for firms to fix on the most appropriate organisational form. This may be a PBO or it may be a project-led organisation. Alternatively, the firm may wish to have a mix of different organisational structures depending on its mix of products. However, while organisational form is important to performance, it is clearly not the only factor. As Engwall (2003) puts it: 'No project is an island.' All projects are situated within a supportive (or non-supportive) environment and many other factors will affect performance (e.g. project leadership). Above all, the firm's experience in particular types of project will have an important bearing on likely success.

This chapter shows that along the spectrum of the six main functional-to project-based organisational forms, the PBO is actually an extreme form, having no functional division of labour or task coordination across project lines. All major business functions, including marketing and finance, are coordinated within the project. The PBO is therefore best suited to very large, risk-intensive projects, where resources have to be combined and shared with other firms. Because of its flexibility and focus the PBO form is able to cope well with emerging properties, enabling project members to respond rapidly to client needs in real time. The case example shows why the PBO form is more effective than the functional form in integrating different types of knowledge and skill, learning within the project boundary and coping with project risks and uncertainties. In short, while the functional and matrix forms embody an inward-looking, linear form of project management, the PBO represents a concurrent, outward-looking model of project management which is able to realise innovation in collaboration with clients and suppliers.

Because CoPS tend to be major new business endeavours, simultaneous product, process and organisational innovation is often required. The PBO is therefore (potentially at least) a highly effective form because it creates and re-creates new organisational structures around the needs of each product and each major customer. Unlike functional departments, the PBO is temporary and is therefore not subject to the anti-innovation bias of functional organisations with their strict demarcations and core rigidities. This chapter demonstrates that, other things being equal, the PBO boasts significant economic advantages over the functional form in the execution of CoPS projects.

On the negative side, the PBO is inherently weak in coordinating processes, resources and capabilities across the organisation as a whole. Individual project success and efficiency, although important, do not necessarily enable a firm to perform well as a whole. Indeed, the case study revealed a problem of learning closure around major projects, as there were no structures or incentives in the PBO for cross-project learning or communications. The learning silos, represented by functional departments, are absent in the pure PBO. As a consequence, PBOs can suffer from a lack of technical leadership and direction, roles typically played by engineering and R&D managers in functional and matrix organisations. PBOs can also breed insecurity over career development, especially among new recruits, because of the dispersion of technical leadership across projects. By contrast, functional departments provide space (and often time) for the sharing of knowledge and experience. In short, the PBO is inherently weak where functional forms are strong: in executing routine production and engineering tasks, achieving economies of scale and meeting the needs of volume production.

Cross-project integration and management control can also become a problem in PBOs if projects 'go their own way'. Systems may come to vary from project to project as heavyweight project managers exercise a high degree of discretion over which tools to apply and how to apply them. It may become difficult for senior managers to track, control and respond to the activities of project teams and directors, limiting the firm's overall capacity for effective corporate strategy and business coordination. To be most effective the PBO requires that projects are coherently directed towards company-wide market and technology targets.

The case example identifies various strategies for dealing with PBO weaknesses, particularly the problem of project isolation. To improve coordination in areas such as overall company strategy, regular reporting channels into company directors can be set up. To enable and encourage organisational learning, cross-project communication and technical leadership, a company can move one stage back from a pure PBO to a project-led organisation. In this arrangement, project managers retain their senior positions but new resource and task coordinators along functional lines are appointed, cutting across project interests and incentives and helping to coordinate, monitor and improve performance across the organisation as a whole. This move back from a pure PBO to a project-led organisation shows the variety of choices involved and the need to match organisational form with the product mix in question.

6 | *Managing software-intensive projects*

I N many high-technology industries embedded software and information technology more generally are the core technologies that must be mastered for competitiveness in project business. In the past 20 years or so these technologies have become a major technical challenge to project business. Firms need to acquire deep capabilities in software engineering and learn how to efficiently manage large, complex software projects to their advantage. IT-based management systems and tools are essential not only for managing software and IT projects themselves but also for most types of complex project. Today, it is difficult to find any large complex project which does not utilise software and IT one way or another.[1]

Focusing on the case of flight simulation, this chapter examines the particular difficulties generated by the management of software-intensive projects in CoPS.[2] One of the accepted international best-practice instruments for managing and improving software development is the capability maturity model developed by the Carnegie-Mellon Software Engineering Institute in the US. This is now widely adopted by professional software firms in many countries and operates rather like the ISO9000 quality system. However, our case research shows that CMM, on its own, cannot improve the quality of software or efficiency in design or production. This is because it does not sufficiently address the human or soft side of an organisation's capability. We show in the case of flight simulation that, while the CMM approach to software development is useful for establishing engineering systems, rigorous

---

[1] However, it is not impossible. In some areas (e.g. the cores for nuclear submarines) software is not used or used sparingly due to the need for safety and the perception of software as being, to some extent, unreliable. In other projects where complex mechanical technologies determine project success (e.g. cryogenic magnets), embedded software is kept to a minimum. But even in these projects IT is used to help manage project operations.

[2] The chapter is based on Hobday and Brady (2000).

business processes and detailed working procedures, it can actually divert attention away from the human side of software development. However, it is the soft side which is so important for software success and underpins many of the wider failures in projects in all types of industries.

While the chapter recommends the kind of sensible and efficient procedures put forward by CMM, it also stresses leadership, good communications, motivation and teamwork in software and IT projects. These soft factors are often ignored and yet they can make or break major projects. They need to be taken seriously in project management, training investments, human resource assessment, promotion and in the day-to-day management of project business at all levels.

Rational vs soft approaches to management

The rational approach to management

To understand why so many projects fail to meet performance expectations it is helpful to focus on the difference between how project management (including software) is *actually* undertaken, compared with views, models and recommendations on how the process *should* proceed (or the rational approach to management). In CoPS, because of design and production complexity and the wide variety of knowledge and skills involved, there is often a lack of certainty on how best to proceed from stage to stage. Not surprisingly the frequency of unexpected events is quite high and sometimes large gaps emerge between 'actual' and 'should be' processes.

In software, the overwhelmingly dominant approach is to try to impose *rational* processes, regardless of the informal *soft* realities which lie behind the formal procedures and systems. Indeed, the denial of soft, informal practices is sometimes seen as a virtue in software development and engineering practice (Parnas and Clements, 1986). If we turn to the project management field (or indeed management in general), as Brown and Duguid (1991) point out, very little attention is given to the implications of the soft vs rational gap (which they term non-canonical and canonical, respectively) for work, learning and innovation. Building on the work of Orr (1987, 1990) they show that the soft vs rational gap challenges conventional management thinking and points to deep practical problems in managing organisations.

Indeed, Orr's evidence shows that attempts to impose rational practices often force practitioners to mask their real activities, driving actual work practices underground, leading to an ever-widening gap between formal company policies, values and procedures and real or soft behaviours. As a result, sometimes rational job descriptions, manuals, organisational charts, training programmes, tools and values of management become ridiculed by intelligent shop-floor practitioners as bureaucratic, unhelpful and detached from reality.

Orr and others show that problem-solving engineers often have to 'break the rules to get the job done'. During this proces, important organisational learning and innovation occur, centred on real or soft work practices. Given the intrinsic task complexity and uncertainty involved in software-intensive projects, these findings are especially relevant to this book.

Taking an historical management perspective, many scholars have long recognised the soft vs rational distinction, arguing that the rational approach is appropriate only for stable environments and relatively simple tasks which lend themselves to centralised, hierarchical organisational forms (or 'machine-like bureaucracies' as Morgan puts it, 1986: 56). Burns and Stalker (1961) show how the most appropriate organisational form, ranging from organic to mechanistic, is contingent on the task at hand, with organic organisations best suited for complex tasks. Similarly, Woodward (1958) shows that the organic – or project – form is most appropriate for complex, one-off production tasks. Mintzberg (1979) argues that adhocracy is best suited to perform complex and uncertain tasks in turbulent environments. As Morgan (1996: 52) notes, the adhocracy usually involves project teams which are constituted to carry out particular tasks and then disband when the work is completed. In CoPS projects, the team often involves members from several different firms, further complicating organisational dynamics.

Management theorists have not only shown that the most effective organisational form is contingent on the task at hand but also that in all organisations an informal soft reality exists which is central to performance, efficiency and effectiveness. Indeed, as early as 1918, the originator of scientific management Frederick W. Taylor (1911) was taken to task by Mary Parker Follett (then a member of the Taylor Society) who argued that firms were social as well as economic units and that human relations and motivations could not be separated from operating tasks.[3] Later, in the classic *The Functions of the Executive*, Chester Barnard (1938) also criticised Taylor and other rationalists, by demonstrating the importance and functioning of informal organisations and their significance within formal organisations. As Barnard showed, although soft informal practices are often overlooked or neglected, they are central to organisational communication and cohesion, as well as to the personal integrity of practitioners.

Many other scholars have challenged the rational approach. Herbert Simon criticised the rational decision-making view of humans, pointing out that actual decisions are taken under conditions of bounded rationality, involving perception, judgement and intuition (Simon, 1955). At the organisational level, Lindblom (1959) argued that under conditions of uncertainty and incomplete information, 'muddling through' in a step-by-step manner is (ironically) the only real rational way to proceed.[4] Writing in the same era, Klein and Meckling (1958), Marshak (1962) and Klein (1962) made similar points in their research into US military systems, concluding that under conditions of uncertainty the decision-making process involves substantial learning and a progressive narrowing of options, very different from the normal production task of scheduling and resource allocation. More recently, Hilmer and Donaldson (1996) show why management systems need a soft accompaniment of practical guidance and informal human support.

Despite such findings, many prominent management thinkers and practitioners continue to treat organisations and people 'as if' they were rational (e.g. Parnas and Clements, 1986, in the software project field). A recent version of the rational view is embodied in business process re-engineering (Hammer and Champy, 1994; Davenport, 1993, 1996). Its popularity in the US and Europe in the 1990s shows that the scientific, rational approach continues to run deep in theory and practice.

In software and IT projects, rational tools and systems can emerge which are diametrically opposed to real human practices. As Sapolsky (1972: 94–130) showed in his study of the American Polaris missile system, PERT, which was developed within Polaris, was not actually used to build the system and, despite its subsequent proliferation, was

---

[3] The debate between Taylor and Parker Follett (1918) is discussed by Peter Drucker in Graham (1995: 24–31).
[4] Lindblom's insights were later developed into 'Logical Incrementalism' by Quinn (1980).

a deeply flawed management tool. Instead, Polaris's success was the result of inspired leadership, good management and a shared spirit of commitment across the organisations involved. PERT, according to Sapolsky, was too complicated to use and a complex computer system used primarily to impress visitors (especially government funders) to justify the programme and build up a myth of managerial effectiveness. In this interpretation, PERT was a deliberate rational smokescreen, masking soft, real practices.

Given the above findings, it is surprising that such management insights failed to reach a wider audience of theorists and practitioners, especially in software and IT where the rational approach dominates. In a review of the literature, Huber (1996: 124) argues that the failure of academics to reach practitioners is partly because scholars do not present their work in forms and formats which give it 'social or administrative value'. Another possible reason is that sensible rational systems *are* in fact required – they need to be put in place alongside support for soft, human practices.

According to our view, rational systems can have a positive and significant value in project business only when they are acceptable to and shaped by practitioners – not imposed top down by management.

Software and the limits of rational management

As noted earlier, many high-cost products, systems, networks and con-structs are today software and IT intensive, such as flight simulators, telecommunications exchanges, high-speed trains, air traffic control sys-tems, avionics systems and intelligent buildings. Since the 1980s the use of embedded software has improved the control, flexibility and performance of many high-technology capital goods, while mastery of software devel-opment and IT systems has become central to the ways in which projects are managed. For example, in the case of flight simulators, the design and production of major system components is carried out mainly by software engineers using predicted data and complex computer models. In many project engineering environments we find rows of engineers and project managers working on computers in offices rather than on the shop floor with mechanical and electromechanical technologies as in the past.

The task of understanding, managing and improving software and IT processes poses particular difficulties in CoPS and in the software packages required for computer games and many consumer products. Software is a major obstacle to the execution of projects, leading to delays, cancellations and cost overruns. It seems that software has accentuated the human, craft-based elements of design and manufacture, making the control of costs and time ever more difficult.

Software engineering in CoPS brings the rational vs soft management debate into sharp focus. The term software engineering implies that software has progressed to a systematic and predictable discipline. Large programmes of research (e.g. on metrics, structured programming, formal methods, computer-aided tools and integrated project-support environments) are all attempts to devise ways of developing software programs systematically and scientifically from a precise *a priori* statement of requirements.

Despite huge efforts to rationalise software development, there is abundant evidence that software remains a major stumbling block to the successful execution of high-technology projects (e.g. Gibbs, 1994; Peltu, 1992; Littlewood and Strigini, 1992; Flowers, 1996; Paulk, 1995b; Collins and Bicknell, 1997). In software, the term complex usually indicates a large and ambitious project with a high risk of designing the user interface incorrectly (perhaps due to unclear or changing customer needs). It also implies stringent performance requirements (including a low presence of errors in the operational task of the software), a high risk of incorrect budgeting and scheduling, and major systems integration challenges (Boehm, 1988: 69 and 71).

The term rational, which has a specific meaning in software, is defined as the systematic development of a program from a precise initial statement of requirements in a reasoned, logical and documented manner (Parnas and Clements, 1986). In the company discussed below, as in many others, rational-type procedures are captured in company manuals and various process flow charts used to guide engineers.

In software the rational approach dominates and it appears that few, if any, of the soft management insights have informed software thinking or training. However, the importance of soft issues such as organisational learning, informal processes, leadership, team building and conflict (Senge, 1990; Leonard-Barton, 1988 and 1992; Garvin, 1993; Stata, 1989) apply as much to software as they do to any other domain of project management and organisation.

Software tends to be analysed within its own, engineering-centred domain and many attempts have been made to improve software performance by recommending rational processes and procedures, regardless of the real working environment. Among the most widely cited prescriptive models are those of Boehm (1988, 1989a and 1991) who introduced both the waterfall and spiral models of software development.[5]

Some authors express concerns over some aspects of the rational approach. For example, Emam and Madhavji (1995) question the reliability of numerical measures of organisational maturity, while Baker and Rouse (1995) point to the dangers of over-formalistic adoption of ISO9001 for software, especially for smaller firms. However, most of the field tends to ignore soft issues, focusing on rational should-be processes. Indeed, CMM, now an internationally accepted approach to quality standards (see Table 6.1), assumes (a) that organisations mature through various stages towards rational, controllable processes, and (b) that this progress can be measured and assessed (Paulk, 1995a; Rout, 1995). The fully controllable rational process (Level 5 CMM) is the Holy Grail of software quality.

The basic idea behind CMM is that the quality of software output is determined by the quality of the organisation's software processes. CMM is based on the application of Shewart/Deming's statistical process control (SPC) and total quality management (TQM) techniques to software. As a company's capability matures, software becomes better defined and more consistently implemented throughout the organisation. The promise of CMM is improved productivity, quality, predictability and reputation. CMM is now a fully defined model, backed by the US Department of Defense. The five basic CMM software process levels are described in Table 6.1.

Of course, many software analysts realise that theory deviates from practice. However, the response to problems is normally to strengthen

[5] DeMarco (1979) and Yourdon (1978) provide early reports on how to control software through formalised design reviews (called code walkthroughs) within firms. Abdel-Hamid and Madnick (1991) analyse software productivity and reflect on common mistakes made in software project management. Smith (1994) analyses the causes of software failures from a quality and reliability perspective. Humphrey (1989a) examines how individual software practitioners might improve their engineering skills, while Culver-Lozo (1995) assesses the difficulties in scaling up best practices from small to large software projects. Kellner (1996) provides a formal method of software process analysis, based on computer simulations, quantitative analysis and predicted estimates of impacts of changes. Similarly, Pulford et al. (1996) provide a purely quantitative approach to managing software. Some authors tackle the issue of how to integrate software into complex products, again from a rational perspective (Humphrey, 1989a and 1989b; Paulk, 1993; Boehm, 1988; Buxton and Malcolm, 1991).

Table 6.1: The capability maturity model (CMM)

CMM *software process – Levels 1 to 5*

- Level 1 *Initial* – ad hoc/chaotic – few processes defined for developing and maintaining software – success depends on key individuals
- Level 2 *Repeatable* – basic project management techniques used to track cost, schedule and functionality – previous (similar) project successes can be repeated
- Level 3 *Defined* – documented processes for both management and engineers – accepted standard software practices across all projects – tailored versions possible
- Level 4 *Managed* – detailed measures of both software process and product quality collected, quantitatively understood and controlled
- Level 5 *Optimising* – quantitative feedback allows continuous process improvement from the process and from innovative ideas and technologies

Levels 1 and 2 focus on project management. Levels 3 and 5 focus on understanding and improving the process with feedback data.

and impose more rigid rational controls, formal systems and procedures (Jones, 1996) rather than to support and recognise soft processes (and damaging gaps between soft and rational processes). In fact, some leading software analysts accept that the design and development of software is not and cannot be rational, but go on to claim that great benefits can be gained if you proceed as if the process was rational (Parnas and Clements, 1986; Paulk, 1995a).

In recent years, problems of software project management have led to unease among many leading software writers. In review articles on large-scale, complex software projects published in *IEEE Software*, two highly respected writers on software conclude: 'If past is prologue ... we might expect the following: ever more concern with building healthy corporate culture; increasing awareness of teams and workgroups as sociological entities; continuing emphasis on good methods, controls and communications; and finally perhaps even a bit of Zen' (DeMarco and Miller, 1996: 27).

It is fair to conclude not only that management studies have failed to inform the software field but also that, despite concerns over many project failures, the software profession retains a highly rational approach to work processes. The dominant software approach is consistent with the Taylorist scientific approach, which is applied even (and perhaps especially) in the uncertain, organic settings of high-technology capital goods software. Curiously, while rational processes underpin the dominant CMM approach to software quality, there is an underlying current of concern for human beings and real group dynamics.

Case study of complex software processes: lessons from flight simulation

Research approach

To show how software managers can analyse and address the rational problem, we set up an experimental exercise with an outward-looking firm which needed to improve its software project performance.

The study involved developing a real-time method for analysing both soft and rational practices in order to feed back information to our case company (called Dynamics) for verification, analysis and improvement purposes.[6] As shown in Appendix B, the approach used techniques from the field of organisation development to analyse one project in depth to gain detailed empirical insights and then to verify the accuracy and generalisability of findings in structured workshops with a sample of software practitioners (Hobday and Brady, 2000). Our approach compared rational procedures about (a) how processes should proceed with (b) the processes that actually occurred in practice in one particular project (examined below) and identified problems that occurred as a result of any divergences between the two.

A complex software product

The main components and subsystems of a typical civil flight simulator include the image generator, host computer, cockpit, visual display, platform, motion system, cabin, instructor station, projectors, back projection screen, off-simulator electronics, training facilities and other components. The trainee pilot sits in the flight simulator cockpit and 'flies' the aircraft to a destination entered into the computer, rather like a real aircraft. Unlike a real aircraft, an instructor is able to monitor and test the pilot as he or she simulates dangerous flight events such as engine failure. Today, most pilots receive the majority of their training on

---

[6] The real name of the company has been changed for confidentiality purposes.

simulators for reasons of cost and efficiency. Some civilian pilots obtain a licence without ever having flown a real aircraft (so-called zero-flight-time training).

Most of the flight simulator functioning depends on software, involving complex models and existing or predicted data on flight behaviour and performance. The latter (so-called data packages), generally supplied by the aircraft makers, are central to the building of the flight simulator. Software development occurs in the normal way with the capturing of general customer requirements, followed by a series of more detailed design stages, coding, testing, hardware–software integration and maintenance.

Stages of development in a rational world

During our research we identified the rational, formal processes and stages in the building of a typical simulator in Dynamics ('what should occur') and attributed average times to each phase (see Table 6.2). A flight simulator project takes on average two years to complete. Most of the stages involve software activities of one kind or another, ranging from systems analysis, engineering, code writing, testing and systems integration. Special software skills are needed for avionics, computer-generated imagery, flight performance (e.g. aerodynamic modelling) and systems interfacing. In large firms like Dynamics, engineering is supported by R&D into human factors (e.g. ergonomics and psychology), new hardware systems (e.g. special printed circuit boards, microprocessors and multimedia interfaces), flight environments and many other fields.

Skills and knowledge required

In flight simulators, as in many other real-time software systems, the kinds of knowledge required are varied and complex. Flight simulator producers are required to master at least four difficult knowledge and skill sets:

1. the skills to integrate hardware and software components (motion, visual, computer and cockpit) into a coherent whole (the simulator);
2. the knowhow to use and develop the mathematical simulations which replicate the behaviour of the aircraft;

Table 6.2: Typical life cycle stages of a flight simulator project (civil and military)

Key stages	Duration*
Bid stages	
1. Price bid in response to RFP**	4 weeks civil (16 weeks military)
2. Negotiations with the buyer	1 week civil (52 weeks military)
Development stages	
1. Programme launch and communications	Up to 8 weeks
2. Systems requirements analysis	
3. Provisional design work	
4. Detailed design specification	
5. Software structuring and coding stages 2–5	26 weeks civil; up to 52 weeks military
6. Power-on phase	6 weeks
7. Hardware commissioning	6 weeks from power phase
8. Hardware/software integration	8–12 weeks civil (24 weeks military)
Post-integration stages	
1. Quality testing (in factory)	6–12 weeks (military only)
2. Customer testing (in factory) (factory acceptance certification)	3–6 weeks
3. Breakdown and shipping	3–6 weeks
4. Re-installation and re-commissioning on customer premises	6 weeks
5. Customer acceptance on site (regulator certification)	2–4 weeks
6. The full flight simulator is ready for training (RFT)	
Post-delivery activities	
1–5 years' warranty and service	
Post-delivery support and services (up to 20 years' life)	
Spare parts delivery	

* Several stages of military systems take longer due to customisation, performance and testing requirements.
** Request for proposal.
Source: compiled from interviews at Dynamics in 1995 and 1996.

3. the detailed knowledge of client requirements for training, checking and pilot-quality programmes;
4. precise knowledge of the rules and regulations (especially the acceptance test guides) which specify the requirements for simulator approval.

Core technical competence of the flight simulator producer

In recent years the core technical capability of the modern flight simulator producer, as with many CoPS producers, has become one of systems integration (see Chapter 4). With increasing complexity and technological advance, many of the subsystems previously built in-house by flight simulator producers are today contracted out to specialist suppliers. These include visual systems from Evans and Sutherland, the computers which drive the flight simulator (e.g. from Concurrent Computer Corporation and Silicon Graphics) and several other key components. While other major suppliers (and aircraft makers) can produce key parts of the simulator, the one major activity the flight simulator producer can perform (which others would find extremely difficult to imitate) is the integration of the various parts of the system.

Systems integration operates at two main levels: physical components and knowledge. At the component level, companies such as Dynamics take the aircraft maker's data package, as well as parts and subsystems produced in-house and by the specialist suppliers, and combine them using engineering and integration skills, involving each of the main hardware and software domains described earlier.

At the level of knowledge and experience, the capability to integrate the various sets of engineering, regulatory and training knowledge is needed to produce a flight simulator which delivers the feel of the real aircraft. Systems knowhow enables the engineers to convincingly mimic the behaviour that human pilots expect from an aircraft and also to meet the regulators' safety requirements. Many of these skills are tacit, embodied in specialists who use their judgement and experience to approximate a convincing replica of the real aircraft. Human pilots play an important part in advising the software and systems engineers, not only at the early stage of requirements capture but also during the latter stages of final testing, revisions and trial. Despite the apparently technical and codified environment, producing a faithful replica of a real aircraft involves a substantial craft input and relies on highly skilled individuals in subject domains such as fuel systems, avionics operating systems, performance modelling and visual technology.

The Triumph project

Project characteristics
Although Triumph was a fairly typical project, it had some unusual features and posed some technical difficulties. The customer, the Ministry of Defence, took a direct role in Triumph, insisting on formal systems engineering tools and procedures.[7] There were several technical challenges (see below), notably the use of ADA, a highly structured programming language developed for real-time, embedded systems (which contrasts with the more widely used FORTRAN language).[8]

The Triumph flight simulator, developed for military pilot training purposes, was to mirror the operation of a modified, wide-bodied civil aircraft about 25 years of age which went out of service in the mid-1980s. The MoD purchased a fleet of these old aircraft for conversion into military tankers/troop carriers. A firm based in Cambridge was responsible for modifying the aircraft and supplying relevant data (e.g. installing new flight re-fuelling tanks, engine updates and a rear cockpit/visual system). An American firm, Lockheed, the original aircraft producer, was to supply the all-important data package needed to drive the simulator.

Triumph, a one-off project, began in July 1994 and was due to be completed and in service by 9 September 1996 at the MoD. Engineers

---

[7] Systems engineering, like software engineering, can be viewed as an effort to achieve a rational production process. The systems engineering discipline originated in the 1950s and 1960s within the US Department of Defense major military and space programmes (Sage, 1981; Shenhar, 1994a; Boardman, 1990). It provides a highly technical, formal, engineering-based approach for the management and integration of large-scale complex projects. A review of DoD standards and their impact on industry is provided by Lake (1992), while Fairburn (1995) deals with multi-company projects. Although the approach has given rise to a huge literature (Chambers, 1986), it has little to say on how to deal with emergent, unexpected properties or soft, informal issues. A study by Walker et al. (1988) shows that large civil projects share many of the characteristics of military ones.

[8] ADA's development was sponsored by the US military (in the mid-1970s and early 1980s). It began to be used in flight simulation in specialist applications in the mid-1980s and became the dominant military language during the next ten years, displacing FORTRAN. ADA is a highly structured language developed for real-time operations (as opposed to atemporal systems).

were drawn mostly from the military division of the company. The latter had been an independent firm recently acquired by Dynamics and amalgamated with Dynamics' civil operations. However, the contract had originated in the civil division and this led to continuity difficulties between the bid and early design stages. Another complication, discussed below, was that the two amalgamated companies were expected to operate under a new formal management system imposed by Dynamics.

Triumph project technology

The project cost was around £11 million, which is average for a flight simulator. According to Dynamics engineers, Triumph was not unusual in terms of duration and risk and there were no radical technical requirements which demanded new R&D. Around 20–25 engineers worked directly on Triumph at any one time. In addition, indirect company-funded managers and administrators from operations departments contributed to the project.

As with most flight simulator projects, Triumph had some special features which had to be accounted for. It was not typical of a military aircraft because it was a conversion from civil to military, as noted. This meant that it had many civilian aircraft features as well as military ones. The actual jet was a large civil one compared with the more usual, smaller military jets.

The host computer and interfaces, based on a standard platform developed by the civil wing of the company, were to be tailored to meet Triumph's needs. The aircraft was fairly old and some of the original software was to be re-used. Around 50 per cent of the flight simulator was new, including novel software which had to be designed using ADA. Although no novel technology had to be developed, some was new to the firm and various parts of the system were leading edge and had to be configured in new ways. The most important technical challenge to the project team was the ADA language. This was the first time Dynamics had used ADA and this necessitated both formal training programmes and the learning of new skills and techniques on the part of several engineers.

Project organisation and key responsibilities

The Triumph project was integrated into the company's traditional organisational structure: a project matrix organisation, with project teams cutting across functional lines (see Chapter 5). Functional departments supported the projects with services such as R&D, purchasing, marketing, finance, training and quality assurance.

The project team was led by a project manager and a systems engineer. The project manager, whose main responsibility at the time was Triumph, like most project managers was not a technically qualified engineer but carried out the business, financial and day-to-day management of the project. He was in charge of overall milestones, plans and budgets and had to ensure schedules were kept, finances were in order and team communications functioned well. He was the main interface with the client, dealing with customer problems, new requests and external communications. The systems engineer was in charge of overall engineering, including systems integration, and all the hardware and software. His role was inward looking. He was responsible for ensuring all the engineering tasks were carried out according to specification, schedule and budget. The systems engineer worked alongside the project manager in what was by all accounts a good and effective working relationship.

It is worth noting that neither the project manager nor the systems engineer, as often occurs in matrix organisations, had a direct staff and worked mostly by facilitation and persuasion. Project team engineers reported up through functional lines to their respective group managers in charge of the four main engineering departments. However, considerable power of influence resided in the project manager who reported regularly to company directors on progress and problems.

The engineering team leaders, in charge of work packages (further broken down into modules), negotiated with the PM and interpreted what the plans meant. The team leaders then reported to their respective group managers to request resources (mostly people and machinery) to carry through fairly large work packages. Team leaders had between two and eight engineers reporting to them at any one point. Some had more responsibility than others. There were nine team leaders in charge of avionics, tactics, radar, engines, controls, flight, systems integration, the instructor operating system and computer systems.

In addition to the above, several senior engineering specialists had design responsibility for specific areas such as aircraft systems (including fuel, hydraulics and landing gear) and environmental control systems. Highly skilled and respected, they typically worked on several projects at a time, reporting to both team leaders and group managers. Group managers, the functional heads of the engineering departments, were responsible for resourcing Triumph and other projects. Although highly influential, they were not formally a part of the project structure. In Dynamics' military division there were four group managers responsible for the four main functional engineering areas.

Pressures on formal processes

At least three possible sources of strain on formal systems were evident in Triumph. Each could have potentially caused a deviation between soft and rational processes: (i) industrial turbulence; (ii) a new management system; and (iii) technical difficulties. First, general industrial turbulence and company transition affected Triumph as they did most other projects. For several years the flight simulator industry had been subjected to extreme distress, caused by market recession following the Gulf War and the decline in civilian aircraft travel, coupled with military cutbacks following the break-up of the Soviet Union. Recession had resulted in widespread lay-offs across the industry and total employment in Dynamics had fallen by more than 50 per cent in the previous 2–3 years. Morale was low and job insecurity high.

The bid phase of Triumph had been caught up in Dynamics' takeover of the civil company which entailed a physical site relocation. Constant change affected the company, as did the loss of senior managers and key engineers, both before and during the Triumph project. In Triumph neither the project manager nor the systems engineer had been involved in the bid phase of the project due to the merger of the two companies which coincided with the early stage of the contract.

Second, the merger caused some confusion due to the coming together of two companies under a new management system, called MSA.[9] Following the takeover by Dynamics, the parent company began imposing MSA, a worldwide corporate system adapted to suit local circumstances. MSA covered company strategy and positioning, bidding procedures, project implementation, specific management tools, scheduling procedures, budgeting, cost control, risk management and purchasing. MSA was in the process of being introduced and some aspects had been adopted by Triumph.

Third, technical difficulties confronted the project. Triumph relied on a standard platform developed for civil flight simulators, but the

---

[9] The name is changed to protect confidentiality. MSA was contained in a worldwide corporate toolbook, analysed during the research.

engineers were drawn mostly from a military background, causing some difficulties at the early stage. Other technical difficulties, including unexpected requirements, are analysed below. As discussed below, each of the above three factors played an important part in shaping the progress of the project.

Software tools and procedures

Rational tools and procedures
In theory, the rational software tools and procedures mandated by the company should have been embodied in and supported by the firm's formal processes. During our research we therefore identified hard management tools which were used, and/or supposed to be used, by software engineers and managers.[10] Our aim was to assess how tools were used, if any tools were not used (and why) and what else, if anything, was being used to help get the job done.

We found it useful to divide management tools into three broad categories: (a) hard mandated tools, including computer-aided software engineering (CASE) tools, MoD requirements, PC-based tools and formal MSA reporting systems; (b) soft mandated tools such as software reviews (so-called code walkthroughs) and monthly coordination meetings to measure and communicate progress; and (c) soft informal tools (unofficial measures used on Triumph), including paper reports, ad hoc meetings and other forms of group interaction.

Many of the hard tools were defined by MSA which outlined procedures for bidding, project implementation, scheduling, software design and testing, budgeting, risk management and subcontract management. Several hard tools, used in all UK military flight simulator projects, were contained in MoD standard 2167A. This called for Triumph to conform to a detailed design format to be sent to the MoD for approval. Similarly, formal software test procedures had to be followed and specific documents were to be used to record the project's history and track any changes. 2167A defined and documented the project life cycle in a fairly rigid manner, with some tailoring permitted for flight simulation. In fact, 2167A provided a route map

---

[10] For an analysis of different types of management tools, procedures and systems see Brady et al. (1997).

for Triumph, a work breakdown structure, high- and low-level design stages and documentation standards (called MoD JSP188 issue 4).

Other hard tools included ILS (Integrated Logistics Support standard SLIC 2B), adopted by the MoD from the US DoD (discussed below). Interleaf, a rigid documentation software package, provided a template to ensure a common design format across the project. Matrix X V4, a rapid prototyping tool, was to produce real-time ADA code of the model and then automate the documentation. In addition, there were many other hard tools and procedures in evidence in the large rule book for MSA.

How formal tools were actually used

As noted, we compared rational tools with what actually took place in practice and identified problems in the use of tools. One finding was that some elements of MSA had been adopted by Triumph engineers (e.g. job titles and roles) and several engineers believed they were deploying MSA. However, it later emerged in discussions with directors that Triumph was not a designated MSA project, a confusion which had resulted from the transition from one management system to another and somewhat unclear communications from top management.

Severe problems were reported with some IT-based tools (e.g. ILS). In theory, Triumph engineers should have fed into the ILS system all the items to be purchased, including data on repair advice and delivery information. The computer system would then place orders for the components just in time for their use. Triumph, like other projects, had to rely on ILS for the delivery of spares as the former manual system of order processing and chasing had been abandoned in favour of ILS. However, ILS was not capable of ensuring that some important spares (with lead times of 8–9 months) would be delivered on time. The just-in-time approach of ILS prevented ordering for inventory. In this case, based on his long experience, the project manager took the decision to bypass the system unofficially (and against company procedures) to order spares directly. Similar events regularly occurred in other projects in the company.

In Triumph the computer-based system, Compass Contract/MRP11, was (like ILS), according to engineers, not flexible enough for tailored, one-off projects. MRP11 was imposed on project teams and in some cases engineers decided to bypass the formal system to 'get the job done', as they put it. Interleaf, the documentation template, was generally viewed as useful, but engineers still had to draw many detailed arrows and lines by hand because it was not flexible enough to encompass all the detail needed. The ways in which such lines were drawn differed from engineer to engineer.

One common complaint among engineers was that meeting the required standards entailed a great deal of time, effort and post hoc paperwork. Some felt too much engineering time was spent on form-filling and bureaucracy which did not add value to the final product. However, the hard requirements mandated by the MoD were seen as part of the overall task funded by the customer and were by and large planned for and implemented.

Soft tools and management discretion

The third category of tools, soft discretionary tools, was widely used. Indeed, the most important real triggers for action listed by Triumph engineers were informal tools, ranging from regular meetings to immediate responses to panic phone calls. One of the most cited and most useful tools was a two-page weekly written report by each engineer, introduced to Triumph by the project manager. Although informal, it provided most of the basic data for managers and engineers to control and track Triumph's progress. By contrast the project management master schedule, which should have driven activities, was mostly used infrequently as a high-level reference point by the project manager.

Another important tool for communication and problem solving was the weekly meetings which allowed regular interactions between individual software writers, different teams and managers. These meetings, which facilitated the exchange of data, the triggering of important actions and information feedback from the customer, were viewed as critical to Triumph's progress. They followed an open format, allowing conflicts to be identified and resolved. These weekly meetings, which were optional from the project management perspective, did not take place in all projects in Dynamics because they were not mandated.

Evidence of discretion and human initiative abounded in Triumph and in the other company projects we studied. In Triumph, some of the most important project management features resulted from personalities rather than formal tools and systems. Regardless of official procedures, the systems engineer and project manager had substantial degrees of freedom in the styles and methods with which they pursued their goals. Both initiated new procedures and chose how to deal with risk, communications and team motivation in a manner which suited their team, their experiences and what their immediate bosses expected of them.

At the systems integration level, the Triumph systems engineer believed that the best way to meet both software and hardware goals was to work closely with the engineers on a day-to-day basis, leaving customer interfacing (and other outside business tasks) to the project manager.[11] This division of work appeared to work well, according to interviewees.

At the software practitioner level, team leaders, engineers and specialists exercised a great deal of discretion as to how to implement software tasks and how to approach the detailed design and testing of modules. Practitioners had complex choices to make and were responsible for managing not only their own work packages but also the interface between their work and that of other engineers. To some extent, software engineers were also managers, selecting, choosing and adapting management tools and documentation in order to complete their tasks effectively.

In short, Triumph relied heavily on personalities and discretionary choices. While high-level formal procedures established a broad framework for operating, as well as deadlines and milestones, personal qualities (especially inter-personal skills) were also important. Detailed procedures were less important and sometimes seen as a hindrance. In Triumph, as in other projects, the tacit skills of the project manager, systems engineer and other team members played an important part in the project's progress and problems. To understand why unofficial soft tools appeared so important to the project it is helpful to turn to actual software work processes in Dynamics and to compare these with rational ones.

---

[11] In much larger projects (e.g. those with hundreds of engineers) more formal approaches usually have to be adopted. For an account of how to scale up effective informal systems while maintaining the benefits of smaller groups, see Culver-Lozo (1995).

Table 6.3: Deviations between soft and rational processes. *

1. Overall project management processes
2. The requirements capture process
3. The detailed design process
4. Testing procedures
5. Managing outside organisations
6. Measuring and monitoring of progress
7. Learning processes

* Each heading, apart from overall processes (number 1), refers to project sub-processes.
No order of priority is implied.

Soft vs rational processes – case study interpretation

Seven major deviations between rational and soft processes

Our research revealed seven major deviations between soft and rational processes, most of which created uncertainty and caused risks to the project. Here we briefly describe the rational process as contained in official company manuals and procedures and then show how the actual processes differed, pointing out the causes of major differences, the outcomes and how risks were being managed in Dynamics. The seven major deviations in the software process are presented in Table 6.3 and commented on below, in turn. Many of these problems were general difficulties, common both to Triumph and to other projects at Dynamics.

1. Overall project management processes
According to the formal system, Triumph software processes were to follow the overall requirements of MSA and 2167A, including a formal requirements analysis, monthly reports, detailed design, off-line module testing and detailed documentation. A general high-level representation of the software life cycle is presented in Figure 6.1.[12]

---

[12] Also see Table 6.2 for a detailed breakdown of project stages and timing. The company had its own proprietary, detailed flow chart which cannot be shown

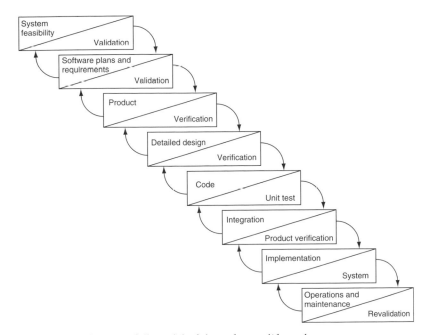

Figure 6.1 The waterfall model of the software life cycle
Source: Amended from Boehm (1983: 7).

The typical waterfall model includes requirements analysis, preliminary and detailed design, coding, testing, hardware–software integration and customer acceptance.

As shown below, what actually occurred was that tasks were not all completed according to schedule. Nevertheless, other parts of the project moved forward, leading to variations in progress within the project. Incomplete information and unexpected feedback loops from later to earlier stages necessitated major revisions to plan. Not all changes were properly documented and new requirements emerged which could not have been foreseen.

One main reason why actual events proceeded in a more haphazard way than the rational process was the intense work pressures placed upon engineers and managers because of market recession and redundancies. This context had, to some extent, depressed morale and

here. However, Boehm's standard waterfall model is close enough for the present purposes.

introduced risks to both schedule and technical targets. Software testing was rushed and informal as insufficient time was available for code
walkthroughs. Cross-programme scheduling loops occurred as key
engineers were pulled out of Triumph to engage in bursts of problem
solving in other projects.

Other reasons for variation between soft and rational processes were
the organisational tensions inherent in the matrix structure. In
Triumph, as in other projects, the project manager and systems engineer had high levels of project responsibility but no direct staff. They
relied on group managers for key people and had to compete for
resources with five or six other large military projects under way in
the company – 'too much responsibility but too little power' as the
project manager put it.

In response, the project manager and systems engineer fell back on
soft, informal tools to track events, control budgets, ensure progress
and deal with unexpected risks. Most problem solving was conducted
amicably through informal discussions with team leaders and their
group managers; within engineering, there existed a culture of positive
problem solving, fairly typical in engineering environments. Because
the project manager reported monthly to a group of company directors,
this enhanced his status in relation to group managers and provided a
final source of backup in case of severe problems or conflicts.

2. The requirements capture process

In theory, according to company procedures a major engineering
effort should have gone into the requirements capture process to
ensure all major customer needs were costed, understood and
planned for. In practice, too little engineering input took place at
the bid stage. Promises were made to the client which were difficult to
fulfil and not fully budgeted for – due to stiff competition, company
negotiators believed they had to grant concessions to the customer at
short notice to secure the order (a common problem with bidding in
flight simulator and other industries).

In addition, some early requirements were captured but not communicated sufficiently well from the bid team to the project team. Because
of the company takeover, neither the project manager nor the systems
engineer was involved in the bid phase, causing problems in both
technical and managerial continuity between the bid and requirements
analysis stages. Staff shortages, the company merger and site relocation

meant that delays and uncertainty had occurred for three or four months and the requirements analysis phase had been rushed.

Later on, other new requirements emerged which could not have been captured at the early design stage. Such emergent properties often complicate the rational project cycle in flight simulation. For example, in Triumph, a malfunction in the rear visual system was picked up by a pilot only at a late stage and this called for revisions to the overall system design. The risks to the project were being managed through close cooperation between engineers and the customer, and with the help of specialist engineers the team was able to ensure that revisions to other design modules could be kept to a minimum.

3. The detailed design process

According to the rational procedures of the company and the client, once the requirements were captured and broken down into modules, engineers should then move to the detailed design stage. However, some software engineers jumped straight from the requirements analysis and preliminary design stages to software coding. This occurred not only in Triumph but in other projects as well. Pressures of work caused some to skip the formal design steps. Some experienced engineers felt they knew how to produce the code directly and did not need to conduct detailed design. Others were not sufficiently aware of detailed design procedures. In general, too few engineers used tools (e.g. CASE) to do detailed design. Practices varied across departments and projects. One of the risks caused by the lack of attention to detailed design was that the number of coding errors could increase and that these might not be picked up until a later stage where corrections would be difficult and costly. A similar problem cropped up in testing.

4. Testing procedures

In theory, all testing should have followed requirements, formal test procedures and code walkthroughs of software modules.[13] However, most testing was informal and self-administered, where engineers typically set up and ran a few testing parameters. A large amount of testing went on during later stages (e.g. hardware–software integration) when correction costs were high and technically difficult to conduct. Existing formal procedures (e.g. the customer Acceptance Test Schedule) were

---

[13] See Yourdon (1978) for an analysis of the benefits of code walkthroughs.

too general to ensure the testing of individual software components. Managers were attempting to resolve the detailed design and testing problems by defining the processes for both more clearly in Dynamics. Requirements for the testing of modules were being made more transparent and, in some cases, more stringent. Also, simple metrics for tracking and measuring the impact of good test practices were being developed.

5. Managing outside organisations

The process of managing outside suppliers of software and data fell into two categories: (a) customer interactions, and (b) subcontractor and supplier management.

(a) Customer interactions

Although the formal system made allowances for customer interactions in the design and development process at the early phase, most engineers believed that customer feedback was central throughout the project life cycle and not just at the early requirements capture stage. As Triumph progressed, new needs emerged and client requirements were changed. Software practitioners had to respond to these changes and this complicated the rational software life cycle. However, in Triumph as in other projects, there was insufficient customer interfacing planned at the engineering level, as requirements were supposed to be captured early on. Engineers responded to difficulties as they arose, used their experience and judgement to pre-empt problems and employed their discretion in deciding on particular courses of action to resolve problems.

(b) Subcontractors and suppliers

Along with customers, major suppliers were on the critical path of software development and systems integration, a feature not recognised in the formal company process chart, nor in the simple model of Figure 6.1. In Triumph, some difficulties (e.g. delays and technical problems) resulted from problems with suppliers. Engineers responded by working more closely and regularly with suppliers on a co-engineering basis to help identify and manage supplier risks.

Such difficulties were compounded in the case of Triumph by the rigidity of the formal ILS system for purchasing. This rigidity convinced the project manager that the best way to ensure the necessary spare parts were obtained from suppliers on time was to bypass the formal system. Managers felt forced to take unsanctioned actions to mitigate the risks introduced by ILS.

6. Measuring and monitoring of progress

A variety of data-collection and metrics tasks were called for in the formal company manual. However, little data on software performance and productivity were actually collected. The data which were available could not be used to track and improve performance in software. In addition, the accounting practice in Dynamics of booking general infrastructural work to specific projects tended to mask true project costs. Although engineers recognised that simple, clear and useful metrics were needed to track and improve software performance, these were not available, nor was there any agreement on what form such metrics should take and how they could be developed and used.

7. Learning processes

As Chapter 7 shows, one very important task in project-based organisations is to capture and transfer knowledge from one project to another, thereby increasing learning, ameliorating risks and raising productivity. The formal system involved a post-project review contained in the company toolkit. While Triumph had a brief review, in many other cases post-project meetings were not conducted. Overall, there was no basic system in place for analysing and reflecting on projects and feeding back key lessons (positive and negative) into the organisation. Constraints on time and resources prevented more practitioners from engaging in post-project learning assessments. Knowledge sharing was largely informal as individuals gained experience and moved from one project to another.

A market for experienced people had developed with capable, knowledgeable and experienced individuals in high demand from competing project managers and departmental heads. Because learning was haphazard and focused on individuals, there was a risk that good practices and successes might not be repeatable.

Is the Triumph case generalisable?

The above evidence indicates considerable deviation between rational and soft processes in Triumph. It should be noted that Dynamics is a highly respected, successful world leader in flight simulators for both the civil and military fields. As such, it is reasonable to ask: (1) why did actual processes differ so much from rational ones? and (2) are the underlying causes particular to Dynamics or flight simulation or can they be expected to occur in other products, companies or sectors?

From the Triumph case we can identify at least seven causes of divergence between soft and rational processes:

- first, the turbulent, high-pressured business environment;
- second, the complexity of the product and project tasks;
- third, difficulties in precisely capturing customer requirements at the start of, and during, the project;
- fourth, the need to progress with incomplete information due to feedback loops between later and earlier stages of production;
- fifth, new, unpredictable requirements emerging during production;
- sixth, heavy work pressures among staff;
- seventh, the role of outside organisations with conflicting business goals and motivations.

The high-pressured work environment, itself partly caused by industrial turbulence, is by no means uncommon. Indeed, many firms face fast-changing technologies and markets, even in sectors once noted for their stability (e.g. aerospace, the utilities, military and shipbuilding). Other causes of work pressure in Triumph included employee redundancies (downsizing) and new management processes, again not uncommon, especially in high-technology fields.

Regarding product and task complexity, although in many industries products are much simpler than in flight simulation, in others they are equally or more complex, requiring multiple sets of components, skills and knowledge – for example, hospital information support systems, air traffic control systems, avionics systems, intelligent buildings, oil drilling equipment and aircraft engines. As with simulators, these are complex systemic products involving an important component of embedded software. Most are project-based and the user is often involved in design, installation, maintenance and post-delivery modifications. Although issues of this kind may not apply to the production stage of low-cost, mass-produced goods based on standard components (e.g. cars, TVs and camcorders), they are likely to apply to the design and development stages.

In short, similar difficulties are likely to present themselves in high-technology project businesses of all kinds. Uncertainty, incomplete information, difficulties in fully capturing user requirements and the emergence of new, unpredictable system requirements during production are all closely related. Such properties are to be expected in high-technology systems with multiple interfaces and varied knowledge bases, although they probably do not apply to very simple, low-cost products.

The failure of suppliers to deliver key inputs is fairly common in major projects which involve many firms, but less common in projects carried out largely in-house. The trend in some CoPS industries is for large systems integrators to outsource production (e.g. in aeroengine and warship production). As Chapter 4 showed, this has occurred in response to increasing product complexity, the rise of innovative input manufacturers from, for example, the semiconductor and computer industries (Miller et al., 1995) and the strategic desire to focus on core systems integration capabilities by restricting the range of in-house component production activities.

External suppliers may not share the project or business goals of the prime contractor and may have different company cultures and ways of working. It may not always be possible (or even desirable) to attempt to force outside organisations to comply strictly with rational formal internal processes. In major projects, soft factors such as trust, goodwill, negotiation skills and persuasion are likely to be the critical factors in project success.

When all or most of the above causal factors apply, deviations between soft and rational processes of the kind witnessed in Triumph are likely to be replicated in other sectors, as might be the outcomes in terms of project risks and difficulties. If the above factors apply with less force (e.g. because production occurs largely within one firm or because there is industrial stability and little work pressure), the deviation may be expected to be less intense and actual soft processes may approximate the rational more closely. Conversely, in large projects with very high levels of technical complexity and novelty, with many subcontractors involved, we might expect to find more severe divergencies between rational and soft processes – and *more* intense problems in completing projects on time and within budget.

In major high-technology projects, it is highly unlikely that rational systems alone will be adequate to the task at hand. The need for speed, flexibility, human initiative, rapid problem solving and adjustment to new technical circumstances will place great pressures on these rational processes. In response to uncertainty, engineers are likely to fall back on soft methods to enable them to resolve and avoid problems, mitigate risks and possibly even turn circumstances to their advantage.[14] We observed that experienced engineers do not fully trust elaborate rational systems, particularly if they are imposed from above. Instead, they use their experience and judgement to make discretionary choices. Such actions do not reflect a failure to follow company rules but rather a failure of the procedures themselves and, in the case of Triumph, a strong desire to meet the customer's requirements and secure follow-on orders.

Representing soft processes

A partial representation of process stages

To highlight typical problems faced in managing complex software processes, it is helpful to outline the interdependencies and feedback loops found in Triumph and which occur in other complex, multi-firm projects we have observed. The simple model does not attempt to illustrate all informal soft processes but focuses on stages through time to illustrate the progressive narrowing of options and reduction of risk/uncertainty found in engineering projects involving a major software component.[15]

The waterfall model of the software process in Figure 6.1 fails to illustrate the overlap between stages and the feedback loops between users, suppliers and other projects.[16] In practice, key engineers were pulled out of their allocated projects to solve problems on other projects, causing cross-project scheduling loops, technical problems and knock-on delays. Figure 6.2 provides a rough approximation of actual simulator software progress, to be contrasted with the neat formal process of Figure 6.1. Figure 6.2 is developed in four stages to show

[14] For example, in one software module in Triumph person-hours had been over-estimated so engineers were able to transfer hours to a module which was lagging behind.

[15] The idea that projects follow a process of option/uncertainty narrowing through learning was first put forward by authors such as Lindblom (1959) and Klein (1962).

[16] More sophisticated models such as the spiral model also tend to ignore overlaps, inter-company feedback loops and informal processes (Boehm, 1988). An excellent exception is also provided by Boehm (1989b), who addresses the need for negotiation skills in multi-company software projects.

6.2.1 Main stages (a) including overlaps (b)

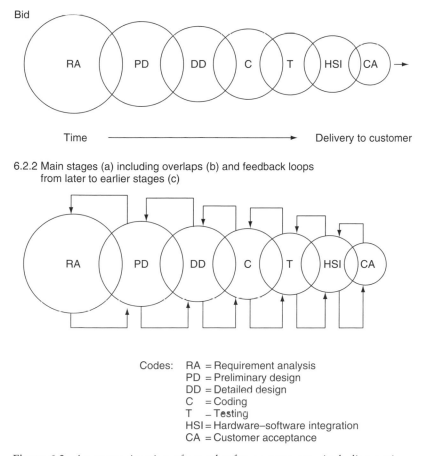

Codes: RA = Requirement analysis
        PD = Preliminary design
        DD = Detailed design
        C   = Coding
        T   – Testing
        HSI = Hardware–software integration
        CA = Customer acceptance

Figure 6.2. An approximation of actual software processes, including option narrowing and feedback loops

how the layers of process complexity build upon each other, resulting in a complicated set of feedback loops between stages, with suppliers and customers and other projects proceeding simultaneously in the organisation.[17]

---

[17] To keep the representation manageable we omit other important connections, notably links with the functional departments which often support projects.

6.2.3 (a) (b) (c) plus customer feedback loops (d) and key supplier feedback loops (e)

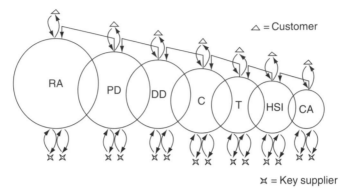

6.2.4 (a) to (e) plus feedback loops from other projects (f)

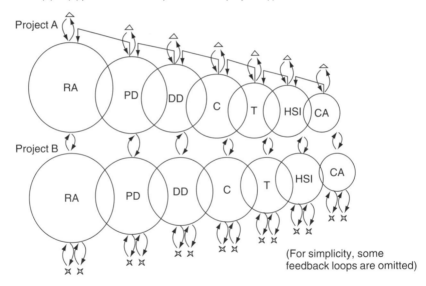

Figure 6.2. (cont.)

Figure 6.2.1 shows the main stages (a) and their overlaps (b). This corresponds to Figure 6.1 but highlights the overlap between stages in terms of both time and technical feedback. Often, for example, the detailed design will begin before the preliminary design is finished and will feed back valuable information to the preliminary design. The spheres, which represent each main activity, become smaller and smaller as the final stage of customer acceptance is approached. The size of the sphere indicates the degree of imprecision and uncertainty (and risk) in relation to the final output. As the project proceeds, uncertainty and risk diminish, options are narrowed and learning occurs until the simulator is completed successfully.

Figure 6.2.2 includes (a) and (b) and adds feedback loops (c) from later to earlier stages. In simulators new unforeseen requirements can emerge fairly late on in the project cycle (e.g. from input from the human pilot), which requires revisions to the preliminary design or indeed the requirements analysis. Such changes, if major, can have system-wide knock-on effects and require changes in several software modules and their interfaces.

Figure 6.2.3 adds customer feedback loops (d) and key supplier feedback loops (e). The customer, represented by a triangle, is able to feed in at all stages of the work, and especially at the early and late stages. During the requirements analysis, very close customer interaction is expected. During testing, often the client will wish to see, approve and comment on test procedures and schedules. In the case of civil simulators the regulator may also play a part during these activities. Equally, the key suppliers, represented by x, are critical to the project's progress. In the case of Triumph, Lockheed supplied the data package, Evans and Sutherland the main visual system, and Concurrent Computer Corporation the computer systems and training in the ADA language. Thus, the process is one of co-engineering as the partners work with each other, share data and feed the systems integrator with key components.

Finally, Figure 6.2.4 draws back to show how one project also has feedback loops with other projects (f) proceeding at the same time in the organisation. In some cases, key engineers are withdrawn from projects (as in Triumph) to work on other projects. Equipment and other resources have to be shared. Despite the efforts of project managers to retain a coherent project team, emergencies arise on other projects and new bids occur which draw resources and priority away from the project in question. In fact, Figure 6.2.4 understates the complexity of cross-project scheduling loops. There may be several projects which relate to each other in a variety of ways. Some of the engineers on Triumph, for example, worked on four or five projects at any one time, although these individuals were exceptions.

Possible benefits from a representation of actual processes

Viewing the project in the light of Figure 6.2.4 points to the causes
and some of the implications of actual software processes at work,
although it does not capture the soft processes themselves. Constant
human actions and reactions have to take place to deal with uncertainty, emergent properties and multiple feedback loops. Figure 6.2.4
suggests the importance of informal communications, meetings,
workshops, motivation and good team relations for the effective
completion of complex projects. Without these, despite highly elaborate rational procedures, projects will stand little chance of successful
completion.

The representation in Figure 6.2.4 also points to potential areas of
difficulty for those involved in flight simulator projects and other
projects facing uncertainty, turbulence and technical difficulties. The
real process model implies that informality is likely to come into play
and that healthy soft processes such as team building, communications,
decision making under pressure and uncertainty, time management
and human motivation are essential to project efficiency and effectiveness. The model can help to alert senior managers and software
analysts to some of the real problems facing project teams and help
initiate new engineers into the complicated real world of software
engineering.

Conclusions

This chapter underlines the importance of both soft and hard management tools in the management of CoPS. As noted in Chapter 3 these
capabilities and tools are critical to effective project management in
general and not just to software-intensive projects. The software and IT
project challenge is particularly daunting because of the craft-based
nature of production, extreme design complexity and the difficulties
of integrating large numbers of subsystems. Because of the lack of
certainty on how to proceed from stage to stage and the high frequency
of unexpected events, the gap between soft and rational processes is
often high, leading to major problems in design, manufacture, delivery
and cost control.

Our case study shows that the gap between rational and soft (or
real) processes has significant implications for project success as well

as for management. We identified seven major causes of variation between soft and rational processes. Under these circumstances, rational systems were inadequate and project managers and practitioners fell back on informal soft practices. Even though soft practices were often hidden from upper management and ran contrary to formal processes, they were needed by the project team to 'get the job done'. Many high-technology projects face similar conditions of uncertainty and risk. Under these conditions, human initiative, tacit knowledge, soft tools and fast informal communications are essential to task completion.

Given the divergencies between soft and rational processes in high-technology projects it is actually *irrational* to proceed with rational, formal tools and procedures 'as if' they are adequate to the task at hand. Nevertheless, contrary to the assumptions of some organisation analysts, rational processes have their place. In the case study, rational systems provided a useful (if inaccurate) route map to completion and a series of logical steps and targets to initiate actions (e.g. requirement capture and detailed design). They provided common software standards to aim for, both within the project and across the company. They also presented an ideal benchmark for measuring progress, including a detailed timetable with milestones. Without this official, rational model of how to proceed, software engineering could descend into chaos, with individuals acting independently of team goals.

Formal procedures provide a single deterministic (if unrealistic) way forward where, in reality, there are perhaps dozens or hundreds of possible ways forward. The rational process also provides some constraints on the creativity of individuals – and helpful rules for the less creative to follow. These are both necessary for the successful management and completion of complex projects.

However, the rational approach *on its own* is insufficient. It palpably cannot deal with the many real-world difficulties which occur in most high-technology projects and is therefore insufficient for the task at hand. The rational approach is virtually silent on vital issues such as how to delegate and empower project managers and how to manage and capture informal learning. It has little or nothing to say on how to build effective project teams, how to communicate well, how to deal with and motivate suppliers, and how to understand and meet the changing and unpredictable needs of customers. Most importantly, the rational model could not cope with the reality of discretionary choice among software engineers. In the real world it is both necessary and desirable that software engineers exercise a degree of discretion over procedures for task completion when they are facing conditions of task complexity, uncertainty and work pressure. Unlike standardised hardware manufacturing production, a large proportion of the software task is a highly skilled, design-intensive, individualistic activity which does not lend itself to a Taylorist, rational division of labour.

The most important point about rational processes is that it is *the manner in which they are created, valued, perceived and implemented*, which determines their usefulness or otherwise. If rational processes are developed by senior management and treated as rules which must be followed, they will fail to accommodate the messy reality of much of the software task – they will also play their part in the failure of projects. Over time a widening of the soft vs rational gap is likely to lead not only to a lack of knowledge of real-world problems on the part of senior management but also to the imposition of unhelpful, time-consuming, bureaucratic procedures which hamper rather than assist real processes. Nevertheless, much of the software field proceeds by ignoring soft realities and instead seeks to impose even more rigid rational systems (e.g. Pulford et al., 1996; Jones, 1996) or proceeds 'as if' real processes were rational (Parnas and Clements, 1986; Kellner, 1996).

The lessons from software and IT for managing project business more generally are clear. Firms must pay equal attention to the development of rational and soft dimensions of their project capabilities. Rational practices must be treated as necessary but insufficient conditions for success and designed to support real processes of value to practitioners. This implies that practitioners must play a significant part in developing procedures so that they become rooted in real practices rather than being rational theories. For CoPS suppliers of all kinds, this implies a continuous effort by senior management to improve processes by identifying divergencies between soft and rational processes and narrowing gaps which exist. This requires a senior management commitment to questioning official values, routines and organisational culture ('this is the way we do things around here'). By ensuring that rational processes are useful and flexible guides to action, it is possible to reduce the soft vs rational gap and improve productivity and effectiveness in project business. While this issue comes into sharp relief in software-intensive CoPS projects, it is also relevant to other types of project (e.g. R&D, new product development and IT projects) in high-volume industries. Without due attention to soft management issues, these projects too are likely to fail to live up to expectations.

7 | *Learning in the project business*

T HIS chapter examines the learning processes that must occur for a project business to develop the capabilities to move into a new technology and market position.[1] The long-term profitability, survival and growth of the project business depend on its ability to learn from new base-moving projects and to convert the knowledge gained into new organisational capabilities and improvements in project performance. However, research has emphasised the challenges that firms face when they attempt to capture the learning gained through projects and transfer it to their wider organisations (Middleton, 1967; Gann and Salter 1998 and 2000; DeFillippi, 2001; Grabher, 2003). There is a risk that the knowledge and experience gained are lost when the project finishes, the team dissolves and its members move on to other projects or are reabsorbed into the organisation. Unless lessons learnt are communicated to subsequent projects, there is also a risk that the same mistakes are repeated.

Despite the difficulties of project-based learning, several studies show that firms can and do achieve organisational learning through projects (Keegan and Turner, 2001; Ayas and Zeniuk, 2001; Prencipe and Tell, 2001). However, research on project-based learning has tended to focus on snapshots of learning practices within a single project or learning between projects, with few examples of 'enduring engagement in learning and profound large-scale transformation' as firms succeed over time in generating and diffusing the knowledge gained throughout their organisations (Ayas and Zeniuk, 2001: 61).

This chapter provides evidence to show how successful firms learn profoundly and continuously from projects. We present a model which shows that the project-based learning that occurs when a firm diversifies into new technology and market positions should be analysed and understood as a dynamic process of project capability building.

---

[1] This chapter is based on a paper by Brady and Davies (2004).

184

Drawing upon the broader literature on organisational learning (Nelson and Winter, 1982; March, 1991), the model shows that initial moves into a new technology or market base are characterised by 'exploratory learning' when the firm experiments and innovates with new bid and project practices. A firm's traditional project management routines may have to be abandoned or radically revised in order to move successfully into the new type of project. Efforts are made to capture the learning generated by the initial exploratory base-moving projects and to transfer the knowledge and experience gained to subsequent projects and to the wider organisation. In a growing market, the emphasis switches over time to 'exploitative learning' as the firm capitalises on the knowledge and learning gained to develop the company-wide capabilities, resources and routines needed to execute an increasing number of projects.

To explore and explain these dynamic processes of project-based capability building, the chapter uses case studies of project-based learning in two leading international suppliers of CoPS – Ericsson and Cable & Wireless (C&W). During the period 1994 to 2003, these firms engaged in a process of capability development to carry out radically different types of base-moving projects: C&W moved into global outsourcing solutions for large corporate customers and Ericsson moved into turnkey and other service-intensive projects for mobile phone operators.[2] The chapter reveals how these firms developed and exploited project-based learning to build organisational capabilities. It also shows how the firms developed their business-wide organisational capabilities in order to improve their wider project processes and performance.

Based on our empirical findings, a model of project capability building is introduced consisting of two interacting and co-evolving levels of learning.[3] First, from the bottom-up, are the project-led phases of learning that occur when a firm moves into new technology or market base: an exploratory vanguard project phase; a project-to-project phase to capture lessons learnt; and a project-to-organisation phase when the organisation increases its capabilities to deliver many projects. Second,

---

[2] Under contracts for turnkey solutions, the supplier is responsible for the entire set of activities involved in the design, integration, construction, testing and delivery of a fully functioning system. In theory, all the customer has to do is turn a key.

[3] The inductive method and longitudinal case study used to construct the model are described in Appendix C.

from the top-down, is the business-led learning that occurs when top-down strategic decisions are taken to create and exploit the company-wide resources and capabilities required to perform increasingly predictable and routine project activities.

The model can be used as a tool to help managers and researchers analyse and improve project-based learning in their organisations and benchmark their performance with other firms, sectors and industries. The phases of learning have become increasingly important to the strategy of a growing number of firms which, like C&W and Ericsson, have been developing a new base of project capability to perform activities outsourced to them by their customers, by entering into long-term strategic partnerships to provide high-value integrated solutions to their customer needs (which we discuss in Chapter 8).

Learning and project capability building

Penrose's (1959) resource-based theory of firm growth discussed in Chapter 3 has been described as a 'learning theory of the firm' (Best, 1990: 127). She argued that the possible paths of direction a firm can follow are shaped by its previously acquired managerial knowledge and experience as well as its ability to absorb valuable new learning and build new capabilities. In addition to the different sets of strategic and functional capabilities, we argued in Chapter 3 that project capabilities are an increasingly vital source of competitive advantage. Studies of organisational capabilities in the resource-based literature have emphasised the importance of knowledge gained from learning, but have largely neglected to examine adaptive organisational learning processes that occur as a firm moves its capability base or adapts to a rapidly changing external environment.

The knowledge that organisations possess through learning can be divided into four distinct types, shown in Table 7.1, associated with explicit/tacit and individual/group distinctions (Cook and Brown, 1999). These four types of knowledge refer to knowledge that both people and organisations possess. According to Cook and Brown, this 'epistemology of possession' cannot account for the knowing associated with concrete individual and group action, which calls for an 'epistemology of practice'. The experience gained through 'knowing in action' produces ongoing changes in the knowledge of particular individuals and enables a collection of individuals to work together in a

Table 7.1: Typology of learning and knowledge

Explicit knowledge	Explicit knowledge can be codified, formally expressed and learned from other people (Nonaka and Takeuchi, 1995). It refers to 'objective' knowledge contained in manuals, guides and procedures (Penrose, 1959: 53). Explicit knowledge is independent of individuals and can be transmitted to others by formal teaching or the written word.
Tacit knowledge	Tacit knowledge refers to the learning gained from personal experience. This form of knowledge is embedded in firm-specific methods, the 'best ways of doing things', skills and teamwork (Best, 1990: 127; Nonaka and Takeuchi, 1995). It 'cannot be articulated' (Nelson and Winter, 1982: 76) and cannot be separated from particular individuals or groups of individuals working in teams. Although 'experience itself can never be transmitted to others' (Penrose, 1959: 53), the results of experience can be converted into objective knowledge and learned from other people or from the written word.
Individual learning	Individual learning occurs when a person gains experience and knowledge.
Organisational learning	Organisational learning happens when groups of individuals use their collective knowledge and experience to perform activities. As Penrose emphasised, a firm is more than a collection of individuals: 'It is a collection of individuals who have had experience in working together, for only in this way can "teamwork" be developed' (Penrose, 1959: 46). The experience possessed by teams of individuals helps to draw attention to the unique organisational capability base of the firm.

group or organisation (Orlikowski, 2002). Cook and Brown (1999) argue that the interaction – or 'generative dance' – between knowledge and knowing is a powerful source of organisational innovation. The interaction does not 'convert' tacit into explicit knowledge as Nonaka and Takeuchi (1995) suggest. Rather, it generates new knowledge which may be tacit or explicit in nature.

Organisational learning

Studies of organisational learning distinguish between resources allocated to routine and innovative learning processes (Nelson and Winter, 1982; March, 1991). Organisations make explicit choices about how to use scarce resources for alternative investments and competitive strategies. They can continue to invest in their current technology and market base by exploiting existing capabilities that are predictable and routinised. Alternatively, they can respond innovatively by exploring unknown technological and market alternatives and by developing new capabilities.

As we discussed in Chapter 3, a firm's organisational capabilities are based on routines. Built around previous patterns of learning, routines refer to repetitive and predictable patterns of productive activity involved in producing products and services that are 'visibly "the same" over extended periods' (Nelson and Winter, 1982: 97; March and Simon, 1958: 13). A firm's tacit knowledge is embodied in well-defined routines and stored in its organisational memory. Formal memories such as written records and other explicit knowledge play a role, but are not sufficient to maintain a firm's organisational memory. Organisations can remember only by exercising routines (Nelson and Winter, 1982). Conversely, innovation refers to the incremental and radical changes in a firm's routines required to develop new technologies or explore new markets (Nelson and Winter, 1982: 128).[4] Innovation is required for a firm to break away from existing routines and branch out in new strategic directions. But routines are required to improve operational performance as a firm develops and consolidates its new technology and market base.

March (1991) develops this theme in relation to organisational learning by making a similar distinction between exploitation and exploration. Exploitation refers to the routine behaviour involved in refining or extending a firm's current capabilities and improving the performance of existing routines. Exploration refers to the innovative behaviour involved in risk taking and experimenting with unfamiliar alternatives. Short-term returns obtained by exploiting a firm's current capability base may appear unprofitable when compared with the longer-term

---

[4] Routinisation and innovation are closely connected. Innovations in routine consist of new combinations of existing routines and reliable routines provide the best components for new combinations.

rewards obtained by exploring new fields of technology or attacking new market spaces. However, firms that engage in the exploration of new possibilities at the expense of exploitation may suffer from 'too many undeveloped ideas and too little competence' (March, 1991: 71).

Each type of activity has distinct implications for learning. The learning gained from exploitation is tied more closely to its consequences through efforts to feed back the learning gained as improvements to current processes. The learning gained from exploration through 'the search for new ideas, markets, or relations has less certain outcomes, longer time horizons, and more diffuse effects than does the further development of existing ones' (March, 1991: 73).

Efforts to strike a balance between exploratory and exploitative learning are closely connected to the rate of change in the environment. In stable environments, where established routines and patterns of behaviour rarely become obsolete, there may be little interest in learning or improving processes through exploration (Hedberg and Wolff, 2001: 537). There is a risk that the learning that does occur – 'single-loop' learning – employs defensive routines to resist change and supports self-sealing and self-repeating patterns (Argyris, 1977). Cyert and March (1963) suggest that when actions improve performance, organisations tend to repeat them until they become standardised or routine operating procedures. However, adhering to standard operating procedures can encourage organisations to behave unreflectively and automatically (Starbuck, 1983 and 1985) which prevents them from adapting to a changing environment.

In changing or unstable environments, firms face the challenge of exploring new alternatives, re-deploying their existing resources and developing new capabilities and routines. The survival of an organisation in a changing environment depends on its ability to exploit successful routines and practices and to generate alternative ones. Individuals and organisations have to engage in self-reflective 'double-loop' learning by confronting previously held assumptions and creating new, more appropriate routines (Argyris, 1977). Time for reflection on the outcomes of learning is essential in order to transform tacit experience into explicit knowledge (Schön, 1983).

Generally, firms increase their capabilities by developing skills, learning new routines and standardising tasks at two different levels (Adler and Clark, 1991). First-order learning involves the incremental development of capabilities which enable existing activities to be repeated more effectively.[5] Second-order learning requires explicit decisions to transform the goals of the enterprise and to change technologies, products, processes and skills in ways that deliberately augment capabilities. The advantages of both levels of learning are cumulative, resulting in increasing returns to experience. Indeed, each increase in an organisation's capability to perform an activity increases the potential returns for engaging in that activity (March, 1991: 73).[6]

Project-based learning

Some important recent studies recognise that learning through projects – a subset of organisational learning – is one of the main ways in which firms develop the capabilities required to improve their performance. The central problem of maintaining project capability is that unless the knowledge and experience gained on one project are transmitted to current or succeeding projects, learning may be dissipated and the same mistakes repeated (Middleton, 1967: 81). When a project finishes, members of the disbanded team often have little time or motivation to reflect on their experience and document transferable knowledge for recycling in future projects (Coombs and Hull, 1997).

The perception that projects perform only unique and non-routine tasks often conceals many potentially transferable lessons. Knowledge creation and learning can occur at several different levels (such as the individual, project, business unit, firm or industry) and often as an unintended by-product of the project activity (DeFillippi and Arthur, 2002). Many firms create organisational learning mechanisms as deliberate attempts to capture the experience gained through projects (Prencipe and Tell, 2001). Such organisational learning mechanisms are the

---

[5] Arrow proposed the counter argument that 'learning associated with repetition of essentially the same problem is subject to diminishing returns' (Arrow, 1962: 155). He argued that learning can produce increasing performance only if the 'stimulus stituations' that induce attempts to solve a problem are 'steadily evolving rather than merely repeating'. By contrast we show below that the repetition of a project activity gives rise to a series of evolving problems involving second-order learning. These are problems of growth and change which organisations *have* to develop the capabilities to solve.

[6] Similarly, Teece et al. (1994) distinguish between static routines which, like first-order learning, enable firms to replicate previously performed activities in a stable environment and dynamic routines which, like second-order learning, are directed towards applying and developing new knowledge and experience.

institutionalised, structural and procedural arrangements that allow organisations to systematically collect, analyse, store, disseminate and use information (Popper and Lipschitz, 1995; Lipschitz et al., 1996). Our colleagues in the CoPS Centre carried out a survey of inter-project knowledge capture and transfer in 43 firms in the UK, Europe, North America and Japan. They found that many learning mechanisms have been developed and adopted, ranging from formal post-project appraisals to informal face-to-face exchanges of project-related news (Brady et al., 2002).

Several studies have emphasised that compared with the high-volume production processes based on standardised and routinised tasks, the one-off and unique nature of project activities provides few opportunities for performance improvements based on routinised learning and systematic repetition (Winch, 1997; Gann and Salter, 1998 and 2000; Turner, 1999). The problem with this widely held view of project-based learning is that it equates all project-based activities with non-routine behaviour. As we discussed in Chapter 3, firms carry out different types of projects ranging from the unique to the repetitive. Unique projects provide fewer opportunities for cumulative learning because project tasks are rarely repeated in the future. In repetitive projects, by contrast, firms can learn from experiences because the tasks performed are repeated in many similar types of projects. Although each project is tailored to a customer's specific needs, they are repeatable because they use the same bid and project management routines and share common components.

The efficient reuse of tacit and codified knowledge is essential to project efficiency in both unique and repetitive projects. On the one hand, firms that deliver one-off or unique projects that do not have clear solutions at the outset rely heavily on tacit knowledge built around the needs of a specific project. The process of sharing and recycling tacit knowledge is difficult, time consuming and costly. Although it is difficult to systematise tacit knowledge, there are opportunities to exploit it by reassigning key members of the project team to other similar projects that require a highly customised solution to a unique problem.

On the other hand, the efficient reuse of codified knowledge is essential in repetitive projects where firms have to solve similar problems over and over. Firms that follow a codification strategy depend on the economics of reuse: 'Once a knowledge asset – software code or manual, for example – is developed and paid for, it can be used many times over at very low cost, provided it does not have to be substantially modified each time it is used' (Hansen et al., 1994: 69–70). By reusing and recombining its knowledge and experience, a firm can utilise its resources more efficiently and take on more projects.

As Chapter 3 showed, firms that move base into a new line of projects that can be repeated in future may realise economies of repetition and recombination. They achieve this by recycling tacit and codified knowledge across an increasing number of projects. The knowledge created by performing tasks that recur frequently over many projects can be reused and recombined in a number of ways to serve different types of customer problems. However, the opportunity to exploit such recurrences may be missed if the knowledge gained is not codified, resulting in a need to create the knowledge from scratch each time a new project is undertaken.

A firm's ability to improve its project efficiency depends on a process of project-based learning and capability building over time. In this way, a firm can grow from the first-of-its-kind project in the new technology and/or market base to a position where it can execute a large portfolio of standardised projects more efficiently and effectively. Programme management techniques can help firms run multiple projects more efficiently, enabling them to share resources and capabilities.

Project learning and capability building

It is clear that a model of project capability building (PCB) is needed to describe the organisational learning that typically occurs when a firm moves into new technology and/or market bases. The PCB model, shown in Figure 7.1, builds on Middleton's (1967) original insight that the establishment of a new project can initiate an organisational cycle leading to far-reaching changes to the capabilities and organisation of the firm.[7]

---

[7] Like suppliers of CoPS, high-volume producers experience a similar process of growth and capability development. The key difference is that in high-volume production growth is driven by product sales rather than project repetition and the emphasis is on developing functional rather than project capabilities. Galbraith's (1982) model of venture start-ups and growth shows how firms evolve through distinct stages from the initial business idea towards high-volume production. Burgelman's study of internal corporate venture projects emphasises that fast growth towards a sizeable business organisation depends on functional efficiency gains obtained by 'the development of routines, standard operating procedures and the establishment of an administrative framework for the new venture' (Burgelman, 1984: 38).

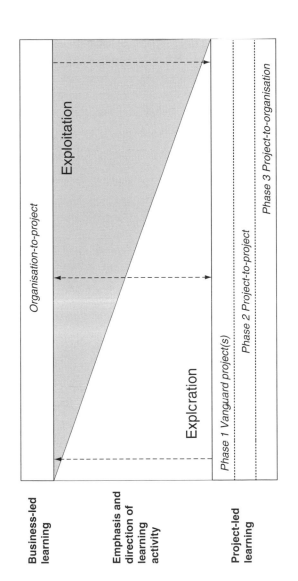

Figure 7.1. Project capability building (PCB) model
Source: Brady and Davies (2004).

The model applies only to projects that have the potential for becoming major new lines of repeatable business, such as turnkey, outsourcing, Design-Build-Operate or Public-Private Partnership projects. It consists of two co-evolving processes of organisational learning, each emphasising the different direction and levels of project capability building within the firm. First, project-led learning occurs when a firm initially moves into a new technology or market base and develops new project capabilities typically through three different phases of project-based learning. Such project-based learning endeavours, undertaken by individual project organisations, units or divisions, are embedded in the wider business and strategic context of the firm.

Second, business-led learning refers to the knowledge that a firm uses when it takes strategic decisions to focus on new project business activities. Whereas project-led learning is largely gained from the bottom up through the activities of the customer-facing project businesses, business-led learning requires deliberate top-down strategic decisions to bring about the changes that occur when a firm creates organisational structures and systematically develops the corporate-wide resources required to exploit a new base of project capability.

Project-led learning

Typically, in phase one, a new project is established at the forefront of a firm to explore strategic opportunities to move into new technology or market bases or to adapt to a changing market environment. These vanguard projects lead the way by anticipating progress as well as gaining experience about the new activity. Because existing routines can be an obstacle to innovation, vanguard projects are responsible for developing new routines outside of the traditional recipe. They are often set up as a separate pilot group to explore the new opportunity on a trial basis and to provide room for new ways of thinking and acting at a distance from the mainstream organisation (Brown and Duguid, 2000: 154).

Project members use their existing knowledge to help guide their action, but gain understanding of the new type of project by carrying out their specific work in a group context (Cook and Brown, 1999). In this phase of within-project learning (Keegan and Turner, 2001: 79), the experience gained is held in common by the group involved in the project. In a process of double-loop learning, project participants must often be prepared to break the rules to invent new routines and ways of working more effectively (Ayas and Zeniuk, 2001: 63). Such deviations from established project procedures and past routines represent a powerful source of learning and organisational innovation.

In phase two, project-to-project learning is predominant as attempts are made to capture and transfer the experience and insights of participants in the vanguard project to subsequent project teams who can benefit from them. Key members of the vanguard project team may be reassembled to work on a subsequent project. Reflective practices, such as project accounts or 'war stories', team learning, lessons-learnt exercises and organisational learning tools, help to communicate the lessons learnt. In this process of between-project learning, formal learning mechanisms (e.g. post-project reviews, intranets and databases) are developed to capture the learning gained on projects, codify it and make it available to other project teams.

Once a sufficient number of the new types of project have been undertaken there is an opportunity in phase three for project-to-organisation learning. In successful organisations, attempts are made to consolidate the initial learning and to systematically spread this accumulated knowledge throughout the department, business unit or division responsible for delivering projects. These project business organisations have to grow or create specialised units with the capabilities required to support the increasing volume of projects. Attempts are made to capture the cumulative learning from previous projects and to institutionalise new routines, information and processes based on those learning experiences. New standardised processes and IT tools have to be put in place to run multiple new bids and projects. This helps to ensure that the knowledge gained from bidding and executing such projects becomes embedded in the organisation's memory.

Business-led learning

These project-led learning processes are embedded within the wider business organisation and strategic context of the firm. Senior management can intervene at any time to actively promote far-reaching organisational changes or withdraw from the new line of projects. Strategic decisions to move forward, such as the creation of divisions, are designed to re-focus the core activities of the firm on the delivery of the new type of project. Customer demands for new technologies, products or services, which require adaptation for existing or new markets, can encourage the emergence of numerous bottom-up project initiatives. The creation of a business unit or venture division provides a place to concentrate resources, capabilities and projects that are scattered throughout the firm. Strategically, top management can gain greater control of the new project activities while continuing to exploit its current mainstream base business. Indeed, previous research on corporate ventures has shown that the creation of a separate division preserves some of the autonomy required to meet the new business opportunity, provides greater focus on the external market environment, and the distance from the mainstream business facilitates a global and cross-divisional strategic perspective (Tidd et al., 1997: 292–3).

Attempts can be made to ensure that important project-based learning is fed back to senior management involved in formulating the overall strategy for the new business opportunity. Ideally, resources and capabilities need to be created which can easily be exploited by the firm as a whole. Processes should be put in place so that the new project activities can be 'routinised for day-to-day performance' (March and Simon, 1958: 26). The objective of business-led learning is to refine and extend a firm's entire organisational capabilities, including its strategic, functional and project routines, in order to fully exploit its new technology or market base.

The interacting levels of the PCB model illustrate the changing direction of organisational learning and triggers for capability building associated with exploratory and exploitative activities. Whereas March (1991) emphasises the 'trade-offs' between the two types of organisational learning, the PCB model attempts to identify the 'transition' from exploration to exploitation as firms advance through the phases. Firms that are quick to enter and capitalise on their experience with a new type of project can gain first-mover advantages. Pioneers in new technology or market positions have a head start in generating new organisational capabilities (Chandler, 1990: 34–5). They can move quickly down the learning curve for each of the different areas of project capability before the challengers go into operation.

Case studies of project capability building

To explain the dynamics of project and business learning it is helpful to illustrate the PCB model by examining episodes of learning and project capability building in two large firms. Because the case studies are from the same sector they provide a fruitful source of comparison. C&W is a service-based firm moving into a new market and technology base for global outsourcing solutions. Ericsson is a product-based firm also moving into higher value-added solutions markets, but without significantly altering its technological base. Both cases show how the initial engagement with a new type of solutions-based project led to transformation of the capability base and organisation of the firm.

Traditional project capability base

C&W is an international telecoms operator and service provider. At the start of our collaboration in 1994 C&W had just moved from a holding company for diverse telecoms services to a federation by developing stronger ties and synergies between its regional business units located in more than fifty countries. Our case study concentrates on the Business Networks (BN) unit within the C&W group. In the mid-1990s, BN was responsible for providing multinational corporate customers with customised voice and data services. The business unit was involved in one main type of project called managed network services (MNS). Drawing upon the resources and networks of C&W's regional business units, BN had developed the capabilities to plan, design and manage MNS contracts using traditional circuit-switching technologies in partnerships with key equipment manufacturers. Where the group was unable to provide coverage using in-house facilities, circuits were leased from third-party operators.

For several decades Ericsson had focused mainly on manufacturing telecoms equipment used in fixed networks operated by traditional public telecommunications operators. Between the late 1970s and mid-1990s, Ericsson gradually moved base to provide mobile communications technology for a new type of customer, namely mobile phone operators. By 1997 Ericsson had become the world's leading manufacturer of mobile systems with 42 per cent of the world market. The following case study is centred on Ericsson Telecommunication Limited (ETL) in the UK (now part of Ericsson Mobile Systems division). In the mid-1990s, ETL and Ericsson's market-facing local companies elsewhere in the world had established the capabilities to perform two types of projects: development projects to improve or refine technologies in each generation of mobile products, and mature product line or implementation projects to design and install equipment (based on existing technology) to meet individual customer specifications for standard equipment supply contracts.

The bid and project management processes performed by both firms were based on the execution of standardised routines which formed part of each organisation's existing project capability base. Project teams in both firms worked to procedures laid out in in-house documents or manuals. For example, C&W used a *Bid Document Preparation Process* which described in detail the procedures involved in preparing MNS proposals (C&W, 1993). Ericsson has used PROPS (the name given to the company's in-house project manual) since 1988 to set up and manage projects in a multi-project environment (e.g. Ericsson, 1990).

It is insightful to illuminate the specific dynamics of capability building that occurred in the two case study firms as they explored departures from their traditional capability base.

Moving the business base: C&W's global outsourcing solutions

Our research with C&W focused on the bidding component of project capabilities. The case shows how C&W moved its entire business base (a technology and market shift) in response to customer demands for a new type of outsourcing project incorporating new internet protocol technologies. The lessons learnt in bidding for two outsourcing contracts were fed back into subsequent projects, led to changes in the organisation of the business unit and contributed to major changes in the strategic direction of the entire C&W group.

Project-led learning

Phase 1: Vanguard project – initial global outsourcing bids
In 1997, some of C&W's largest multinational corporate customers (Standard Charter Bank, Citicorp, Andersen Consulting, Chase Manhattan and Compaq) began to demand more complex and higher-value global outsourcing solutions. They wanted to outsource responsibility for many activities previously performed in-house (e.g. network planning, management and business processes) and wanted their entire IT and telecommunications requirements met using new IP packet-switching technologies. To avoid having to negotiate with numerous operators in different national markets, they also wanted to deal with a single point of contact for their global communications requirements.

C&W's opportunity to move base into the global outsourcing markets and IP technologies arose at a time when the competitive survival of the group was under threat. The uncertainty surrounding several attempts to take over the C&W group affected BN's performance. The unit had failed to win major bids for some time, had undergone several reorganisations and been unable to resolve the difficulties it had experienced in leveraging the resources of C&W's regional business units.

In 1997, BN was galvanised into action by the arrival of two global outsourcing bids: from Citicorp and Andersen Consulting. BN already had some experience with outsourcing bids, but the two new ones involved a long-term partnership with the customer and provided a clear indication of how BN would be working with its customers in future. The Citicorp bid team realised that a new flexible approach of partnering with the customer had to be forged to develop a successful bid. BN's chief executive recognised that established routines and processes developed for less complex MNS projects were inappropriate for outsourcing bids. With the support of senior management, the bid team ignored traditional bid document preparation procedures. Several members of the team had worked together on unsuccessful bids and, unwilling to go through the same process again, felt they had nothing to lose by following their instincts rather than the established methods.

In contrast to the hierarchical management and matrix structure used in standard MNS bids, the team adopted an approach characterised by flexibility, informal team dynamics and a willingness to break the rules if this was required to win the business. Whereas bid teams were usually located in BN's London head office, the outsourcing bid team co-located with the customer in the United States. The creation of what the team called a 'war room' helped to develop a close relationship with the customer as well as among team members. The personal involvement of BN's chief executive in the bid helped enthuse the team and create a desire to win the bid and future business.

Despite Citicorp's advisor recommending the BN bid, Citicorp opted for its incumbent telecoms supplier. However, the knowledge generated and experience gained during the preparation of the unsuccessful bid proved instrumental in winning the next one. In August 1997, BN was invited by Andersen Consulting to tender for another outsource opportunity. The advisor to Citicorp who had been impressed by the

BN approach was also an advisor to Andersen Consulting and recommended that C&W should be invited to put forward a tender. A decision was taken by C&W's board to bid for this high-value contract, which was worth several hundred million dollars, because the global outsourcing market was seen as vital to the survival of the C&W group.

Under the recommendation of BN's chief executive, key members of the Citicorp bid team were reassembled to run the Andersen bid. With the same account director and bid manager, it was possible to build on the experience of the first bid and carry forward the same partnership approach. The BN team again worked closely with the customer to produce a bid document covering all the novel features required by the outsource solution: design, installation, network management and service-level agreements.

After months of negotiation, the final proposal was submitted in March 1998. C&W and GTE, its main American subcontractor, were notified verbally that they were the customer's preferred supplier. In October 1998 the contract was signed and the project moved into implementation.

Phase 2: Project-to-project

BN attempted to build on the knowledge and experience generated during the unsuccessful Citicorp bid by immediately reassigning key members of the team to work on the Andersen Consulting bid. In turn, the knowledge gained from the Andersen Consulting bid proved valuable in bidding for a large outsourcing solution for General Motors, as well as subsequent bids. To capitalise on the experience gained from previous bids, BN adopted a new policy of keeping members of core teams together for two years to work on a series of major outsourcing proposals. In this way, knowledge was enhanced and consolidated.

BN used other learning mechanisms to facilitate project-to-project learning during this phase. For example, there was an independent review of the lessons learnt in the two vanguard outsourcing bids. As part of our research process we interviewed and videotaped key members of the bid teams and senior managers in BN (CEO and vice-presidents) in order to produce a CD-Rom learning tool called *Winning Outsource Bids*. The learning tool outlined the new flexible approach required to develop outsourcing bids and was used by subsequent bid teams.

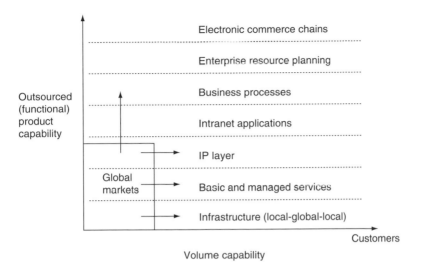

Volume capability

Figure 7.2. Global Markets needs to develop its portfolio
Source: C&W internal bid management presentation (2000).

Phase 3: Project-to-organisation

To accommodate growing demand for outsourcing, BN was reorganised to provide global rather than regionally based solutions.
Previously BN had set up small bid teams organised in a matrix structure to deliver standard MNS contracts from the London head office.
Global outsourcing required a new and larger organisation. BN
increased in size from around 200 staff in 1994 to 700 by 1999.
Large, dedicated teams had to be co-located with each new outsourcing
customer and organised as a pure project-based organisation for a
prolonged selling cycle. As shown in Figure 7.2, BN had to develop a
broader set of capabilities to address the activities being outsourced by
its customers (e.g. intranet applications, business processes and enterprise resource planning) and create partnerships with a new breed of IP
suppliers (Nortel and Cisco Systems) to provide equipment that C&W
installed, maintained and supported.

Business-led learning: the creation of C&W Global Businesses

The experience of winning the Andersen Consulting outsourcing bid
was instrumental in the C&W group's strategic decision to move out of
low-value-added consumer markets and re-focus the entire organisation

on the delivery of global IP solutions to business customers. By 1998, revenue from outsourcing contracts was growing at over 25 per cent each year, reflected in a 155 per cent increase in the division's turnover (Cable & Wireless, 1999). C&W Global Businesses, which operated under a single global brand with a single point of contact for the customer, was formed in 1998. BN was reorganised into a division called Global Markets (GM), responsible for bids and managing global solutions for multinational customers. In 1999, 30 nominated accounts for global customers were transferred to GM from the group's regional operations.

In May 1999, C&W withdrew from consumer activities (e.g. One-2-One and Mercury in the UK) in order to concentrate on business-to-business markets. In June 2000 a new global business, C&W Global, was launched to help GM leverage the resources and capabilities of C&W's regional business units spread around the world. C&W Global developed a global portfolio of products and services divided into simplified groupings to provide business customers with end-to-end solutions for internet protocol and data services.

However, C&W's global strategy was difficult to implement, partly because of the collapse in global telecoms markets, but also because C&W Global failed to gain the full support of the group's regional business units, which were reluctant to cede control over revenue streams from their multinational accounts. Although the group made a decision in 2003 to revert to its traditional regionally based structure, it continues to provide outsourcing solutions through its national and regional business units.

Moving the market base: Ericsson's turnkey solutions
The Ericsson case study also illustrates the ways in which the knowledge generated by conducting a new type of project in a new market base led to far-reaching changes in the strategic focus and structure of the firm's organisation.

Project-led learning

Phase 1: Vanguard project: One-2-One turnkey project
In 1995 Ericsson won a contract to supply a turnkey solution (defined as a fully operational system conceived, built and supplied by Ericsson) to One-2-One (O2O), the UK mobile phone operator then owned by

Mercury (a Cable & Wireless subsidiary). This was the firm's first turn-key project in an industrialised country. By early 1995, O2O was under increasing competitive pressure to respond to its main UK competitor's (Orange) highly successful marketing strategy to achieve nationwide coverage. The idea that a turnkey contract would help O2O achieve its strategic objective of comparable coverage was originally proposed by Nortel (one of O2O's equipment suppliers).

O2O's invitation to tender for the turnkey project was issued in March 1995. Under the contract, O2O announced its intention to outsource all of the network implementation activities it had previously performed in-house, such as cell planning, site acquisition, civil builds, network design, installation, test, acceptance and project management. Due to the high value of the O2O project, the decision to proceed with the turnkey bid had to receive high-level approval from Ericsson's senior management team in Sweden. They recognised that the O2O contract represented a strategic opportunity to move early into what they believed would be a growing market for turnkey solutions in industrialised countries.

The contract was awarded to Ericsson's UK market division (ETL) on 31 July 1995, with an initial goal to achieve 90 per cent coverage of the population of England and Scotland by December 1997. A Turnkey Projects Group was set up to manage the project and to develop the additional and new capabilities required to manage subsequent turn-key projects. It operated relatively autonomously from the rest of the ETL organisation to provide the room needed to experiment with new forms of project organisation, management and capabilities. Given the strategic importance of this project, its progress was monitored closely by top management in Ericsson's Swedish headquarters.

The original plan was to set up the turnkey project organisation and processes using PROPS and existing IT tools. But these approaches proved unable to cope with the size and complexity of the turnkey project. Over twenty different changes were made to the project organ-isation during the first six months to cope with unfamiliar activities and unforeseen events before finally settling on a modified version of the matrix structure defined in Ericsson's PROPS manual. To carry out the O2O turnkey project, ETL had to acquire or develop many new capab-ilities, such as cell planning, site acquisition and civil engineering and other functions. The turnkey group had to develop new project capabil-ities as it learnt to manage longer-term partnerships with the customer and its subcontractors and to provide solutions based on Ericsson's and its competitors' products.

Phase 2: Project-to-project

Members of the vanguard project team continued to work on subsequent turnkey projects for O2O and other mobile phone operators in the UK. They also provided expert advice to Ericsson local-operating companies in Germany, Belgium and Poland beginning to win orders for turnkey projects. However, in general Ericsson's project managers had little time to reflect on their initial turnkey experience beyond standard post-project reviews and documentation.

Our research team, with managers from Ericsson, codified the lessons learnt from the O2O project in a project book called *The Turnkey Project Start-Up Guide* which captured the learning from the vanguard project and drew generic lessons to assist in the future establishment of turnkey projects across all of Ericsson's corporate divisions (Morgan et al., 1997: ix). The guide was intended for Ericsson's senior decision makers (in the company's headquarters and the other business units) and project, commercial and marketing managers in the local-operating companies. It discussed the nature of the opportunities presented by turnkey projects, the implications for Ericsson's organisation and project phases and the types of problems likely to be encountered in turnkey projects.

Phase 3: Project-to-organisation: Turnkey Solutions Services

During 1996 and 1997, Ericsson experienced a rapid increase in the number of turnkey projects undertaken in the UK and elsewhere in Europe. As the managing director of ETL explained: 'We were the first within the Ericsson group to move into turnkey solutions in such a big way. Now the knowhow we have built up can be exploited in other markets' (Brian Barry, quoted in Linx, 1997). But as another senior manager in ETL recognised: 'The trend towards turnkey contracts will require additional competence in the company, not only in certain areas of cellular networks but also in project management' (Richard Whittaker, quoted in Linx, 1997).

To address this capability gap, ETL created an organisation called Turnkey Solutions Services, with key project managers involved in the first turnkey project at its core. Established in 1997, this consultancy unit developed project capabilities in critical areas lacking in the initial turnkey project and acted as a silo for knowledge that the Ericsson's functional departments were unable to provide. It was responsible for supporting the preparation of turnkey bids and projects undertaken by Ericsson's local companies throughout Europe and provided a mechanism for capturing and transferring the knowledge gained from previous projects.

Turnkey Solutions Services personnel were assigned to different turnkey projects to ensure that the knowledge and experience gained from previous and concurrent projects could be used more systematically in the setting up and execution of subsequent turnkey projects. By carefully analysing and codifying the distinct project processes and routines required to deliver turnkey solutions, the unit was able to identify the four main phases of the turnkey project life cycle shown in Figure 7.3:

1. the front-end 'identify and qualify phase' to consult and understand a customer's needs;
2. the 'bid and contract phase' to respond to invitations to tender, prepare proposals and win and negotiate contracts;
3. the 'deliver and implement phase' to manage project execution from network design to integration; and
4. the 'support and enhance phase' to provide services to operate, support and maintain the network.

By 2000, Thomas Vesterlund, Director of Turnkey Solutions Services, recognised that Ericsson had already established strong bid and project-execution capabilities (phases 2 and 3) but needed to develop its capabilities in front-end business consulting (phase 1) and post-project operational services (phase 4) to successfully cover the entire life cycle of activities involved in turnkey solutions projects. The unit also created its own portfolio of increasingly simplified and standardised services to assist in the set-up and execution of the growing number of turnkey and service-intensive projects run by Ericsson's local companies throughout Europe (see Figure 7.4).

Business-led learning: the creation of Ericsson Global Services

While Ericsson's product divisions and local operating companies were launching bottom-up initiatives to meet customer demand for turnkey projects, the company's corporate management team was formulating a far-reaching top-down strategy to reorganise the company around the delivery of turnkey solutions and services. In 1996, Ericsson's Corporate Executive Committee completed the largest planning study

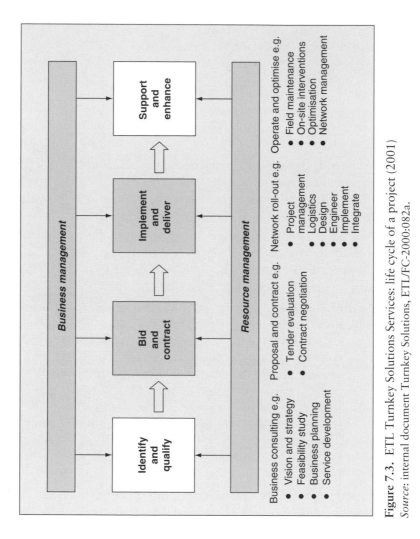

Figure 7.3. ETL Turnkey Solutions Services: life cycle of a project (2001)
Source: internal document Turnkey Solutions, ETL/FC-2000:082a.

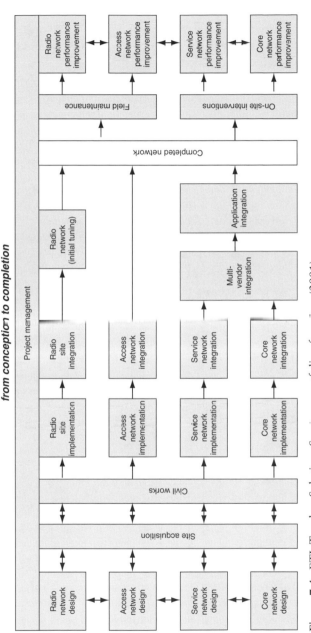

Figure 7.4. ETL Turnkey Solutions Services: portfolio of services (2001)

Source: internal document Turnkey Solutions, ETL/FC-2000:017b

in the company's history. It outlined Ericsson's strategy to create an organisation which could provide mobile operators with solutions and services in response to increasing customer demand from operators like O2O in the UK for mobile networks to be designed, built and managed on a turnkey basis.

It was not until the late 1990s, however, that Ericsson began to implement the strategy by creating organisations with the capabilities to support turnkey solutions and services. In 1999, Ericsson brought together the dispersed turnkey and service activities performed by the various product divisions to form a large central consultancy organisation called Ericsson Services, 'thus strengthening Ericsson's position as complete supplier, system integrator and partner' (Annual Report, 1999: 7). A new division – Ericsson Global Services – was created in 2000 to support the delivery of turnkey solutions and services throughout Ericsson's global operations. In September 2001, Global Services became one of Ericsson's five business units. The Turnkey Solutions unit in the UK and similar initiatives conducted throughout Ericsson were closed down in 2001 as a result of the decision to place all service activities such as portfolio development under the centralised control of Ericsson Global Services.

Ericsson continues to revise its organisation and strategy in response to evolving demand for turnkey solutions and services. In 2003, 120 local Ericsson companies in 140 countries were reorganised to form 28 market units (MUs) and several customer-facing units (CFUs) – such as Ericsson Vodafone – to deal with the largest global customer accounts. Under this new streamlined organisation, all business activities with the customer are undertaken by the MUs and CFUs, providing a single channel to the customer.

Ericsson Global Services is responsible for developing the global service portfolio and supplying resources, capabilities and personnel to help the MUs and CFUs sell and deliver projects for solutions. By 2000, Global Services had reduced the proliferation of 250 service offerings previously developed by Ericsson's product divisions and local companies, such as ETL (see Figure 7.4), to seven Service Solutions families, which addressed each mobile operator's life-cycle requirements from the initial business idea and planning through project execution to service start-up and technical operations. By 2003 Ericsson had further reduced and simplified its service portfolio to three families called AIM (advise, integrate and manage), as shown in

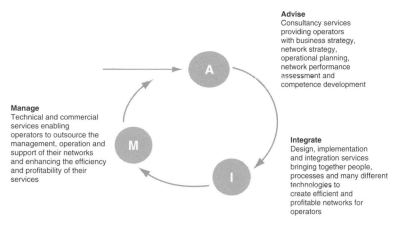

Advise
Consultancy services
providing operators
with business strategy,
network strategy,
operational planning,
network performance
assessment and
competence development

Manage
Technical and commercial
services enabling
operators to outsource the
management, operation and
support of their networks
and enhancing the efficiency
and profitability of their
services

Integrate
Design, implementation
and integration services
bringing together people,
processes and many different
technologies to
create efficient and
profitable networks for
operators

Figure 7.5. Ericsson Global Services – AIM portfolio
Source: Ericsson Annual Report 2002: 22.

Figure 7.5. The target was to have 75 per cent of the services offered as part of Ericsson's solutions to be ordered off the shelf from the AIM portfolio. At the same time, systematic efforts have been made at the corporate level to develop standardised project management routines and business processes for service and solutions-based projects. For example, PROPS, Ericsson's in-house project management guide book, has been substantially revised in recent years to help project organisations inside and outside of Ericsson develop the capability to manage large portfolios of solutions-based projects.

Cross-case analysis

This section shows how the emphasis of learning processes behind the project capability building in the two case studies switched from exploration to exploitation over time. This was achieved by linking the interacting levels of learning to key contextual factors and strategic decisions that triggered either the search for an expanded repertoire of capabilities or the exploitation of existing ones.

Project-led learning

Phase 1

In this phase, the emphasis was on exploratory learning. C&W's bid team and Ericsson's turnkey project organisation needed to gain a detailed understanding of their customers' changing demands. They found that existing in-house project processes and procedures were unable to cope with the scale and complexity of the new types of projects demanded by their customers. Where possible they relied on existing routines and capabilities, but had to develop new areas of knowledge and expertise to meet the changing requirements of their customers.

Senior management in both firms created an open and flexible context which encouraged vanguard project members to question existing routines and styles of management. The vanguard projects operated at a distance from the larger organisation to encourage experimentation and innovation. They developed new management approaches and organisational structures which deviated from established routines and frames of reference. This created some tensions between the vanguard projects and some parts of the parent organisations, which often occurs when pilot groups are isolated from the mainstream organisation (Senge, 1999: 321). In other words, the new ways of thinking pioneered by the vanguard groups represented a threat to the core values and mainstream culture of the larger organisation.

Strategic management in both firms recognised that the rewards from exploration could be realised only in the longer term. They were willing to accept the short-term risks of cost overruns, delays and other problems associated with conducting unfamiliar vanguard projects on the expectation that any losses would be recovered by the future revenue streams.

Phase 2

As other projects were undertaken, the learning shifted from within-project to between-project exploratory learning. Project capabilities were developed without altering existing organisational structures. Rather than simply encouraging a proliferation of alternative practices, deliberate attempts were made to select successful routines and practices and carry them forward into subsequent projects.

Key participants on C&W's bid and Ericsson's turnkey project were largely kept together as a team when assigned to the next project. This ensured that new routines and team-based knowledge that worked well on the first bids and projects were adopted in subsequent ones. However, learning tended to be on an ad hoc basis, with few systematic attempts to spread the initial learning throughout organisations. Although attempts were made to exploit the learning gained, key members of the first bids and projects had little time to reflect on their experience before moving to another project.

Phase 3

In this phase of repeatable project activities, learning from projects was fed back into the project businesses. These organisations changed their structures to accommodate an increasing number of the new type of projects. C&W's business unit employed many new staff and developed new bid, project and functional activities to support global outsourcing bids and projects. ETL created an internal consultancy unit to support the growing volume of turnkey projects executed in the UK and elsewhere in Europe.

As in the first two phases, project capabilities continued to be built from the bottom up by the project business organisation. Emphasis switched from exploration to exploiting what had been learned from previous projects. Attempts were made to refine and institutionalise routines so that knowledge gained from bidding and executing projects became part of their organisational memory. New company-specific routines, processes and IT tools were developed to execute a growing volume of bids and projects more efficiently and effectively.

Business-led learning

The main emphasis of organisational learning implemented by top management in both firms was to move quickly to a position of exploitation. The direction of learning was largely top-down from the corporate organisation to the projects. Attempts were made to simplify, standardise and select among the variety of routines and practices to perform increasingly repetitive and efficient project processes. Company-wide capabilities and resources had to be created to provide a standardised platform of products and simplified portfolio of services as low-cost components that could be used in a growing volume of projects.

Senior management at corporate level in both firms developed strategies to refocus their entire organisations around the new projects. C&W decided to move quickly into the new solutions-based markets by creating C&W Global to focus on the delivery of global outsourcing solutions. Ericsson created the Global Services division and re-focused its entire organisation around the delivery of solutions-based projects.

Both firms continue to engage in some degree of exploratory learning by developing emergent strategies formulated in response to changes in the business environment. Although the organisational learning was mainly top-down, key lessons learnt about the projects were fed back to assist in strategy development and implementation. C&W, for example, has still not settled on a stable structure. In 2003, the firm abandoned its organisation based on global businesses and created a new network of nationally based companies to deliver solutions to business customers.

The case studies show that the organisations followed their own distinctive paths of project and business learning and that the speed of response at which they moved was heavily influenced by their response to the market environment. C&W's senior management believed that the company's survival depended on achieving immediate success in global outsourcing markets. After winning the Andersen Consulting bid in 1998, its aggressive strategy to move quickly to the new base was hampered by the collapse of world telecoms markets and the continuing resistance of C&W's regional business units to the global approach. In 2003, however, the strategic decision to revert to the traditional structure of providing solutions through its decentralised network of nationally based organisations underlines the importance of emergent strategy formulation.

By contrast, Ericsson moved into turnkey solutions from a position of strength as the world's leading mobile equipment supplier. Considerable time and effort has gone into developing, revising and refining strategies to achieve sustainable and long-term growth in this new market base. Since the O2O turnkey project in 1995, Ericsson has continued in its efforts to build an organisation that can effectively harness the corporate-wide capabilities required to deliver large numbers of solutions-based projects.

Our case studies show that moving base into provision of integrated solutions is not necessarily an easy or smooth transition. The episodic nature of learning emphasises the continuing challenge of creating, shaping and adapting project and other capabilities to a rapidly evolving business environment. Both firms had to overcome significant tensions and differences of opinion between strategic and operational levels of their organisations in order to achieve progress in this new activity. In C&W's case, the top-down strategy to create a centralised GM division was hampered by the group's regional business units which wanted to retain profit-and-loss responsibilities for their multinational corporate accounts. In Ericsson's case, the creation of Global Services meant that the bottom-up units were required to relinquish control of their portfolio of service and turnkey solution activities. Indeed, the director of ETL's Turnkey Service Solutions unit resigned over this because he felt that the decision to centralise service development activities would undermine Ericsson's ability to create tailored solutions to a customer's specific needs at the local level.

Conclusions

The project capability building model developed in this chapter illustrates the dynamics of organisational learning and capability building that occur when firms move into a new line of projects which are likely to be repeated in future, such as turnkey, outsourcing and PPP projects. The model describes two co-evolving and interacting levels of learning associated with project capability building. At the project or operational level, an initial engagement with a new type of project can have far-reaching consequences for the strategy and organisation of entire firms. As firms progress through the phases of project-led learning, the emphasis of their activities switches from exploration in the vanguard phase through the transition phases when the exploratory learning is transferred to other projects and exploited by the project business organisation. At the business or strategic level, organisational learning and strategy implementation have to move rapidly to a position of exploitation. Our case firms did this by creating global service organisations with the capabilities and corporate-wide resources needed to perform repeatable project activities. Other firms may deploy other structures to exploit their project-based resources in this way.

For managers, the model presented is a valuable tool for analysing and plotting the position of a firm. In terms of the three phases of project-led learning, a firm whose path is confined to phases 1–2 gains important learning, develops new routines and adds capability, but without altering the existing organisation. Firms that follow a path through phases

1–3 have to extend their capabilities and change their project business organisations to accommodate a growing volume of projects.

It may be that firms rarely conduct business-led learning to refocus their strategy and entire organisation around the new project capability base. However, recent moves into solutions-based projects, such as outsourcing and turnkey arrangements, suggest that a growing number of firms are embarking on long-term paths of project capability building and organisational transformations. The PCB model is designed to provide a framework for analysing and improving these long-term project capability building processes.

As one of the pioneers of this new type of project, IBM's vanguard outsourcing project with Eastman Kodak in 1989 marked the beginning of a long capability building process leading to the creation of IBM Global Services in 1995 and ongoing strategic attempts to focus on repeatable solutions delivery (IBM, 2002). The ability of firms like C&W and Ericsson to emulate IBM's success depends crucially on their efforts to develop and hone their capabilities over many years through phases of exploratory and exploitative learning. The model presented is also useful for researchers as it provides an analytical framework for comparative studies of similar project-based dynamics in other major firms and sectors, through a comparison of first movers, leaders and followers in project capability building. The model applies to other sectors (e.g. software, accountancy, professional services, advertising and corporate finance sectors) that organise their productive activities in projects, especially those types of projects subject to standardisation and economies of repetition and recombination. Furthermore the model can be used to analyse other categories of projects such as new product development and the management of internal capital projects (e.g. factory automation, scientific instrumentation and IT systems) in high-volume consumer goods industries.

8 | *Integrated solutions for customers*

S INCE the early 1990s, a growing number of firms across many industries have been changing their business strategy to focus on the provision of high-value added services, such as distribution, finance, maintenance and other intangible, knowledge-based activities (Quinn, 1992; Oliva and Kallenberg, 2003).[1] Suppliers of CoPS in particular are developing new business models to provide products and services as high-value integrated solutions from a single source that address each customer's business or operational needs.[2] In a shift away from their traditional product or service offerings, firms like Alstom, the train manufacturer, now offer solutions for train availability, Rolls-Royce supplies 'power-by-the-hour', and WS Atkins, the design and technical consultancy company, provides solutions for the life cycle of a building.

Integrated solutions refer to a variety of new types of large capital goods projects supplied by CoPS firms, such as Ericsson's turnkey solutions and C&W's global outsourcing solutions discussed in Chapter 7. Providers of integrated solutions undertake many of the core systems integration and service-based activities previously performed internally by large business or government customers, such as corporate IT users, airlines and telecoms operators. Rather than supplying

---

[1] There are at least two different ways of defining services. (1) The traditional distinction between manufacturing and services assumes that all services reside downstream, such as maintenance, operations and marketing. Services refer to the knowledge-based, intangible activities required for the physical product to add value in ways that are intangible for the user. (2) Many 'functions' performed at the manufacturing end of the value stream can also be seen as services (e.g. product design and engineering) when sold externally (Quinn, 1992: 175).

[2] For further confirmation of this trend see Slywotzky (1996); Slywotzky and Morrison (1998); Wise and Baumgartner (1999); Shepherd and Ahmed (2000); Davies et al. (2001); Davies et al. (2003); Davies (2003 and 2004); Sandberg and Werr (2003).

equipment and software, as in the past, the CoPS supplier specifies, designs, integrates and delivers a fully functioning system and goes beyond this to provide services such as finance and maintenance to meet the customer's long-term needs. The supplier may also operate the system during its life cycle. These solutions-based projects are variously called turnkey solutions, global outsourcing solutions, design-build-operate, Private Finance Initiative (PFI) and Public–Private Partnership (PPP).

Drawing upon new case-study research, this chapter shows that many suppliers of CoPS are developing and implementing strategies for integrated solutions and, as a result, fundamentally altering their positions in the industry value stream. Rather than simply moving downstream from manufacturing to services as some authors suggest (Wise and Baumgartner, 1999; Oliva and Kallenberg, 2003), our research reveals that suppliers are moving into integrated solutions from both upstream and downstream positions to occupy the high-value space situated between manufacturing and services. To implement their strategies for integrated solutions our case study firms have needed to develop or gain access to new sets of capabilities which are often not easily available to firms traditionally based in manufacturing or services. The key element of this new business strategy is the development of systems integration capability which we discussed in Chapter 4. This core capability is required to design and integrate all the component parts of a solution, including the systems hardware, software and services. The detailed understanding of their customer's operational needs and the systems they have designed, integrated and delivered places many CoPS suppliers in a strong position to provide high-value services, including consultancy advice and finance, and to operate and maintain a system during its life cycle.

As we show, systems integration and other service capabilities can sometimes be developed in-house but, often, CoPS producers have to develop new partnerships with external suppliers of the key elements of a solution. Whether originally based in manufacturing or services, our empirical research shows that firms are creating customer-facing organisations to mobilise and integrate the novel combinations of resources and capabilities needed to provide solutions to each customer's needs. This represents a major change in the industrial landscape of major capital projects.

This chapter is based on the findings of a three-year collaborative research project[3] which studied in depth the recent changes in the strategies of five international suppliers of CoPS:

- Alstom Transport – rolling stock and signalling systems;
- Ericsson Mobile Systems – mobile phone networks;
- Thales Training and Simulation – flight simulation;
- WS Atkins – infrastructure and the built environment;
- Cable & Wireless Global Markets – corporate telecoms networks.

A case study method was chosen to analyse strategic decisions and motivations to move into the provision of integrated solutions. Interviews with senior project managers and directors in each of the five firms were conducted in 2000. The managers were asked to describe and explain strategic changes in the focus of each firm's activities between 1995 and 2000. This was followed, during the period 2001 to 2003, by case studies of the business organisation and two major integrated solutions projects in each of the firms to verify the extent and nature of moves in the value stream. The cross-sectoral sample of firms was designed to examine the differences and similarities in firm strategies across manufacturing and services sectors. We then compared these results with a range of other firms, such as IBM, General Electric (GE), ASEA Brown Boveri (ABB) and Rolls-Royce, to identify the different types of strategies and structures firms are adopting to move into the provision of integrated solutions.

The chapter outlines the main features of the integrated solutions business model and develops the value stream approach which is used to examine the strategies our case study firms have been developing to move into integrated solutions. It then describes the core capabilities and organisational structures that these firms have been establishing to implement their integrated solutions strategies.

Integrated solutions: a value stream approach

By examining the evidence we are able to develop some useful tools for understanding the main features of an integrated solutions business model, including a value stream framework. These tools capture the

---

[3] 'Mastering service capabilities in complex product systems: a key systems integration challenge' – funded by the UK's EPSRC Systems Integration Initiative (Grant nos GR/10110 and GR/59403).

ways in which firms are occupying new positions in their industry supply chains to provide integrated solutions.

Value migration

Migration downstream from manufacturing to services took off in the 1990s because of strong East Asian competition in high-volume manufacturing, stagnating product demand and a desire to exploit the growing installed base of major CoPS systems and physical infrastructures, reflected in the accumulation of past purchases and longer product life spans (Slywotzky, 1996). By expanding the scope of the system offering to include services, firms have found that they are able to capture life-cycle profits associated with servicing an installed base. No longer reliant on one-off sales of aircraft engines, Rolls-Royce, for example, earns a growing proportion of its revenues by selling 'power by the hour' services, providing airlines with fixed engine maintenance costs over an extended period of time. Services are attractive because they provide continuous streams of revenue, tend to have higher margins and require fewer assets than product manufacturing. For many large manufacturing firms, services represent an increasing proportion of their total revenues. In 2001, for example, the revenues IBM obtained from services (43 per cent) overtook hardware and technology (42 per cent) for the first time in the firm's history (Gerstner, 2002: 363).

By the late 1990s, revenues from servicing products and systems (e.g. train sales) represented 10–30 times the value of underlying hardware (Wise and Baumgartner, 1999: 134). In other words, the purchase cost of the CoPS represents only a fraction of the total cost of operating and maintaining it during its life cycle. Ericsson, for example, estimates that equipment costs represent a small proportion – only 6 per cent – of the total costs of designing, building and operating a mobile phone network. More than 80 per cent of an operator's costs are in operation, maintenance and network administration and these costs are spread over a ten-year period.

The integrated solutions business model

Several authors argue that the attraction of high-value services is encouraging firms to rethink the focus of their manufacturing strategies (Wise and Baumgartner, 1999; Slywotzky and Morrison, 1998: 249; Oliva and Kallenberg, 2003).[4] They claim that the traditional sources of competitive advantage in manufacturing – backwards integration, developing superior products and scale economies – are no longer sufficient to guarantee competitive success in many industries. Firms are increasingly competing by going beyond their core manufacturing capabilities to move downstream to services (Wise and Baumgartner, 1999) or transitioning (Oliva and Kallenberg, 2003) into the provision of high-value services that address each customer's needs.

The strategies developed by firms to move into services vary widely across industries. Wise and Baumgartner (1999) have identified four downstream business models for integrating forwards into services: (1) embedded services – using software to embed downstream services, such as maintenance or fault reporting, in the physical system; (2) comprehensive services – to finance, operate and maintain a product during its life cycle; (3) distribution control of profitable channel to market activities; and (4) the provision of products and services together as integrated solutions that address a customer's needs.

In consumer goods, cars, domestic appliances and soft drinks, firms have concentrated on moving into highly profitable distribution and after-sales services, offering the final consumer a range of comprehensive services, such as consumer credit, maintenance contracts and short-term warranties. In capital goods, some of the world's leading capital goods manufacturers, including IBM, GE and ABB, pioneered the move into services in the early 1990s and were among the first firms to create the integrated solutions business models that other suppliers are now emulating. Combining elements from each of the various business models (embedded, comprehensive and distribution services), integrated solutions add value by creating unique benefits for each customer.

Beyond bundling

Integrated solutions can be distinguished from traditional bundling strategies. A product bundle is comprised of entirely standardised components, at set prices and offered on the condition that the customer purchases the full line of internally developed products, irrespective of the differences in customer needs or capabilities (Porter, 1985: 425).

---

[4] Regarded as the key measure of firm performance, added value is the difference between the market value of a firm's output and the costs of its inputs (Porter, 1985: 38; Kay, 1993: 23; DTI, 2002).

In the early 1980s IBM, for example, sold low-cost, standardised bundles of internally developed personal computer hardware, software and service support.

Integrated solutions, by contrast, are provided as a bundle of products and services that are customised and priced according to a specific customer's needs (Hax and Wilde, 1999: 13). By the 1990s, firms like IBM had recognised that providers of integrated solutions must be prepared to tailor individual components to each customer's unique requirements and be willing to specify a competitor's product if this provides the best solution to a customer's needs.

To meet a customer's needs for products and services from a single source, solutions providers must take over the risks and responsibilities for performing activities previously handled in-house by their customers and create innovative ways for components to work together as a whole to increase the overall value of the solution for the customer. Integrated solutions providers earn high profits when the value of the integrated package exceeds the value of individual components.

Customer-centric

Providing solutions that address each customer's needs means that firms have to understand how value is created through the eyes of the customer (Slywotzky and Morrison, 1998: 18; Wise and Baumgartner, 1999: 135; Galbraith, 2002a). Under the traditional supply or product-centric approach to value creation, firms focused their efforts on making, selling and delivering products. In many cases, managers concentrated on meeting traditional measures of project success (i.e. within cost, on schedule and to the required specifications) rather than attempting to add value by creating unique benefits for the customer. Beyond the provision of basic technical support and short-term warranties, after the system was handed over on completion of the project the customer took over responsibility for operating, maintaining and financing it during its life span.

Adopting customer-centric thinking involves gaining a detailed understanding of all the activities a customer performs in designing, building and operating a CoPS through its life cycle, from sale to de-commissioning. Engaging in a close dialogue with their customers, suppliers have to identify their customer's business needs and then develop the capabilities to offer products and services that link uniquely well to a customer's priorities. In a move away from its traditional design and build activities, for example, Alstom Transport now offers to provide its customers (e.g. UK train-operating companies) with complete transport solutions for train availability during the life cycle of the system. Its first project of this kind, awarded in 1995, was to renew the train fleet on London Underground's Northern Line. Rather than specify the size of the total fleet, the contract required only that 96 trains be available for service each day for the duration of a 20-year contract. To achieve the customer's targets for train availability, Alstom built 106 trains and set up a maintenance organisation to service them.

As a firm succeeds by learning to provide integrated solutions that address customer needs, it develops a close bonding relationship with the customer (Hax and Wilde, 1999: 13). This relationship is enhanced by proximity to the customer, which allows the solutions provider to antici-pate needs and work jointly in projects to develop and configure new technology, products and services to a customer's needs. Cultivating close relationships often calls for strategic partnerships with the cus-tomer, which may extend to suppliers and competitors linked by their ability to provide a component part of an integrated solution offering. Ericsson, for example, has strategic partnerships with several leading mobile phone operators. Its customer-facing division, called Ericsson Vodafone, which is located next to Vodafone's UK headquarters in Newbury, works in collaborative project teams to develop and commer-cialise 3G mobile technologies, products and applications.

The value stream

A value stream framework, which identifies the entire set of activities involved in making, delivering and using a CoPS to provide services to the final consumer, can be used to analyse, plot and compare strategic moves into integrated solutions provision. Usually, the analysis of the value chain in the literature on solutions is concerned with how an individual firm can manage upstream and downstream activities to that firm's advantage. However, to fully understand how firms change their position in the supply chain to provide integrated solutions, it is neces-sary to examine how value is added within an industry. Indeed, Porter recognises that a firm's value chain for competing in an industry is 'embedded in a larger stream of activities' (Porter, 1990: 42). We use the concept of the value stream developed by Womack and Jones (1996: 19) to identify the activities entailed in creating and producing specific goods and services, flowing from raw materials to the final consumer.

Until the mid-1990s, a traditional capital goods industry such as railways or telecommunications typically consisted of two main vertically integrated value-adding stages: equipment manufacture and operations. In recent years, these sectors have developed more elaborate divisions of labour, as firms specialise in performing an increasingly narrow range of activities in vertically disintegrated value streams. To account for this increase in the type and range of activities performed, our research has identified four main value stream stages in a typical capital goods industry, as depicted in Figure 8.1. The outputs of one value-adding stage are the inputs of the next. Value accumulates at each stage to make up the overall value stream. Each of these stages in the value stream is progressively closer to the final consumer, such as the railway passenger or mobile phone user.

The value stream stages in a typical CoPS sector include:

• *Manufacture*: the first stage is responsible for taking raw materials and subassemblies and transforming them into physical components and subsystems that are manufactured to meet an overall system design.

• *Systems integration*: the second stage adds value through the design and integration of physical components – product hardware, software and embedded services – that have to work together as a whole in a finished product.

• *Operational services*: in the next stage, an operator or business user runs and maintains a system to provide services, such as a corporate telecoms network, baggage handling, flight simulation training and train services.

• *Final service provision*: in some industries services are provided to the final consumer through intermediary organisations called service providers. These firms buy in the system capacity they require from external operators and concentrate on brand, marketing, distribution and customer care activities.

The four stages can be illustrated by the example of mobile communications. Since the mid-1990s, suppliers like Ericsson have been concentrating on becoming systems integrators and outsourcing a growing proportion of their non-core manufacturing activities to specialised contract manufacturers, such as Flextronics. In addition to traditional operators, a new type of service provider has entered the market. For

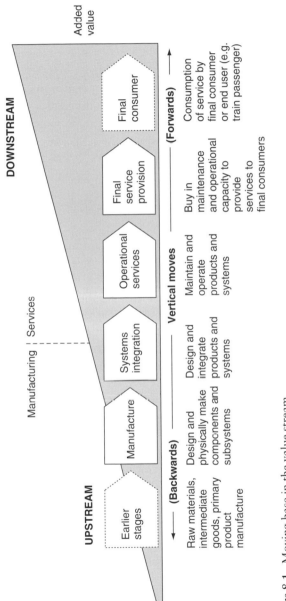

Figure 8.1. Moving base in the value stream
Source: amended from Davies, 2004.

example, as a so-called mobile virtual network provider, Virgin Mobile specialises in developing its subscriber base through brand image, advertising and customer care activities while buying in network capacity from another operator to carry its radio communications traffic.

The line dividing the two segments into upstream and downstream stages corresponds to the traditional manufacturing–services distinction. These segments face different business problems, operate in different market environments and require different organisations and capabilities. Upstream stages add value to the physical product through technology development and manufacture. Downstream stages add value by performing intangible, service-based activities, such as understanding their customers' requirements, maintaining and operating systems and providing services such as customer care, advertising, billing, branding and marketing.

Systems integration is the pivotal activity in the value stream linking manufacturing to the provision of services. Systems integrators have to ensure that the value of the solution for the customer is greater than the sum of its parts. They remove the need for the customer to assemble or integrate the products and services that comprise a solution and take responsibility for negotiating with multiple suppliers of a solution's component parts – hardware, software and services. Because systems integrators have an in-depth knowledge of their customers' operational needs as well as the products they have designed, they are well placed to provide services to monitor, operate, maintain, finance and support a system.

Rather than a simple linear step-by-step process, adding value involves a series of dynamic feed-back loops and iterations between later and earlier stages. Systems integrators ensure that manufacturers in an earlier stage of production are able to produce components as integrated packages that conform to an overall design. Through learning by using (Rosenberg, 1982), operators and service providers can identify opportunities to improve system performance and feed back the experience gained into the design and integration of current and future product generations (Geyer and Davies, 2000).

Moving base in the value stream

The changing activities performed by CoPS suppliers and customers raise questions about the focus of a firm's activities and its core capabilities. As we emphasised in Chapter 3, a firm can gain powerful competitive advantages by developing the organisational capabilities to perform strategic, functional and project activities associated with its evolving technology and market base. In this chapter we show that a firm's capabilities can be identified more specifically in terms of the activities it performs in its industry value stream, such as manufacturing, systems integration, operational services and final service provision.[5]

The concept of a basic position suggests that there is a centre of gravity in the value stream arising from a firm's initial success in the industry in which it grew up. Firms develop their capabilities and create organisations that fit their particular industries and value-adding stage. They can be in the same industry but have different capabilities and organisations because of their different starting positions, experiences and initial successes. A firm's centre of gravity 'establishes a base from which subsequent strategic changes take place' (Galbraith, 1983: 319). When a firm changes position in the value stream by moving upstream or downstream it must develop new capabilities and create new organisational structures. As a firm succeeds by learning to provide integrated solutions that address customer needs, its centre of gravity moves closer to the customer. But a strategic centre-of-gravity move of this kind is difficult to accomplish without rethinking the traditional focus of the firm in the value stream.

Penrose's (1959) analysis of a firm's resource base and growth strategies, discussed in Chapter 3, is particularly useful in considering the changing boundaries between suppliers and customers in the value stream brought about by the emergence of integrated solutions. One of the main competitive problems facing suppliers is that some customers will wish to integrate backwards. Suppliers can prevent this only by providing high-quality products or services and selling at a price that makes backward integration unprofitable for customers. A firm can also strengthen its position by acquiring an intimate knowledge of a customer's technology, business and market needs. However, the customer

---

[5] Richardson (1972) recognised that the various activities in an industry 'have to be carried out by organisations with appropriate *capabilities*, or in other words, with appropriate knowledge, experience and skills ... [O]rganisations will tend to specialise in activities for which their capabilities offer some comparative advantage' (Richardson, 1972: 888). Firms that specialise in performing specific activities in an industry must (as Chapter 3 shows) also develop strategic, functional and project capabilities required to make full use of the firm's internal and external resources, knowledge, skills and experience.

must also make 'special efforts to inform the seller of its peculiar requirements in order to get the seller's help in meeting them and in solving its
own problems' (Penrose, 1959: 117). This close relationship with its
customer enables the supplier to adapt its products and services to a
customer's needs and to learn what new combinations of products and
services can be provided to solve them.

Conversely, suppliers must understand the risks of integrating forwards into activities previously handled in-house by their customers.
Customers may no longer be prepared to open up their businesses and
discuss problems with their suppliers if they have any reason to fear
that the supplier may become a competitor. This is why one of the
pillars of Ericsson's strategy as a telecommunications equipment supplier has traditionally been to stop short of moving forwards into the
operation of its customers' networks.

Integrated solutions strategies

Our case study research shows that rather than simply going downstream, integrating forwards or transitioning from manufacturing to
services, as the literature on business strategy claims, firms are moving
into this new economic activity from upstream *and* downstream positions in the value stream. Table 8.1 summarises the shift in the strategies of the five case firms since the mid-1990s.

Strategic moves

For the product-based firms, integrated solutions do entail a move
downstream from a traditional base in manufacturing. As their traditional centre-of-gravity stage in the value stream – making physical
products – has become less profitable, Alstom, Ericsson and Thales
have outsourced a growing proportion of their manufacturing activities and are focusing on becoming systems integrators and providers of
services to operate, maintain and finance products.

Alstom illustrates the shift in strategies of these product-based firms.
Within the diversified Alstom energy and transportation group, the
Alstom Transport division is responsible for train and signalling system
design and manufacture. Since the mid-1990s, Alstom has developed a
strategy to evolve from a 'seller of goods to a system and service
provider' (Owen, 1997). In 1998, a Service Business was created as a

Table 8.1: The shift to integrated solutions

Company	Traditional product or service focus (1995)	Integrated solutions (2003)
Alstom Transport – railways	Products: • subsystems (e.g. propulsion, traction, drive, electronic information systems) • rolling stock • signalling and train control systems	Transport solutions (e.g. 'train availability'): • systems integrator – turnkey solutions for project management, fixed infrastructure and finance • services for maintenance, renovation, parts replacement and service products – 'Total Train-Life Management'©
Ericsson – mobile communications systems	Products: • mobile handsets • mobile system • subsystem products: radio base stations, base station controllers, mobile switches, operating systems and customer databases	Turnkey solutions to design, build and operate/maintain mobile networks: • mobile systems – complete supplier, systems integrator and partner • global services – services and business consulting to support a customer's network operations
Thales Training and Simulation – flight simulation	Products – standalone flight simulators for commercial and military aircraft	Training solutions (e.g. 'pay as you train'): • systems integration • training services: networked training, independent training centres for training services and synthetic training environments

Table 8.1: The shift to integrated solutions (continued)

Company	Traditional product or service focus (1995)	Integrated solutions (2003)
WS Atkins – infrastructure and the built environment	Engineering consultancy, project management and technical services for infrastructure projects	Integrated solutions for the built environment: • design, build, finance and operation of infrastructure across industrial sectors • Total Solutions for Industry (TS4i) provides one-stop-shop for design, construction, maintenance and finance
Cable & Wireless Global Markets – corporate networks	Provides 'managed network services' for multinational corporations: • network design • supplies telecoms infrastructure and applications • network management	Global outsourcing solutions for a multinational corporation's entire telecoms and IT needs on a global basis: • network design • telecoms infrastructure and applications • network management • ownership of the network • network operation • business process applications • service level agreements

result of a strategic review of Alstom's global activities, which recognised the huge growth in the market for rolling stock services, such as maintenance, technical support, product upgrades and renovation. The Systems Business was set up to carry out major systems integration, turnkey and PFI contracts for complete bundles of train, signalling and infrastructure. By 2000, the Passenger Business, traditionally responsible for the design and manufacture of critical subsystems such as traction systems, was outsourcing the manufacture of up to 90 per cent of components integrated in its rolling stock products and systems.

By contrast, for the service-based firms, providing integrated solutions requires the development of upstream capabilities as well as moving further downstream into operational service provision. C&W and WS Atkins are strengthening their capabilities as integrators of systems using components sourced from external manufacturers.

In the late 1990s, C&W, for example, developed a strategy (which was discussed at length, together with Ericsson, in the previous chapter) to focus on the provision of global outsourcing solutions for corporate telecoms networks, based on internet protocol technology. The strategy entailed building on the firm's core business of operating and managing corporate networks and moving into higher-value network design, systems integration and services. Demand for integrated solutions first arose in 1997 when some of C&W's largest multinational customers began to request that their suppliers provide a single point of contact for their end-to-end global IT and telecoms requirements. In global outsourcing contracts, C&W takes over responsibility for network ownership and service performance for a fixed contract period and a fixed price. As C&W's systems integrator, the Global Markets (GM) division carried out the design, integration and management of corporate networks, using equipment developed in close cooperation with external manufacturers (Nortel Networks and Cisco Systems) and network components provided in-house. To meet its customers' demands, David Sexton, GM's Chief Executive, recognised that 'suppliers must redefine their role as value-generating integrators, rather than low-cost component suppliers' (C&W, 1999: 5).

Whereas C&W's core value stream activity has traditionally been in operational services within a single industry, WS Atkins started out as a specialised provider of design and engineering consultancy services to the systems integration stage in the value stream and provided its services across several industries, such as transport, property management, defence and public health. Under a strategic review in 1998, WS Atkins was reorganised to meet customer demands for long-term contracts that involved the provision of an increasing range of services. At the time, the firm's strategic vision was to be 'the world's first choice supplier for technical services and integrated solutions for the built environment' (WS Atkins, 1999: 4). In April 1999, the group was reorganised again to focus on the provision of integrated solutions across three consolidated UK national business streams – property, transport and management and industry.

Our case study firms' strategic decisions to move into integrated solutions markets have been driven by a combination of internal motivations and changing external conditions. All five firms were attracted by the opportunity to move away from a reliance on one-off, lumpy capital projects procured on an intermittent basis to more continuous revenue streams associated with long-term and highly profitable service-based contracts. The firms have also been driven into these new markets in response to changes in their business environment – customer demand for outsourcing solutions and changes in government policy.

To meet the demand for outsourcing, the case study firms are undertaking systems integration and operational activities previously performed as part of their customers' business. In full outsourcing solutions, this includes the transfer of assets and staff to supplier firms. Buyers of CoPS are entering into long-term partnerships with their suppliers to ensure that solutions providers share the responsibility and risks of performing outsourced activities. For the outsourcing customer, a CoPS no longer represents a fixed cost incurred on an intermittent basis but a variable cost paid for in regular instalments for the duration of a service-based contract. A supplier of capital goods can achieve efficiency gains by spreading the costs of providing solutions over a larger number of customers. These efficiency gains benefit customers that cannot achieve the same cost savings when designing and implementing one-off solutions solely for internal requirements. A supplier can achieve lower unit costs by strengthening its capabilities because these capabilities represent a fixed set-up cost, in which the supplier does not have to reinvest each time it serves a new customer (Domberger, 1998: 78).

The process of customer outsourcing of CoPS has been accelerated by the liberalisation and privatisation of former state-controlled sectors, such as telecoms and railways. For example, Ericsson recognises that its integrated solutions offerings must address the needs of the variety of customers operating in more competitive mobile communication markets. Whereas experienced and vertically integrated mobile operators, such as Vodafone, often want to perform a broader range of activities in-house, less sophisticated and more specialised customers with limited in-house capabilities, such as Virgin Mobile, tend to rely on suppliers for complete solutions to their needs.

CoPS suppliers in the UK, such as Thales, Alstom and WS Atkins, are also being encouraged to move downstream by increasing use of private finance in public-sector projects. Under the Private Finance Initiative, introduced in 1992, private-sector companies design, build, finance and operate public-sector projects, ranging from schools to complex weapons systems. Under the policy of the Public-Private Partnership, adopted in 1997, public projects are financed partly by private firms, while the state shares some of the risk. PFI and PPP suppliers perform activities along the value stream from systems integration to services provision, as well as providing finance and consultancy services.

Strategic imperatives and choices

To move successfully into the provision of integrated solutions, our research shows that in some cases a firm must gain control of the channel to market. In other cases, firms already have channel control. Channel control is imperative where suppliers sell directly to a few large customers in oligopolistic markets because any attempts to move downstream may be blocked if a firm sells its products and services through independent firms that control the channel to the customer. For example, Thales's attempts to move into flight simulation training solutions for commercial airlines have been prevented by the specialised independent training schools which purchase simulators and control channels to market. Performing a role similar to distributors or retailers of consumer goods, these training schools have resisted attempts by Thales and other producers to enter the training market. As major airlines have outsourced training, it has been the training schools rather than simulator producers which have taken on the training tasks, despite the efforts of Thales and other producers to move into the fast-growing and lucrative training market.

Such channel conflicts can be overcome if the firm can develop partnerships with channel controllers or buy into the channel. For example, C&W's initial attempts to move into the high-value end of corporate networks markets were hampered by the presence of global business consultancy organisations, such as Accenture and PriceWaterhouseCoopers, which use their scale and global reputation to exploit and control channels to the business user. To gain a channel to market, C&W actively pursued and finally formed a strategic partnership with Accenture. C&W now provides global data and IP components of outsourcing solutions to Accenture's clients.

Alstom and Ericsson, by contrast, have not faced such channel conflicts as they move downstream because they already have direct and symbiotic relationships with their customers, namely railway and mobile phone operators. They may, however, face conflicts with their customers if they move too aggressively into the customer's territory or move without prior agreement. As long as customers see the value of solutions and request them, there is no channel conflict and moves by CoPS suppliers into customer solutions are mutually reinforcing from both a value-creation and a strategic perspective.

Once channel control has been established, a firm faces two strategic choices about where to position itself in the value stream. The first choice concerns the scope of systems integration. Some firms providing solutions are developing the systems integration capabilities to provide single-vendor and multi-vendor systems. Single-vendor systems are comprised of technology, components and subsystems developed internally by vertically integrated manufacturers, such as Thales's proprietary flight simulation products.

Multi-vendor systems are assembled or integrated from externally developed components. WS Atkins, for example, designs and project manages the integration of systems supplied by external manufacturers across diverse sectors. Its railway division, WS Atkins Rail, buys and integrates equipment from Alstom, Bombardier and Siemens as well as more specialised suppliers. Alstom and Ericsson are developing the capabilities to integrate single- and multi-vendor systems. Alstom, for example, designs, manufactures and builds rolling stock and offers to integrate equipment supplied by its competitors, Bombardier and Siemens, as part of its turnkey solutions offerings.

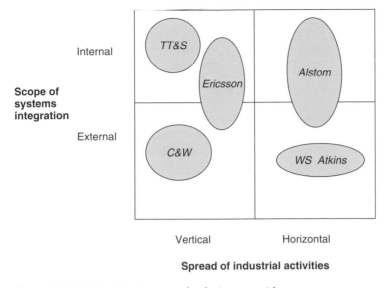

Figure 8.2. Positioning integrated solutions providers
Source: Davies, 2004.

The second choice relates to the spread of a firm's industrial activities, vertically within an industry and horizontally across different industry segments. Vertically focused strategies are built around the provision of integrated solutions to customers within a specific industry, such as C&W's development of global outsourcing solutions for multinational customers. Horizontally focused strategies are concerned with the provision of integrated solutions to customers operating in a range of industries.

Using our case study findings, we can begin to distinguish between different types of integrated solutions strategies, represented as a matrix and shown in Figure 8.2, along two different dimensions: the scope of systems integration and the spread of industrial activities, vertically and/or horizontally. The matrix reveals that there is a great deal of variety in the strategies pursued by the case study firms. It can be used to analyse the strategy of a firm or division within a diversified firm, such as Thales Training and Simulation (which provides single-vendor solutions within a single industry). Some of these firms, like WS Atkins, specialise in multi-vendor solutions and sell their services to horizontal industry segments. Others, like Ericsson, provide single- and multi-vendor solutions within a single industry. As a diversified firm, Alstom provides single- and multi-vendor solutions to customers across a number of energy and transportation sectors.

Integrated solutions capabilities

Our research reveals precisely how different categories of firms have been implementing their strategies for integrated solutions in diverse ways. However, in all cases a firm's original base in the value stream shapes the types of capabilities and organisational structures it must establish when it moves position.

Building integrated solutions capabilities

Table 8.2 summarises the types of capabilities required to compete successfully in the provision of integrated solutions. It is essential that firms build a core capability in systems integration. But to offer complete solutions to their customers' needs throughout the life cycle of a complex product or system, firms will have to be able to offer operational services. In addition to these main value-adding stages, financial services and business consulting services are offered to support and underpin the creation of value by providing inputs at different stages up and down the stream.

Systems integration services

To provide customers with physical CoPS that can easily be deployed with services as part of a solution to a customer's needs, all five case study firms are developing much deeper and broader systems integration capabilities. Traditionally, the product-based firms designed, manufactured and integrated systems using in-house-developed components. By the late 1990s, Alstom, Ericsson and Thales were developing strategies to focus on the systems integration function, while outsourcing a growing proportion of their manufacturing activities.

As service-based firms with no in-house manufacturing capabilities, C&W and WS Atkins are specialised systems integrators. Performing little or no technology development in-house, these firms specialise in providing systems integration services using components sourced from external manufacturers. C&W, for example, is developing

Table 8.2: Capabilities of integrated solutions providers (2003)

Company	Systems integration services	Operational services	Business consultancy services	Financial services
Alstom Transport	Design and build trains and signalling systems (equipment developed in-house or externally). Prime contractor in large turnkey projects	Maintain, upgrade and operate trains	Consultancy-based approach to meet customer needs	Vendor financing and asset management
Ericsson	Design, manufacture and integrate mobile phone systems (equipment developed in-house or externally)	Maintain, support, upgrade and operate mobile networks	Two business consultancy organisations to meet needs of Ericsson and external customers	Considering but not yet offering vendor financing
Thales Training and Simulation	Design, manufacture and integrate flight simulators (extensive use of external component manufacturers)	Provide services to train pilots and manage simulator-building facilities. Joint venture with GE Capital Training	Consultancy organisation to meet customer needs	Revenue-sharing agreement for simulators, e.g. split between TT&S and United Airlines

Table 8.2: Capabilities of integrated solutions providers (2003) (continued)

Company	Systems integration services	Operational services	Business consultancy services	Financial services
WS Atkins	Design and integrate external manufacturers' equipment across diverse sectors, such as railway and baggage-handling systems Coordination of external contractors for product supply	Maintain, operate and provide services to end-users, e.g. setting up independent service provider to design, build, finance and operate baggage-handling services	Consultancy-based approach to meet customer needs	Created joint-venture company, TS4i, with Royal Bank of Scotland to provide integrated solutions for design, construction, maintenance and finance
Cable & Wireless Global Markets	Design and integrate networks (externally supplied products and technology). Developing capability to integrate internet and IT systems. Coordination of external contractors for product supply	Operate and manage a global customer's IT and telecoms needs	Consultancy-based approach to meet customer needs	Sometimes takes on responsibility for ownership of networks for duration of contract

partnerships with new best-of-breed IP suppliers such as Nortel and Cisco Systems to provide corporate customers with systems that C&W designs, installs, maintains and supports.

The range of activities performed by systems integrators is increasing as a result of customer demands for turnkey solutions. If other products, services or capabilities are required to provide complete solutions to a customer's needs, systems integrators cooperate with partners in joint ventures or consortiums to carry out those portions of the work. For example, Alstom Transport has established its Systems Business unit to integrate components, subsystems and services developed internally or externally by partners in a consortium. By combining skills in project management, systems integration, financial engineering, fixed infrastructure and civil engineering, the Systems Business is able to provide track infrastructure, rolling stock and signalling systems as a single turnkey package.

Operational services

Suppliers are building on their base in systems integration and moving into provision of operational services to maintain, renovate and operate a product or system during its life span from sales to de-commissioning. Two product-based firms, Alstom and Ericsson, have set up new divisions to provide these services. For example, Alstom's Service Business unit offers services which it calls Total Train-Life Management. These capture value created during all stages in the operating life cycle of a train, including maintenance, renovation, spare parts and asset management. The typical life cycle extends over thirty years including two years or so to design, build and manufacture rolling stock and twenty-eight years to provide services offering large and continuous revenue streams.

As they take over operational activities, suppliers have more incentive to design systems from the start that are reliable and easily maintainable as they are responsible for these activities. Being involved in services allows firms to routinely tackle in-service problems and generates a stream of new opportunities to improve system performance. Lessons learnt can be fed back directly into the design and build of current and future generations of systems. Because manufacturers like Alstom, Ericsson and Thales develop technology as well as integrate systems and perform operational services, they are able to create new direct feedback loops within different parts of the same firm. System designers and service providers operate in a closed loop, in which responsibility for operational performance and costs remains in the hands of a single organisation. In the case of Alstom's contract for the Northern Line extension of the London Underground, the managers responsible for maintenance and operational services were deeply involved in the front-end design of the rolling stock. As a result of their recommendations, the train designers made more than 250 modifications to create easy-to-maintain and easy-to-use trains.

By contrast, pure systems integrator firms like WS Atkins and C&W that rely on external manufacturers for equipment and technology development are unable to take advantage of these dynamic feedback loops. They have to work in collaboration with external partners if they wish to initiate a cycle of innovative improvements between systems integration and operational service activities. Inevitably, this makes it more difficult to design reliable and efficient systems for current and future needs. However, unlike the product-based firms, service-based firms have more opportunity to compare one system with another and can gain a deep understanding of the advantages and disadvantages of the various competing systems in the marketplace.

Business consultancy services

As part of an integrated solutions bundle, firms are offering customers consultancy advice on how to plan, design, build, finance, maintain and operate systems. Firms are expanding their business consultancy capabilities by creating joint ventures with other firms that have such capabilities, acquiring firms already operating in this field or developing business consultancy skills in-house.

Some of the case study firms, including Ericsson and WS Atkins, have developed these skills internally by establishing specialist business consultancy organisations. Ericsson Global Services helps the company's market-facing units provide customers with consultancy advice on their strategies for mobile communications, such as how to write business plans, produce network designs, finance and manage their assets and develop applications for 3G services. Alstom and Thales have developed a consultancy-based approach within their existing business units. C&W, by contrast, has been seeking a strategic partnership or joint venture with one of the major business consultancy organisations because in global corporate network markets these firms dominate the value stream and control access to the customer.

Financial services

The ability to provide finance is the fourth capability being developed by some integrated solutions providers. Financial services play a vital role in the negotiation phase when customers require assistance with financing the purchase of high-cost CoPS. Firms can offer value-sharing contracts which lower the purchase price of a CoPS in return for a proportion of the future value generated during its operational phase. The supplier is paid in part by sharing in the operational efficiency that it creates for the customer. Value-sharing contracts provide an opportunity to engage in strategic discussions with customers during the negotiation stage and to open doors to many other projects that might otherwise have been unavailable to the firm.

The growing importance of private finance is generally associated with large public-sector PFI and PPP projects. However, demand for financial services has also been driven by industry-led initiatives to provide vendor financing and asset management services in capital-intensive telecoms, railway and other large infrastructure systems. Vendor financing is a form of credit that a supplier extends to its customers so that customers can afford to buy new capital equipment and systems from the supplier. It is valuable to customers because high up-front procurement costs are spread out over the life cycle of the system. In 3G mobile phone markets, for example, vendor financing is being offered to help mobile operators with limited funds build 3G mobile phone networks on expectation of payment at a later date. But suppliers vary in their approach to vendor financing. Whereas Nokia has used vendor financing to gain market share, Ericsson has been less willing to be financially exposed in this way.

Asset management is also of growing importance as a service for customers, such as train operating companies seeking to reduce the costs and extend the operating life of an installed base of products. In 2000, for example, WS Atkins created Total Solutions for Industry, a joint venture with the Royal Bank of Scotland, to provide customers with a one-stop-shop source of integrated solutions for finance together with design, construction and maintenance. Serving contracts with an asset value of between £5 million and £20 million, the joint venture offers to manage assets for customers such as mobile telephone base stations, baggage-handling systems and power stations. The bank supplies the finance and specific financial services such as equity savings and WS Atkins undertakes design, construction management and asset management.

Figure 8.3 conveys the variety of capabilities offered within an integrated solution. It identifies the novel combinations of systems integration and service capabilities that CoPS makers are developing in-house or through strategic partnerships to meet the differing needs and capabilities of various customer segments. In mobile communications, for example, these customer types range from (a) less experienced 'virtual' buyers with limited in-house capabilities (e.g. highly specialised virtual mobile phone operators like Virgin Mobile) that often demand full turnkey solutions to their needs, to (b) more sophisticated 'vertical' buyers with extensive internal capabilities (e.g. large incumbent operators like Vodafone and T-Mobile) that may prefer to buy only selected modules.

Organising for solutions

Several new forms of organisation are being created by the five case study firms to implement their integrated solutions strategies. In moving away from their traditional product- or service-based business units, the firms have been creating customer-focused organisations to use resources and capabilities from both internal and external suppliers to provide efficient and repeatable solutions.

Other observers of customer-focused organisations have studied the ways in which large manufacturing firms have reorganised their activities for the delivery of repeatable solutions (Foote et al., 2001; Galbraith, 2002a and 2002b). They describe a 'front/back' model of solutions provision implemented by firms like IBM, Sun Microsystems, ABB and Nokia. In a shift away from traditional structures with operational units organised along product, brand or geographic lines, these firms are forming 'front-end' units to develop, package and deliver integrated solutions. To do this they refocus their product-based units as 'back-end' providers of standardised solutions-ready components and develop strong 'strategic centres' to manage the interfaces between the two types of operational units. This 'reconfigurable organisation', as Galbraith (2002b) calls it, can adapt and respond to continuous shifts in strategy. It 'consists of a stable functional structure around which projects and miniature business units are continuously formed, combined, and disbanded. These units can focus on products,

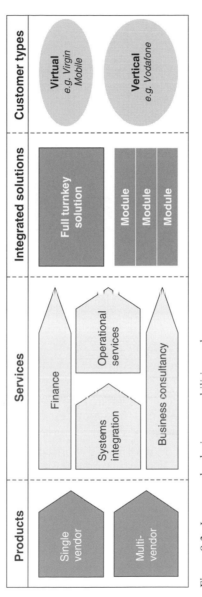

Figure 8.3. Integrated solutions capabilities and customers

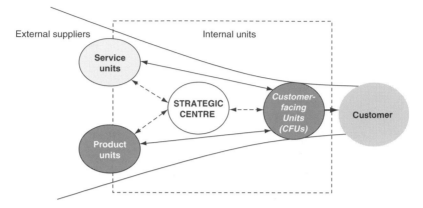

Figure 8.4. Customer-facing organisation

channels, segments, customers, regions, suppliers, technologies, and so on' (Galbraith 2002b: 89).

Figure 8.4 presents our model which identifies the specific organisational structure required for integrated solutions provision. The model can be used as an ideal type to analyse and compare the different structures being set by the case study firms and many other leading suppliers of CoPS. It identifies the operational units in a model of organisation applicable to firms traditionally based in manufacturing and services. The model consists of front-end, customer-facing units set up as project organisations which control the channel to the customer and perform the core systems integration function. Back-end units can be either divisions within the firm or external suppliers. They are responsible for providing CFUs with the product platforms and service portfolios, knowledge and resources they need to provide customers with tailored solutions. The use of common product modules and service components allows integrated solutions to be tailored to each customer's needs, without consuming excessive resources.

Our five case study firms and many other corporations are establishing different versions of this model depending on whether they started out from a base in manufacturing or services. Alstom and Ericsson, for example, have established new operational units in addition to their product-based business units to provide service components of solutions. C&W and WS Atkins, by contrast, already have strong in-house service capabilities and are concentrating their efforts on establishing long-term partnerships with external manufacturers to provide product components of integrated solutions.

Front-end units: customer-facing integrated solutions providers

The front-end CFUs are responsible for meeting each customer's needs for an integrated solution. These project-based units design and integrate the systems and arrange the provision of services during the operational life of a system. Some firms, like Thales Training and Simulation, will attempt to mobilise the additional capabilities required for integrated solutions provision without altering their traditional product- or service-based organisations. However, most firms entering this new market will, like our other four case study firms, create new types of CFUs to meet the needs of different customer segments. CFUs are designed to meet needs of different types of market base including:

• industry-based segments;
• customer groups within an industry;
• single customers;
• single projects.

Several of our case study firms have restructured their entire organisations to focus on different customer or market segments. Alstom, for example, has set up a variety of customer-facing business unit structures such as the Services unit which provides rolling stock operational services and the Systems unit which offers turnkey solutions for rolling stock and signalling systems. In addition, Alstom establishes 'special purpose vehicle' project organisations, such as the West Coast Train Care Company which was set up specifically to meet Virgin Train's needs for the UK's West Coast Main Line. Ericsson has also restructured its entire organisation to create market-facing units for customers in different geographical regions and customer-facing units for individual global mobile phone operators such as its Ericsson Vodafone division which is dedicated to meeting the mobile operator's needs on a global basis.

Service-based firms like C&W and WS Atkins have created front-end structures able to gain access to external sources of best-in-class technology and products. C&W has created partnerships with so-called best-of-breed IP suppliers so that its front-end GM division can meet the needs of different groups of corporate customers with various systems that C&W designs, installs, maintains and supports. WS Atkins has set up a number of front-end units to deliver solutions based on leading-edge technology across different industry-based customer segments.

The front-end units are organised so that the entire capabilities of the firm and its external partners are channelled through the project implementation team at the point of contact with the customer. CFUs are set up as project-based organisations to respond rapidly and flexibly to different customer needs, acting as flexible resource units for constantly forming projects. However, resources from the firm's back-end units and network of external partners may be required when resources cannot be provided internally by the front-end unit. Project teams, composed of people from the front-end unit, its partners and the customer's organisation, can be rapidly assembled, disbanded and reassembled around each customer's needs for a solution. Teams operate in ways similar to professional services and consultancy organisations, moving routinely from one project to another.

The provision of integrated solutions means that CFU project teams have to carry out two essential phases of pre-bid and post-project activities not usually identified in traditional project life-cycle models. As summarised in Figure 8.5, the life cycle of an integrated solution extends through four phases of activities with the customer:

1. strategic engagement phase when high-level business discussions take place to work out a customer's needs or priorities, often before an invitation to tender has been issued;
2. value proposition phase when a detailed proposal or offer is developed that adds value for both supplier and customer;
3. systems integration phase when a system is designed, built, integrated and delivered by a project team and its partner organisations;
4. operational services phase when the system is operated, maintained and supported, often by the supplier's functional line organisation, over a period of time specified in the contract.

The CFU is responsible for engaging with existing or potential customers about their strategic needs and operational priorities, often before the customer has requested formal assistance. In these senior management pre-bid discussions, solutions providers offer consultancy advice on how to improve a customer's operations or develop its business model.

If the customer requests help or issues an invitation to tender, a proposal team is assembled to develop a value proposition. If the

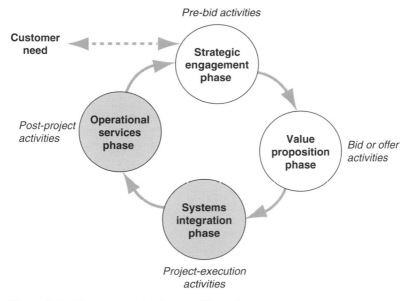

Figure 8.5. The integrated solutions life cycle

customer is a strategic partner, the proposal team makes an offer rather than a bid. The team requires people with skills and expertise in commercial management, technical design and project management. They are responsible for ensuring that the value created by the solution during systems integration and operational service provision will meet the customer's expectations. The team has to work quickly to develop the proposition. The exact degree of customisation specified in the proposal will vary according to the sophistication, size and unique requirements of each customer. Rather than sell solutions from pre-defined price lists, the team has the authority to decide how to tailor products and services to solve specific customer problems. They must break down an integrated solution into its component parts. Each part is then scheduled and assigned to internal or external product and service suppliers.

Unlike traditional arm's-length bargaining over products or services, an integrated solution requires a commercial framework based on cooperation and trust. This helps the proposal team and customer develop a common understanding of how value will be measured in terms of pricing and margins, the volume and mix of products and services, capital costs and the distribution of risk. Part of the skill of the CFU is to identify and target suitable early candidates for an integrated solution. Successful providers develop strategic relationships with leading customers so that the knowledge gained from the initial learning is used to develop product platforms and service portfolios that can be mobilised and integrated at lower costs across a growing customer base, should demand take off.

Back-end units: product platforms and service portfolios

Whereas CFUs work directly for individual customers in temporary project teams, back-end units are organised along functional lines to perform routine and recurring activities. They are responsible for developing and providing common product platforms and service portfolios, resources and other capabilities that can be integrated by CFUs. Several of our case study firms, including WS Atkins, C&W and Ericsson, have been developing structures which prevent the back-end units from having direct relationships with the customer. Product and service units, whether internal or external to the firm, are responsible for developing standardised solutions-ready components that can be shared more efficiently across many projects.

Product-based units supply the common technology and product components of integrated CoPS solutions delivered by the front-end units. In-house product-based organisations often view the creation of front-end solutions providers as a threat to their power base and status within the firm. Under the new organisational arrangements, these internal product units have to become flexible and responsive to the front-end demands for resources and capabilities. They must provide tailored components, products and systems, particularly where the front-end units are developing highly customised solutions based on new generations of technologies for lead customers, such as Ericsson's 3G product platform developed for Vodafone. Product-based units are also responsible for establishing a platform of standardised or modular products that can be easily configured at low costs as part of a solution to each customer's needs.

Service-based units are responsible for developing a portfolio of simplified, consistent and easy-to-understand services that the front-end project teams use to sell and deliver integrated solutions. Rather than develop customised services for each new project, the front-end solutions providers can select pre-developed service offerings from the portfolio. Back-end service units can also provide the front-end with additional resources and support when the required capabilities cannot be found locally. Based on standardised processes, tools, pricing and guarantees for service reliability, the service portfolio is constantly revised to improve the process of selling and delivering solutions.

Services can be provided by internal business units or external service providers. Product-based firms like Alstom and Ericsson have set up stand-alone service divisions to develop service portfolios. Ericsson's Global Services division, for example, was formed in 2000 to develop a portfolio of services (see Chapter 7) that can be used by its front-end units. The division has no direct contact with Ericsson's customers. Instead it provides resources and service portfolios that can be configured as part of each solution delivered to mobile phone operators. Service-based firms may also need to access a broader range of services than they can traditionally provide in-house, such as WS Atkins's joint venture with the Royal Bank of Scotland to provide customers with financial services as part of an integrated solution package.

Repeatability is a measure of a firm's progress and success in integrated solutions provision. The high costs of developing the capabilities to provide initial one-off solutions for lead customers have to be recouped by replicating the product and service components of solutions until they become standardised offerings, sold repeatedly to many customers at lower costs. As discussed in Chapter 3, cumulative learning and improved performance depend on how quickly and successfully firms expand the menu of reusable knowledge. Firms can gain a competitive advantage by obtaining economies of recombination through the development and reuse of common solutions-ready components and economies of repetition through the exploitation of a new base of project routines. Although there are important economies to be gained through standardisation, there is always a need for some degree of customisation to solve each customer's specific problem.

Strategic centre

The strategic centre is responsible for encouraging collaboration between the front- and back-end units and between the firm's internal and external activities. It develops corporate strategies, organisational structures and brand names to support global delivery of solutions. Most importantly, top management in the firm has to strike a balance between the opposing forces of customisation and standardisation. It is responsible for promoting the front-end pull of customisation, while accommodating the back-end push for standardisation.

On the one hand, the front-end CFUs are driven by the necessity to meet their customers' needs for highly tailored solutions. But too much emphasis on front-end customisation can leave a firm without an effective means of providing repeatable solutions based on standardised product platforms and service portfolios. On the other hand, there are limits to the drive towards standardisation and replication. Some of the largest and most sophisticated solutions customers may be reluctant to outsource all of their requirements to an external provider. Because of the complexity of the problems they face, these firms – such as global mobile phone operators, train operators and airlines – may find that their needs and priorities are not fully satisfied by solutions comprised mainly of standardised modules.

Unless a strong centre can provide effective management of the interfaces between the front and back units, these organisations may pursue diverging strategies, becoming deadlocked over priorities, and pass accountability for success and failure back and forth. At Ericsson, for example, the product-based units such as Ericsson Mobile Systems no longer sell directly to customers. In a radical restructuring of Ericsson's global activities, they have become internal providers of technology and solutions-ready products to the firm's front-end market units, which serve customers in different regions, and customer-facing units such as Ericsson Vodafone, which are dedicated to the needs of global mobile phone operators. To manage the interfaces between its internal product and service units, Ericsson has created corporate functions to plan and allocate resources, manage transfer pricing and support competence development throughout the group.

When firms create the customer-facing units with sole responsibility for channels to market and customer relationships, they often face strong resistance from the in-house product or service units. These internal units are reluctant to lose control of their customer accounts and unwilling to accept that the front-end units will propose solutions that incorporate a competitor's technology or products. A senior management team has to be prepared to resolve any conflicts by overcoming resistance to the new structure from the firm's established units. For example, C&W's strategy to create a global structure for integrated solutions provision met strong resistance from its regional business units which were unwilling to relinquish control of their profitable corporate customers. In response to this internal resistance as well as to an unfavourable market environment due to the collapse of the dotcom boom, C&W's senior management team decided to re-establish its traditional structure of delivering solutions through its regional-based business units. Ericsson, by contrast, continues to fashion an organisation for global integrated solutions composed of front and back units overseen by a strong corporate centre.

Conclusions

This chapter presented a set of analytical tools – the value stream capabilities framework and model of organisation for solutions provision – to help researchers and practising managers understand and act on the solutions imperative.

The value stream framework can be used to analyse, plot and compare the strategies of firms moving into the provision of integrated solutions. The framework shows that rather than simply going downstream or transitioning into solutions, suppliers of CoPS can move into integrated solutions from both upstream and downstream positions. Product-based firms, such as Alstom, Ericsson and Thales, are gradually pulling out of their traditional base in manufacturing and focusing on being systems integrators and providing the services needed to operate and maintain their systems. Service-based firms, such as WS Atkins and C&W, are strengthening their upstream systems integration capabilities and moving further downstream into high-value services previously carried out internally by their customers. Many other CoPS producers around the world are engaging in these activities.

To move successfully into the provision of solutions, firms have to first gain control of the channel to market. Failure to do so prevents them from developing the close customer relationships required to provide integrated solutions and can relegate them to a lower-tier provider of solutions components. Others already have this control.

Once channel control is assured, a firm faces two strategic choices about where it should be positioned in the value stream. First, it can specialise in one particular activity, such as systems integration, or integrate forwards and backwards within a single industry's value stream. In addition to these vertical moves, a firm can provide integrated solutions horizontally to customers operating across different industries. Second, the firm must decide whether to provide single-vendor or multi-vendor solutions. Some observers argue that the 'acid test' of a true solutions provider is a willingness to propose a solution that incorporates a competitor's product or technology if this provides an optimal solution to a customer's needs (Foote et al., 2001: 87). IBM, for example, recognises that customers increasingly value firms that can provide solutions that integrate technology from various suppliers and, more importantly, that integrate technology into the core business processes of a customer's organisation (Gerstner, 2002: 123).

A key competitive advantage of service-based firms like C&W and WS Atkins is their ability to specify best-in-class products as multi-vendor solutions, often by forming strategic partnerships with equipment manufacturers. Although many product-based firms, like Alstom and Ericsson, now offer multi-vendor systems, others like Thales and Rolls-Royce remain single-vendor providers. Firms that remain tied to internally developed proprietary technology have to be confident that they can persuade their customers that their products are world class. In many cases, prior involvement in technology development enables product-based firms to benefit from dynamic feedback loops not available to service-based firms: knowledge of operational performance can be used to make technical improvements in current and future product generations.

Many CoPS suppliers are developing new sets of capabilities that distinguish them from the traditional categories of manufacturing or services. Based on our empirical findings it is clear that the provision of integrated solutions requires a fundamental shift in the firm's centre of gravity towards systems integration. An intimate knowledge of their customer's needs and the systems they have designed places systems integrators in a strong position to provide operational services to support a system during its life span. By effective outsourcing and managing of upstream component manufacturers, these firms can concentrate on their core systems integration and operational service activities, while building up their capabilities in business consultancy and financial services to offer entire solutions to a customer's needs.

In a departure from the traditional product- or service-based organisations, leading CoPS firms are creating new customer-facing structures to mobilise the capabilities required to deliver integrated solutions. In our front/back model of integrated solutions provision, front-end units act as a distribution channel to the customer for products (single- and multi-vendor) and services (systems integration, operations, finance and consultancy) supplied by a firm's in-house units or external partners. Back-end units are responsible for developing solutions-ready components that can be incorporated in the solutions designed and integrated by the front end. A strong strategic centre is required to implement strategies for integrated solutions and to coordinate internal interfaces between different units within the organisation and external interfaces with the customer, supplier and other collaborators.

The challenges of moving into integrated solutions provision should not be underestimated. To be able to develop a profitable business, firms have to be very sensitive when attempting to gain control of the channel to the customer. They must avoid moving so far downstream that they begin to compete with their customers and must manage the risks associated with financing life-cycle solutions. They must also demonstrate that buyer firms are able to trust them to deliver the business-critical technology they need over the long term. For many suppliers the biggest challenge is how to develop the capabilities and organisations required to integrate different pieces of a system provided increasingly by an external network of specialised component suppliers, subcontractors and service providers. This is a challenge which may take many years. IBM, for example, is still engaged in the process of implementing a strategy for integrated solutions initiated by its former CEO, Louis Gerstner, in the early 1990s.

9 | Lessons for the project business

THE project business emerged as a major new form of industrial organisation and management practice in the second half of the twentieth century. Since the 1960s there have been numerous studies of project management techniques, specific types of projects (e.g. R&D and new product development) and project activities in particular industries such as pharmaceuticals and construction. But until recently the wider significance of the project for innovation and business strategy has gone largely unnoticed. Managers, policy makers, business commentators and scholars have been preoccupied with understanding, adopting and refining the principles of high-volume production. These principles were pioneered by some of the world's largest and most successful American firms like Ford, General Motors and AT&T and later improved upon by Japanese corporations such as Toyota. These firms created large, top-down, hierarchical, functional organisations, well designed for producing and selling standardised consumer goods and services in high volumes and making repetitive decisions in the comparatively stable industrial environment of growing mass markets.

Efforts to implement and improve high-volume techniques have led to significant advances in management tools in recent years (e.g. lean production, business process re-engineering and mass customisation). Yet the returns from such improvements are diminishing and will continue to do so in the future. Even today, for many firms seeking stability in the face of fragmenting mass markets, accelerating techno-logical change and intensifying global competition in low-cost manu-facturing, the reliance on high-volume management techniques and large, semi-permanent organisations is appealing. But this quest to improve operational efficiency within the constraints of the traditional production paradigm is more likely to postpone the inevitable decline than promote strategic renewal.

252

In recent years a new emphasis on project management and project forms of organisation has grown up in response to this increasingly turbulent business environment. One driver of the project form is the attempt to withstand the onslaught of strong competition in consumer goods (e.g. cameras, cars, consumer electronics and other household goods) and services (e.g. software development and call centres) from low-cost regions such as Asia. A growing number of firms in the US and the EU are outsourcing standardised productive activities to specialised contract manufacturers, using off-shore locations for low-value service activities allowing them to move into higher-value project-based activities. Although advanced volume-based producers like Procter & Gamble and McDonald's are unlikely to reorganise their core productive operations along project lines, they are increasingly using projects to open up profitable avenues of growth and create new sources of competitive advantage and innovation. Unlike semi-permanent functional departments, projects can be assembled, disbanded and regrouped according to the specific needs of a business and in response to dynamic changes in the environment. Projects are used to promote innovation in new technology development and cross-functional product design. The new investments in innovative processes underpinning volume production (e.g. factory automation systems, IT systems and corporate telecoms networks) require deep project management capabilities for their implementation. Moreover, the project is the basic unit of organisation used to carry out many of the high-value-added systems integration, professional consultancy and downstream service-based activities that firms are now attempting to provide.

The project business paradigm

This book shows how and why the project business provides a new paradigm for today's innovative organisation. It highlights how business leaders and researchers can learn from the experiences of the suppliers of high-technology CoPS that have traditionally used projects to manage and organise their core productive activities. These firms have deployed and improved upon the project form for many years for both strategic and innovative purposes. Project business techniques and project forms of organisation were pioneered by the US military and continue to be led by suppliers of CoPS as diverse as General Electric, IBM, ABB, BP, Rolls-Royce, BAE Systems, Arup, BT, Nokia, LogicaCMG and McKinsey. The project-based strategies, management tools and organisations used by CoPS firms differ fundamentally from those traditionally used in high-volume production. Because these complex, high-cost products, services, systems, networks, capital goods and infrastructures are produced in low volumes and tailored to meet a customer's specific needs, they require project strategies, project capabilities, project management techniques and project forms of organisation. The vast project management knowledge and experience of CoPS firms, good and bad, accumulated over several decades, are of great significance for the project business in general. Suppliers of CoPS use projects not just for managing all their routine day-to-day business activities with customers but also for responding to new strategic opportunities such as supplying novel generations of technology, opening new markets and achieving far-reaching organisational transformations.

Drawing upon a ten-year programme of CoPS research on the project enterprise, which analysed management tools, organisational forms, core capabilities and business strategies deployed by large international firms, we have been able to identify the main challenges facing today's project business. In this concluding chapter, we outline the strategic lessons that managers in all types of firms and industries must learn if they are to master the challenges of managing an innovative and efficient project business. The aim is to point the way forward for project businesses operating in today's fast-changing, innovation-driven environment.

Creating competitive advantage in the project business

With a few notable exceptions (e.g. Morris, 1994; Turner, 1999) the large body of project management literature has focused on how to improve the operational efficiency and effectiveness of project management techniques, but neglected the strategic role of the project as a vehicle for competitive advantage and corporate renewal. Managing projects more efficiently is certainly a challenge, but on its own it is insufficient to fully exploit the business potential of project enterprise. To succeed in project business, projects must become the dynamic centre of the firm, driving growth, innovation and competitive advantage. We have identified seven generic lessons which convey how many of the world's leading suppliers of CoPS have met the key strategic challenges facing today's project business.

Lesson 1: Build and use project capabilities for innovation

The first lesson is that a firm must develop its organisational capability to use projects to achieve competitive advantage in the fast-changing innovation environment. In contrast to functional capabilities used in high-volume production, we showed that project capabilities are essential to manage and organise the low-volume, design-intensive and customer-focused activities. Strong project capability is the key to improving operational effectiveness and achieving strategies for diversification.

By increasing its capabilities to develop proposals for major clients, win bids or offers and successfully execute projects, a firm can gain a competitive advantage if it performs these operational activities better than its competitors. The project business can guarantee current revenues and profitability by exploiting its existing project routines and incrementally developing its capabilities to improve the performance of current activities ('what it does today'). As we have seen, the cost advantages of scale and scope economies attributed to functional organisations are difficult to achieve in low-volume project activities. However, firms can realise economies of repetition and economies of recombination, the twin sources of productivity improvements in the project business. Such project efficiency gains achieved by many of the firms studied in our research – such as Thales, Rolls-Royce, Ericsson, C&W, Alstom Transport, WS Atkins, GKN, Oxford Instruments and BAA – stem from their ability to carry out distinct portfolios of standardised projects, performed repeatedly using common components and based on well-tried and tested bid, project and programme management procedures. These procedures have to be embodied in company-specific routines, guide books and the IT-enabled business processes required to successfully manage portfolios of any new type of repetitive project.

Such operational improvements are necessary but not sufficient for creating and maintaining competitive advantage in the project business. More significant advantages can be obtained by using projects strategically to diversify into new technology and/or market positions. The project business can generate future revenues and profits by using its key resources and most talented people to explore and develop the radically new capabilities required to meet tomorrow's innovation needs and challenges. As we have seen, a firm's initial move beyond its traditional base often begins with the establishment of a major project. These strategically important base-moving projects may be implemented by top management to explore new business opportunities. But they can also be established as independent bottom-up initiatives by individual project business units themselves, as they respond quickly and flexibly to market signals and new business opportunities. For example, firms like IBM, GE, Siemens, Ericsson, C&W and Alstom all started out on the path to integrated solutions when their business units set up projects to meet the new outsourcing demands of major business customers.

When base-moving projects are created, project directors, managers and team members must learn about the unique characteristics of a new technology or market opportunity. They need to be given the freedom and support to break the rules of the company, abandon or ignore existing bid and project routines and experiment with new tools and processes. However, the creation of new routines represents a break with past management practices and is often perceived as a threat to the existing power bases of various groups within the firm. In such cases, project teams must be given the high-level support they need to carry through new projects as they see fit and as their project experience indicates. If the new project leads to repeat business, high-level programmes of capability building need to be put in place, resourced and supported by senior management. Today, firms are presented with an increasing stream of opportunities to undertake many new types of projects, such as turnkey, outsourcing and PPP projects, that are likely to lead to a large amount of repeat business for successful organisations.

In an environment driven by rapid innovation and technological obsolescence, the lesson for suppliers of high-volume consumer goods, standard components and services is that they can no longer rely on functional excellence alone to achieve competitive advantage. Although they rarely use projects to carry out their volume-based productive operations, they too must develop the deep project capabilities needed to manage their core innovative activities and use projects to adapt new technologies for product or service applications in the market. There are dozens of major examples which demonstrate that the creation of new business ventures more often than not begins with the establishment of a novel project venture to move quickly into a new market space. Take the early example of IBM's Personal Computer which came to market in 1981. One of the company's renegade independent business units (the Entry Systems division based in Florida) created a separate project organisation called Project Chess which developed the PC in one year (Cringely, 1992: 126). At this time, an IBM project to build the PC using internally developed components was in its fourth year with no end in sight. The willingness of Project Chess to break the rules by buying in components helped to accelerate the product's development time. Vanguard projects of this kind can expand in size to form a new subsidiary organisation.

Top management should recognise that base-moving projects can be an important source of strategic renewal for the firm. A strategy for corporate development should determine the remaining growth potential of existing mainstream businesses and the resource levels required to exploit current technologies and markets. But to achieve growth and profitability in new technology and/or market bases, a resource pool should be reserved for activities beyond the current business base. The existence of this pool of dynamic resources allows senior management to support and promote new project initiatives. By these means, project capabilities can help firms to minimise the risk of branching out in innovative directions and revitalise functional organisational structures. However, this can happen effectively only if the firm learns to build project capabilities as part of its portfolio of top management skills.

Lessson 2: Learn within, between and beyond projects

The second lesson is that firms need to systematically promote learning within and between projects, and iteratively between projects and the wider business organisation. This is how firms like IBM, Ericsson and C&W built project capabilities into all layers of the organisation. The traditional functional organisations used in high-volume production act as silos for learning and knowledge acquisition. In the past these helped to preserve and build a firm's capabilities over time. However, the transitory nature of projects poses a particular challenge for learning and capability development as project teams typically break up after a project is completed and there are no project silos to capture this crucial learning.

Other studies confirm that poor performance and low productivity are widespread in project businesses (e.g. Flyvbjerg et al., 2003). Our research has shown that an important reason for this poor performance is the inability of many firms to capture and utilise the knowledge and learning gained from projects. All too often, commercial pressures to utilise resources fully during the life of the project and to reallocate them quickly when a project finishes prevent systematic learning within phases of a project and from one project to the next. However, as described in this book, leading suppliers of CoPS in the US, Europe and Japan have successfully developed mechanisms and tools to achieve project-based learning, allowing knowledge capture, analysis and feedback into the wider organisation. Innovative firms such as UK-based Oxford Instruments, a maker of advanced scientific and medical equipment, have developed a range of new performance-enhancing tools for learning from project to project.

Learning from project to project and from individual projects to the wider business organisation is essential to productivity, efficiency and growth, where firms carry out standardised projects which are performed repeatedly for many customers. However, such learning is equally important in the case of unique projects (e.g. Heathrow's Terminal 5 project) that are unlikely to be repeated in the future because roles performed by individuals and the specific problems confronted by project teams are often similar in subsequent projects. For example, project risks can be managed more effectively prior to the start of a major new project by learning directly from managers who have dealt with similar risks encountered in previous projects. The technique, deployed by Ford and other major companies, of insisting that new project directors review the experiences of similar projects is a powerful learning tool which is all too often neglected in the heat of the moment. The new project should be used to promote learning in the wider business organisation. By removing people from their usual routines and setting them unusual goals to solve by working in teams with unfamiliar people, the wider, more permanent organisation can be opened up to processes of renewal and organisational change.

As we illustrated with the cases of Ericsson and C&W, entirely new sets of project capabilities have to be developed when firms move base into rapidly growing new markets and/or dynamically changing technologies. Expanding into a new base often begins with the creation of a vanguard project organisation – such as Ericsson's stand-alone Turnkey Projects Group – to explore the technical and commercial viability of the business opportunity. In a process of self-reflective learning with its partners, suppliers and customers, the vanguard project team has to be prepared to abandon traditional project management techniques and routines if they threaten to prevent innovation. The team must utilise the learning gained within the project to experiment with new approaches to project management and organisation. If a firm experiences strong demand for a new type of project, the learning gained from initial projects is needed to underpin the far-reaching organisational transformations and the strategic repositioning of the firm in the marketplace. Without this learning, this transformation cannot take place – or it takes place slowly, ineffectively and inefficiently.

Our model of project capability building identifies two interacting levels of learning: the project and the business organisation as a whole. To grow successfully beyond their traditional business bases, successful CoPS firms carry out bottom-up project-based learning to gain knowledge and experience about the new business opportunities. For example, C&W's first major outsourcing projects were set up in response to its largest corporate customers' demands for global networks based on IP technologies. At the same time, they engaged in high-level business-led learning to establish what kind of corporate-wide capability development and organisation were needed to achieve success in the new line of projects. Senior management was responsible for ensuring that the capabilities were in place to deliver a growing number of increasingly standardised projects based on repeatable processes and routines. When made a priority, the systematic application of project and business learning enables a firm to exploit economies of repetition and recombination. In this way, firms can achieve first-mover advantages by proceeding more quickly down the project learning curve than their competitors.

The major difficulties of learning in project business with multiple partners need to be addressed with the specific tools, structures and processes we outlined in Chapters 5, 6 and 7, which are designed to suit the project business. Many of these findings apply not only to CoPS suppliers but also to volume producers, where organisational learning through projects is an essential first step in improving performance and achieving strategic objectives. However, much of the general advice on organisational learning assumes the existence of permanent or semi-permanent organisations and repeated processes as typically found in high-volume industries. Creating an effective learning organisation involves regular cycles of data collection, reflection, experimentation and organisational improvement, centred on key projects. New learning routines need to be embedded in the business and a culture of learning has to be created, encouraging time for reflection to capitalise on previous project experiences including bidding for new types of business.

Lesson 3: Organise for project business opportunities

The third lesson is to design the right kind of temporary organisations suitable for solving each business opportunity facing the project business. This is a lesson that must be learnt by all types of firms that use projects to drive their businesses. In contrast to the traditional functional organisations, CoPS suppliers typically use various project-based organisations – ranging from matrix to single-project structures – to cope with rapidly evolving technologies, cross-functional product integration and changing customer needs. Chapter 5 outlines some of the tools needed to judge which organisational structure is best suited for a particular activity.

Project-based organisations can be internal to the firm, but they often extend beyond the boundaries of the firm to embrace many different organisations in project consortia, joint ventures, alliances and strategic partnerships. The competitive advantage of the world's most successful suppliers of CoPS increasingly stems from their ability to collaborate successfully with other partner firms and competitors in their core business and innovative activities. For example, Bombardier often participates in joint-venture projects and consortia with its main rivals (e.g. Alstom Transport and Siemens) and customers (e.g. Virgin Trains) to design and build railway and urban transportation systems. Collaboration occurs within different parts of the firm and between the firm and its partner organisations. It is important not just at the early design stage but throughout project execution and, sometimes, afterwards during the operational life of a product, as in the maintenance of rolling stock, aircraft engines and telecoms systems.

Project collaboration in CoPS rarely occurs in a vertical supply chain manner with component and service suppliers feeding into a dominant manufacturer, as in cars and consumer electronics. Instead it takes place horizontally and by mutual adjustment across a project network or web of organisations which can include partner suppliers, regulators, users and specialist small firms. Within the project, firms work closely with customers as strategic partners to realise new markets, develop technologies and deliver innovative products. It is within the project network that supplier positions are upgraded and downgraded according to their performance. Consistently good performance is rewarded over time with new contracts, while poor performance is eventually penalised with the loss of business. In project networks, competition and collaboration occur side by side, sometimes leading to clashes of interest as rival firms seek to win new business.

Project collaboration can be especially difficult where new technology is involved and the inevitable reliance on untested outside contractors becomes a source of risk and uncertainty. Different organisational cultures, problems in contractual relations and the need to integrate different domains of knowledge make collaborative projects very difficult to execute. Even when projects are largely controlled within a single firm, many units which cross national boundaries may be involved, leading to management coordination difficulties. For example, one of the main challenges in managing Ericsson's large development project to create a new platform of GSM technology, undertaken between 1993 and 1996, was the difficulty of coordinating its geographically dispersed design activities in the company's R&D centre in Sweden and design offices located in nine European countries.

In the project business, collaborators often need to share their intellectual property at early stages of the project, sometimes with competitors, in order to realise new markets and agree on how to proceed. Different firms tend to see problems from their own point of view, making it necessary for the overall project director or manager to deploy negotiation skills, agree rules of engagement and ensure these are adhered to throughout the project. Once in place, the project team needs to be protected from the influence of outside interest groups which often attempt to change project goals and rules, especially in large politicised projects. By gaining respect and reputation, heavyweight project managers become successful and trusted members of professional communities involving different firms with shared long-term interests. This building of trust is important, not only for the execution of on-going projects but also for cross-company collaboration in future projects.

Lesson 4: Manage software- and IT-intensive projects

The fourth lesson that today's project businesses must learn is how to deploy the software and IT tools and systems needed to produce high-technology products and services. CoPS, in particular, have a large component of embedded software, while IT systems are often used intensively in the management and day-to-day operations of projects. It is in these types of software- and IT-intensive projects that many projects go disastrously wrong.

The widespread inability of project businesses to accurately estimate and control software and IT costs and to deliver on time and to budget, especially when more than one supplier is involved, is well recognised. It is often the case that, once delivered, the system requires a great deal of further unplanned work to ensure that it functions as originally planned. The evidence shows that, despite the proliferation of elaborate software tools, this situation is getting worse rather than better. One of the reasons for the difficulties in managing software and IT is that, despite the availability of management tools, much of the software activity remains a human-centred, craft-based activity and, as a result, it is difficult to estimate costs, control processes and automate design or production. Major software and IT projects present project business teams with large numbers of alternative design options which cannot be managed by the commonly available (rational) design methods alone.

Our research indicates that although the software and IT community has developed many elaborate tools and process-analysis techniques, these tend to assume that rational, formal processes are the solution to cost, control, quality and productivity problems. These processes treat the organisation as a machine amenable to engineering adjustments and fine tuning. While effective management systems and processes are essential, much software and IT practice (and training) fails to account for the uncertain, informal reality which lies behind the formal processes and systems. For example, our research with Thales Training and Simulation shows that tools and systems alone cannot adequately cope with the most important drivers of project performance such as personal choices and motivations, leadership quality and the complex multi-project work environment facing many engineers and managers. The key to the successful management of software and IT projects is the deployment of sound human judgement and informal management tools which bring experience and skill to bear on the design and execution of projects rather than a reliance on highly elaborate, formal management tools and procedures. These often fail to live up to their promises. This underlines the wider challenge of managing the soft side of projects.

Weaknesses in strategy, leadership and communication skills, as well as a lack of clarity over goals and procedures, plague software and IT projects. Spectacular failures in both the public sector (e.g. the UK's National Air Traffic Services project to design the Swanwick air traffic control centre and the London Ambulance Service despatch system) and the private sector (e.g. the London Stock Exchange and the pan-European Ariane 501 spacecraft launcher) confirm the many studies which show that the overall software problem is getting worse rather than better. In many cases, project managers fail to account sufficiently for the vital human factor which makes or breaks a new project. If the development of this soft dimension is overlooked rather than treated as an essential ingredient of project success, projects will continue to fail. The importance of project leadership and effective communications in particular need to be not only recognised but also backed up with training, management support and investment throughout all levels of the project business, including the top management team.

Many of these lessons apply to complex, high-technology hardware and service projects regardless of their software and IT content. Wherever there is an important, human input centred on expert individuals and groups, a high degree of empowerment and practitioner involvement in project management is called for. In the past it may have been appropriate for decisions to be taken at a high level in project business. However, increasingly, important decisions need to be delegated down to the managers at the operational, project level as these are the people who take the day-to-day decisions vital to project execution and adjusting to customer needs. Project managers are therefore key people in the project business and need to be empowered to take the heavyweight decisions needed to create and execute projects.

Lesson 5: Develop strong systems integration capability

The fifth lesson is that project businesses must learn to master the core task of how to design and integrate various bodies of knowledge and physical components into a well-functioning system. This distinctive capability is essentially one of systems integration: the ability to bring together inputs from within the organisation and, increasingly, from external suppliers of services, systems, software and hardware.

Systems engineering techniques are used to help manage design and integration activities and plan the whole process from the start. In a shift away from the traditional waterfall model of sequential stages, modern systems engineering tools take into account the various feedback loops between later (e.g. manufacturing, integration and testing) and earlier design stages. Techniques such as concurrent engineering and partitioning systems into smaller manageable subsystems help to minimise interactions between subsystems that may result in unpredictable outcomes (sometimes called emergent properties). However, difficulties in achieving design freeze at the outset, changes in customer specifications and design iterations between later to earlier stages mean that emergent properties cannot be pinpointed in advance by using systems engineering techniques, no matter how well executed. To be successful under these conditions of uncertainty, project managers and engineers must recognise that unexpected events and unknown risks will arise and they need to use their tacit knowledge, judgement and experience to cope with them. As in complex software development, soft, intangible skills are central to effective systems integration performance.

Today, systems integration is seldom undertaken solely in-house. In addition to managing their internal tasks, many CoPS suppliers have to coordinate the production and innovation activities of supply networks made up of small firms, major users, other large partner companies and sometimes regulators, standards bodies and government departments. An ability to negotiate with component suppliers and other partners before, during and after project delivery is one of the marks of a successful systems integrator. Traditional arm's-length market transactions as normally defined cannot provide the signals needed to drive product and process innovation forward, which is why negotiation skills are so important.

Many manufacturers of CoPS, such as Thales, Rolls-Royce, Alstom and Ericsson, have recently been outsourcing a growing proportion of their lower-value production in order to focus on becoming systems integrators. As they do so, they have learned how to manage and coordinate external networks of component and subsystems suppliers. Most firms use tried and tested suppliers wherever possible to minimise supplier risk and uncertainty. However, in some cases, the use of unknown partners and suppliers is unavoidable. In these cases it is important that the firm has the ability to assess the capacity of the supplier to deliver to technical design, cost and customer specification targets. Successful systems integrators have to develop the knowledge and experience in-house to evaluate component supplier proposals and check the statements and track records of new suppliers and then monitor their technical and commercial progress.

Systems integration is becoming a core capability at the heart of the strategic management of the major corporation in all types of industries. But there are significant differences in the strategies of systems integrators depending on type of product and technology. For example, in high-technology volume products such as cars, semiconductors and hard disk drives, firms deploy their systems integration capabilities to exploit upstream relations with component suppliers to gain cost and speed advantages in the marketplace. By contrast, CoPS makers are deploying systems integration capabilities to exploit downstream relationships with their customers by incorporating intangible services such as maintenance, training, running business processes, finance and consultancy into their tangible systems offerings.

Systems integration capability underpins the way leading firms are able to move selectively, and simultaneously, up and down stream to gain advantages in the marketplace. This way they exploit the twin, concurrent processes of outsourcing lower-value activities and insourcing higher-value activities. CoPS suppliers which fail to build up the capabilities to integrate forward into services and provide customer-centric solutions are highly likely to fall behind in the marketplace.

Lesson 6: Provide customer-centric solutions

Closely related to the task of systems integration, the sixth lesson for CoPS suppliers is that the successful definition and execution of projects should be driven by the need to solve each customer's business or operational problems. IBM was among the first companies to transform itself from an internally focused, functionally driven organisation into one that drives all of its activities backwards from the customer. When Louis Gerstner became chief executive of IBM in 1993 he believed 'there was a very important role for some company to be able to integrate all of the pieces and deliver a working solution to the customer' (Gerstner, 2002: 60). Similarly, as CEO of General Electric, Jack Welch reinvented GE's business model during the 1980s and 1990s in a move away from a traditional product-centric manufacturer to a customer-centric solutions model (Welch, 2001).

Suppliers of CoPS in all types of industries – such as Accenture, LogicaCMG, Rolls-Royce, Ericsson, C&W and Alstom – are now following IBM and GE into integrated solutions by occupying new strategic positions in the value stream centred on systems integration. To do this, they are developing new service capabilities (e.g. operations, maintenance, finance and consulting skills) and creating customer-facing organisations. This shift into high-value customer-centric solutions has three wider implications for the project business.

First, the need to organise integrated solutions projects around individual customers' requirements has done much to elevate the role and status of the bid and project managers within the managerial hierarchy of the firm. Because of the strategic importance and high value of such projects, super-heavyweight bid and project managers, who are inevitably in very short supply, are needed to drive sales negotiations with senior managers up to and including CEOs if their involvement helps to close the deal. Traditional forms of project management based on hierarchical control, vertical lines of communication and functional specialists are being replaced by flatter, horizontally managed and commercially focused team-based structures which are organised to respond flexibly and rapidly to each customer's needs at the highest level.

Second, the traditional triple constraints model of project success (within cost, on schedule and to exacting technical specifications) has been extended to include a new measure: customer satisfaction. Although it is a decade since Pinto and Kharbanda (1995) first identified this fourth measure of project success, the growth of integrated solutions means that a project is now regarded as successful only if it solves an individual customer's immediate and longer-term business problems. Solutions providers must work closely with their customers to identify, create and share in the value added generated by each project. Solutions-based contracts are often underpinned by detailed service level agreements (SLAs) to guarantee performance levels. SLAs are used to measure the progress of specific project phases which are linked to improvements in a customer's operational processes or competitive position. To satisfy a customer's needs, a solutions provider has not only to respond to detailed contractual specifications but also to be able to respond flexibly – even during late stages in the life of a project – to changes in a customer's needs and priorities.

Third, demand for integrated solutions means that the traditional project life cycle now extends over many years or even decades. As we have emphasised, the solutions life-cycle model includes four main phases: engaging with the customer in high-level strategic negotiations, often before an invitation to tender has been issued; working closely with the customer to develop a value proposition during a bid or offer phase; project managing the systems integration process; and operating the product or system during a specified contractual period. Suppliers and customers need to establish long-term strategic partnerships and create co-located organisations to foster the kind of close cooperation and innovative environment required to ensure that a customer's problems are solved. To avoid being held accountable to established bureaucratic procedures, virtual project businesses are needed which can operate independently from their parent companies so that they can come up with creative solutions to a specific business problem or market opportunity.

Suppliers of consumer goods, such as domestic appliances and cars, are also moving into the high-value-added services along with physical products. These volume-based organisations are unlikely to need the types of capabilities required to offer the highly customised and unique solutions provided by CoPS firms. However, they also need to understand these solutions-based activities as they are buyers and users of CoPS, such as IT systems, corporate telecoms networks, factory automation systems and mobile phone networks. Managers in volume-based organisations, as customers, need to learn how to ensure that their needs for solutions are met by working jointly with their suppliers in bid and project teams. They too need to learn from the experience of successful CoPS enterprises.

Lesson 7: Lead the project business

The seventh lesson is that strong and flexible leadership is essential in order to build and sustain an innovative project business. If project leadership is not provided, then none of the previous lessons outlined in this chapter can be learnt and acted upon. Leadership is important at all levels within the project business organisation, including senior managers and executives responsible for deciding the overall direction of the firm, managers and directors responsible for running business units or divisions, and the heavyweight bid, project and commercial managers charged with developing new projects and programmes.

Strong and versatile leaders in senior management, including the CEO and heads of business units or divisions, are at the centre of the successful project business. Leadership is required to decide when to move into a new technology or market base and to know the right time to abandon a firm's traditional base business. For example, it is only those firms with entrepreneurial, creative and determined senior management teams, such as IBM, GE and Ericsson, that have been able to make the far-reaching changes to move into integrated solutions markets by driving change throughout their organisations. As Louis Gerstner recognised, the hardest part of turning IBM into a customer-centric, integrated solutions provider was changing the values and mindsets of thousands of people who had grown up in a highly successful product-centric organisation (Gerstner, 2002: 177).

As we have seen, however, the opportunities facing a project business are seldom simply driven by top-down strategic plans. Projects set up to meet new customer demands and adapt technology for novel market applications are often a product of decentralised initiatives led by the many project-based organisations within large firms. Strong leadership of individual project business units or divisions is essential to provide a quick and successful response to new market signals. As we saw with C&W, for example, David Sexton, CEO of the Global Markets division, was quick to identify the importance of the new business opportunity presented by global outsourcing solutions for corporate telecoms networks. His leadership of the first global outsourcing negotiations with the customer helped to galvanise the bid team into winning the business.

Because managers involved in bids and projects are individually responsible for such high-value contracts, they too must be leaders. Leadership in projects is about focusing on the overall project objective and progress, being flexible and adapting to changing conditions and to the needs of project team members. Leaders of projects have to be able to exercise different leadership styles. They should be able to motivate team members as circumstances change, appreciate the value of different experiences and skills and manage multiple interfaces between team members and with external suppliers, customers and other project stakeholders. An enthusiasm for knowledge and learning and an ability to focus on solving a particular customer's problems is an essential personal leadership skill for bid and project managers.

In the business of projects it is often necessary for the lead firm to engage at multiple levels with external organisations including users, purchasers, regulators and other large and small suppliers of components and services. These organisations may well be involved in key design tasks as well as engineering, production, delivery and operations. Because of the multiple organisations engaged in project business the leadership role becomes one of lateral consultation and negotiation rather than vertical interaction and hierarchical management. The function of the chief negotiator needs to be performed by a highly skilled and heavyweight project manager to ensure that conflicts are quickly resolved and any obstacles to progress of the project are removed.

The project business paradigm: facing the future

Some of the individual lessons described above will be known to some chief executives, directors and managers of successful CoPS businesses. Using projects to drive innovation and achieve business objectives has been their core activity for many years. However, even the most successful project businesses have yet to develop a coherent, integrated and strategic approach to projects.

Unlike mass-produced goods where well-known management tools such as lean production, total quality management and continuous improvement are embraced as best practice, in the project business, including CoPS industries, there is much less agreement about what constitutes good competitive practice, no well-understood learning curves, and only a few widely available management tools. Often the tools which are available (e.g. PERT and concurrent engineering) fail to meet the strategic project challenges we have identified. In many cases, project businesses struggle to adapt systems designed for high-volume production (e.g. MRP11). Although managers are often fully aware of project management practices in their own firms and industries, there is too little cross-fertilisation of ideas about good practice from one industry to another.

Yet it is this lack of knowledge about what constitutes success in the emerging project business paradigm which creates a window of opportunity for firms that are able to learn the strategic lessons outlined in this book. By rapidly overcoming the challenges involved in building an innovative and dynamic project business, they can move ahead in the competitive race. Managers in high-volume industries, with much less experience of project management and project modes of organising, have a great deal to gain by familiarising themselves with the experiences of successful project businesses.

As projects become more central to corporate strategy, innovation and competitive advantage in many industries, managers must be prepared to reject mainstream business models designed for high-volume production and develop the new ones required to add value through projects. However, there is no one way or single best practice in the business of projects. New projects are a way of exploring how to enact competitive strategy and branch out in new directions of innovation. Major new projects are the way business leaders formulate strategic moves and create new business ventures.

In facing the future, firms need to understand how and why the innovation environment is driving them to build project businesses to cope with changing markets and technologies. In CoPS, firms face the particular challenge of developing service-intensive solutions, often for inexperienced customers, in increasingly competitive markets, such as newly licensed mobile phone operators. New projects arise daily because of globalisation, large public infrastructure investment, de-regulation, liberalisation and privatisation. In consumer goods, leading firms are attempting to cope with shortening product life cycles, product commoditisation and strong Asian competition by using projects to migrate downstream into higher-value-added services. High-technology component producers are embarking on new projects to outsource production and, sometimes, design activities to partner suppliers.

In deploying projects to achieve strategic business goals, firms must move beyond the traditional discipline and mindset of project management which focuses on operational efficiency. Projects are not merely part of the operational side of business, they are central to business innovation, capability building and corporate strategy. Each successful project has its own distinctive features – and it is, collectively, these features which constitute the competitive advantage of the project business. By treating projects as the key to market creation, exploiting technology and customer-centric solutions, more firms will be able to capture the rewards of the innovative project business.

Appendix A: Project-based organisation: case objectives, method and limitations

The purpose of the case study in Chapter 5 is to examine the nature, strengths and weaknesses of the PBO in comparison with the functional form through the lens of two major projects carried out within a single firm: one in a PBO division and one in a functional division. The case is a study of a firm that produces a wide range of advanced, high-cost scientific, industrial and medical equipment. The senior management in the firm wished to learn from the operating experiences of PBD, which had been in pure PBO form for around two years. PBD had proved highly successful in meeting customer needs and project performance targets. A key strategic decision was whether or not to implement a pure PBO in FMD, a larger division. The management felt that there were lessons to learn from the good and bad experiences of both organisations. Although both PBD and FMD produced similar CoPS equipment, for geographical reasons the physical merging of the two sites was not an option in the foreseeable future.

The research method involved examining the experience of two similar, complex projects (termed project P in PBD and project F in FMD) in order to review and compare project processes, problems and performance and to draw lessons for both organisations.[1] One of the problems of case study research of this kind is the counterfactual difficulty of knowing what would have happened (e.g. in terms of performance) if another organisational structure had been applied. It is also difficult to attribute particular behavioural and performance attributes (e.g. flexibility, effectiveness, efficiency and return on

---

[1] Project processes refer to patterns of managerial, technological and operational practice: the 'way things are done' within the project, including both formal and informal routines. At the broader firm level, processes occur within and across the various functions of the firm (e.g. marketing, production, finance, engineering, R&D and personnel) and occur both formally and informally, shaping the efficiency and effectiveness of a firm.

investment) to particular factors such as organisational form rather than to other factors (e.g. project leadership, company culture, product market differences and senior management support). The method adopted here to overcome at least some of these difficulties is to take the case of a single large CoPS supplier which, for particular historical reasons, operates a mix of both project-based and functional/matrix forms, addressing similar product markets and clients with the same senior management team. This way we are able to analyse and compare two major projects of similar value, duration, technology and customer, in the two distinct strategic business units, one PBO and one functional/matrix.

The research involved three stages: first, a structured questionnaire was used to gather the views of a sample of practitioners in each project, including scientists, engineers, draftsmen, technicians and project managers. Views were sought on the detailed, actual experiences of PBD project P and FMD project F and on perceptions of the wider strengths and weaknesses of both organisations. Second, interviews were carried out with senior managers and directors on their perceptions of the projects and each organisation's strengths and weaknesses. Third, a workshop was arranged with both groups to feed back results and check the findings were consistent with the experiences of the staff, many of whom had worked for both parts of the organisation and other strategic business units within Complex Equipment Inc.

Twenty interviews were conducted for each project. Information was gathered on origin, history, structure, management, client relations, supplier links, project processes and performance. The sample consisted of a 'slice group' (i.e. representatives of most main functions and seniority levels of the two projects). Within the case, the research focused on:

- organisational structure;
- project management and leadership;
- team identity and coherence;
- client and client management;
- risk management;
- formal and informal tools and procedures;
- organisation-wide learning and coordination;
- project performance;
- organisational strategies and solutions.

We report on each of these issues in Chapter 5 by contrasting the functional matrix with the PBO division.

Regarding scope and limitations, the research took a bottom-up look at two real projects, but did not systematically research the broader company processes or functions (e.g. corporate strategy, quality systems, bid processes, production, purchasing and cross-departmental communications). Nor could the study look systematically at the relations between project and wider company business processes. Both projects were carried out largely under the control of the firm (e.g. the degree of co-engineering was low), so although other partners and users were actively involved, the case is not an example of an extensive multi-firm project where developments are shared more equally between partners. In addition, the case refers to the type of PBO conducting a small number of major CoPS projects rather than the case of a PBO carrying out large numbers of smaller projects simultaneously. Even within this category, the case issues cannot claim to be generally applicable to other large firms producing small numbers of elaborate, high-value CoPS.

Accepting these limitations, the case was able to illustrate some of the features of the PBO for CoPS compared with the functional matrix and major differences in project processes, advantages and disadvantages of the two organisational forms. The case also yielded insights into some of the wider organisational issues, especially organisational learning which featured as a major problem in the case of PBD.

Appendix B: Applying organisation development techniques to software processes

Our approach is based on intervention techniques from the field of organisation development, which tries to improve the way organisations work in practice. The tradition of organisation development, which spans both management strategy (Mintzberg, 1989) and implementation (Mullins, 1994; Handy, 1993; French and Bell, 1973; Tyson and Jackson, 1992), tends to treat strategy, management and work as iterative processes which are 'crafted', informal and sensitive to organisational style and human motivation rather than top-down, scientific or rational. These authors show how selective outside interventions can sometimes be helpful in surfacing issues, identifying problems and stimulating new working practices in firms (French and Bell, 1973). Underpinning this approach is the belief that dealing with soft, informal, human processes is essential to organisational improvement.

The method, described in detail in Hobday and Brady (2000), involved five basic steps, each with more detailed subprocesses and outputs (see Figure B.1).[1] In Step 1 we agreed with management and practitioners the scope, aims, outputs and timing of the exercise, and identified a structured group of interviewees. In Step 2 we collected data on rational processes as contained in toolkits, manuals, flow charts, formal procedures – and from interviews with senior managers on how the process 'should' proceed. Process analysts at Dynamics contributed to the questionnaire design and to capturing, diagrammatically, the formal company processes.

Data were then gathered from practitioners on how the process *actually* proceeded in project Triumph, using a structured questionnaire. Step 3 involved comparing soft with rational practices for divergencies using the data and we generated a list of major 'hot spots' (problem areas) and 'beauty spots' (solutions and best practices).

---

[1] Hobday and Brady (2000) provide several other case examples across a range of technology domains.

❶ Set up programme: identify structured group for interviews and workshops

❍

❷ Data collection: ideal processes (management) vs actual processes (practitioners)

❍

❸ Benchmark analysis: identify key variances and hot spots – prepare workshop 1

❍

❹ Workshop 1: (a) verification (b) establish causes of problems (c) identify solutions (d) proposals on implementation

❍

❺ Workshop 2: report back to senior management and agree actions/ support needed for implementation

Figure B.1. Software analysis and improvement method: five basic steps

In Step 4 (workshop 1) the findings were presented back for verification, analysis of causes of hot spots, discussion of possible solutions to problems and proposals for implementation. Step 5 involved reporting to senior management to feed back findings and agree an implementation plan.

Our interviews took place in three phases: shortly after the start in 1995, during the main period of design in 1996 and just after the project finished in 1997. A total of 40 interviews were carried out, involving 28 individuals, at most levels of seniority across all relevant departments.

The rationale for choosing flight simulation and project Triumph was as follows. First, flight simulation provides an example of a high-technology capital good, involving highly complex software engineering tasks, several supply organisations and the user in design and development. Second, as a safety-critical area, the software is subject to a great deal of formalised rational systematic controls and specific management tools are utilised to control processes in order to ensure a high-quality product. Third, the sample project Triumph was chosen because (a) it was a significant project, just at the start of its development and could be tracked in real time; (b) as a military project, rational tools and procedures were mandated and could be relatively easily identified; and (c) the project, although challenging, was fairly typical in that it contained a moderate degree of technical complexity and novelty and an average involvement of outside suppliers and users. In the event, during the project major efforts were made to deliver a rational software process to conform to UK Ministry of Defence (the user) procedures and documentation requirements.[2]

---

[2] Note that a second civil project, not reported on here for space reasons, was also analysed for purposes of comparison.

Appendix C: Research leading to the project capability building model

The PCB model presented in Chapter 7 was a product of inductive research (Eisenhardt, 1989: 535) based on the empirical findings of three successive research projects undertaken between 1994 and 2003. As shown in Table C.1, Project 1 identified Ericsson's move into a new category of projects. It proposed the hypothesis that Ericsson's new 'turnkey project' represented a generic move taking place across industries. But there was little evidence to support this claim until Project 2 which found that Cable & Wireless was also moving into the provision of a new category of projects which Project 3 referred to as 'integrated solutions'. It was not until Project 3 that in-depth case study evidence was collected to confirm that five firms operating in different industries were developing the capabilities to move into the provision of integrated solutions projects.

The process of theory building was highly iterative and the long gestation period for the emergence of the theory reflects the empirical evidence. It has taken a long time for the organisations to build capability and to overcome organisational inertia as they move from a focus on exploring new possibilities to full exploitation of a new line of projects. Throughout the three research projects, data were collected in a variety of ways. The authors conducted 126 data-gathering interviews (lasting around two hours each) with strategic managers (including current and former CEOs), senior project managers, heads of functional departments and managers involved in project and line activities.

In addition, action research was undertaken with Ericsson and C&W to produce tools that aimed to improve the performance of the organisations (Eden and Huxham, 1996: 527; Dickens and Watkins, 1999). Project 1 produced a Turnkey Project Start-up Guide, designed to help Ericsson capture the lessons learnt on the new type of turnkey project and improve future performance in similar projects. Project 2 helped C&W develop a CD-Rom learning tool to help other teams put

Table C.1: Empirical research project leading to the PCB model

Research projects*	Research focus	Method	Tool development
Project 1 (July 1994 to June 1997)	Technology and innovation management	Multiple case studies – business case studies and two project case studies in each of three participating firms	Turnkey Project Start-up Guide book developed for Ericsson
Project 2 (July 1997 to September 2001)	Project-to-project learning	Interview-based survey at three levels – senior management, project management and practitioner with 43 firms in UK, Europe, North America and Japan	CD-Rom learning tool developed for Cable & Wireless Project Handbook developed for an aerospace company
Project 3 (May 2001 to July 2003)	Developing services capabilities	Multiple case studies – business case studies and project case studies in six collaborating organisations	Generic web-based organisational capability model developed Customised for Ericsson

* The three research projects were all funded by the UK's Engineering and Physical Sciences Research Council under four separate grants: GR/K31756, GR/L97377, GR/N10110 and GR/R59403/01.

together major outsourcing bids. Project 3 created a web-based tool for Ericsson which was designed to raise awareness of the organisational changes required to provide integrated solutions.

The first two interventions aimed towards capturing and transferring the lessons learnt from their vanguard projects (Phase 2 of the PCB) and the third towards developing an organisation which could fully exploit the new market for integrated solutions (Phase 3 and business-led learning). The process of developing these tools provided a rich source of data about the practicalities of project capability building which was used to construct the PCB model.

References

Abdel-Hamid, T. and Madnick, S. E. (1991). *Software Project Dynamics: an Integrated Approach*, New Jersey: Prentice Hall.

Abegglen, J. C. (1994). *Sea Change: Pacific Asia as the New World Industrial Centre*, New York: The Free Press.

Abernathy, W. J. and Clark, K. B. (1985). 'Innovation: mapping the winds of creative destruction', *Research Policy*, 14, 3–22.

Abernathy, W. J. and Utterback, J. M. (1978). 'Patterns of industrial innovation', *Technology Review*, 80 (7), June–July, 41–47.

Acha, V., Davies, A., Hobday, M. and Salter, A. J. (2004). 'Exploring the capital goods economy: complex product systems in the UK', *Industrial and Corporate Change*, 13 (3), 505–529.

Adler, P. S. and Clark, K. B. (1991). 'Behind the learning curve: a sketch of the learning process', *Management Science*, 37 (3), 267–281.

Allen, T. J. (1977). *Managing the Flow of Technology: technology Transfer and the Dissemination of Technological Innovation within the R&D Organization*, Cambridge, MA: The MIT Press.

Amsden, A. H. and Hikino, T. (1994). 'Project execution capability, organizational know-how and conglomerate corporate growth in late industrialization', *Industrial and Corporate Change*, 3 (1), 111–147.

Ansoff, H. I. (1957). 'Strategies for diversification', *Harvard Business Review*, September–October, 113–124.

Arena, R. (1983). 'Méso-analyse et théorie de l'économie industrielle', in *ADEFI*, *Economica*, Paris.

Argyris, C. (1977). 'Double loop learning in organizations', *Harvard Business Review*, September–October, 115–125.

Arora, A. and Gambardella, A. (1999). 'Chemicals', in D. Mowery (ed.) *US Industry in 2000: Studies in Competitive Performance*, Washington: National Academy Press.

Arrow, K. (1962). 'The economic implications of learning by doing', *Review of Economic Studies*, June, 155–173.

Arthur, W. B. (1993). 'Pandora's marketplace', in *New Scientist Supplement*, 6 February, 6–8.

Augsdorfer, P. (1996). *Forbidden Fruits: An Analysis of Bootlegging, Uncertainty and Learning in Corporate R&D*, Aldershot: Averbury.

Aviation Week and Space Technology (1991). March 18 issue.

Ayas, K. and Zeniuk, N. (2001). 'Project-based learning: building communities of reflective practitioners', *Management Learning*, 32 (1), 61–76.

Baden-Fuller, C. and Stopford, J. (1999). *Rejuvenating the Mature Business*, 2nd edn, London: International Thomson Business Press.

Baker, M. and Rouse, A. (1995). 'Getting and keeping software quality certification: some associated issues', in G. Doukidis, B. Galliers, T. Jelassi, H. Kremar and F. Land (eds.) *Proceedings of the 3rd European Conference on Information Systems*, Athens, Greece.

Balconi, M. (2002). 'Tacitness, codification of technological knowledge and the organisation of industry', *Research Policy*, 31, 357–379.

Barnard, C. I. (1938). *The Functions of the Executive*, Cambridge, MA: Harvard University Press.

Barney, J. (1991). 'Firm resources and sustained competitive advantage', *Journal of Management*, 17 (1), 99–120.

Baumgartner, J. S. (1963). *Project Management*, Homewood, IL: Irwin.

Bennis, W. G. (1966). *Changing Organizations: Essay on the Development and Evolution of Human Organization*, New York: McGraw Hill.

Bennis, W. G. and Slater, P. L. (1968). *The Temporary Society*, New York: Harper & Row.

Best, M. H. (1990). *The New Competition*, Cambridge, MA: Harvard University Press.

(2003). 'The geography of systems integration' in A. Prencipe, A. Davies and M. Hobday (eds.) *The Business of Systems Integration*, Oxford: Oxford University Press, 201–228.

Bijker, W. E., Hughes, T. P. and Pinch, T. (eds.) (1987). *The Social Construction of Technological Systems*, Cambridge, MA: MIT Press.

Boardman, J. (1990). *Systems Engineering: an Introduction*, New York: Prentice Hall.

Boehm, B. W. (1988). 'A spiral model of software development and enhancement', *IEEE Computer*, May, 61–72.

(1989a). *Software Risk Management*, Washington, DC: IEEE Computer Society Press.

(1989b). 'Theory-w software project management: principles and examples', *IEEE Transactions on Software Engineering*, 15 (7), July, 902–916.

(1991). 'Software risk management: principles and practices', *IEEE Software*, January, 32–41.

Bonaccorsi, A. and Giuri, P. (2000). 'When shakeout doesn't occur: the evolution of the turboprop engine industry', *Research Policy*, 29 (7–8), 847–870.

Brady, T. and Davies, A. (2004). 'Building project capabilities: from exploratory to exploitative learning', *Organizational Studies*, 26 (9), 1601–1621.

Brady, T., Marshall, N., Prencipe, A. and Tell, F. (2002). 'Making sense of learning landscapes in project-based organisations', presented at the 3rd European Conference on Organizing, Knowledge and Capabilities, Athens, Greece, April.

Brady, T., Rush, H., Hobday, M., Davies, A., Probert, D. and Banerjee, S. (1997). 'Tools for technology management: an academic perspective', *Technovation*, 17 (8), 417–425.

British Aerospace Annual Report (1998). Farnborough, Hants.

Brown, J. S. and Duguid, P. (1991). 'Organizational learning and communities of practice: Towards a unified view of working, learning, and innovation', *Organization Science*, 2 (1), 40–57.

   (2000). *The Social Life of Information*, Cambridge, MA: Harvard Business School Press.

Brusoni, S., Prencipe, A. and Pavitt, K. (2001). 'Knowledge specialization and the boundaries of the firm: why do firms know more than they make?', *Administrative Science Quarterly*, 46, 597–621.

Brusoni, S., Prencipe, A. and Salter, A. (1998). 'Mapping and measuring innovation in project-based firms', SPRU mimeo, June.

Burgelman, R. A. (1984). 'Managing the internal corporate venturing process', *Sloan Management Review*, Winter, 33–48.

Burns, T. and Stalker, G. M. (1961). *The Management of Innovation* (reprinted 1994) Oxford: Oxford University Press.

Buttrick, R. (2000). *The Interactive Project Workout*, 2nd edn, London: Financial Times-Prentice Hall.

Buxton, J. N. and Malcolm, R. (1991). 'Software technology transfer', *IEEE Software Engineering Journal*, 6 (1), 17–23.

Cable & Wireless (1993). 'Bid document preparation process', Cable & Wireless Document CW/BN/BM/BMSP001.

   (1999). 'Global outsourcing and the networked economy: telecoms' opportunity to deliver real competitive advantage', Cable & Wireless.

Carlsson, B. and Eliasson, G. (1994). 'The nature and importance of economic competence', *Industrial and Corporate Change*, 3 (4), 687–711.

Castells, M. (1996). *The Rise of the Network Society*, Oxford: Blackwell Publishers.

Cawson, A. (1986). *Corporatism and Political Theory*, Oxford: Basil Blackwell.

Chambers, G. L. (1986). 'The systems engineering process: a technical bibliography', *IEEE Transactions on Systems, Man and Cybernetics*, Vol. SMC–16, No. 5, September/October, 712–722.

Chandler, A. D. (1962). *Strategy and Structure*, Cambridge, MA: The MIT Press.

(1990). *Scale and Scope: The Dynamics of Industrial Capitalism*, Cambridge, MA: Belknap Press.

Charette, R. N. (1989). *Software Engineering Risk Analysis and Management*, New York: Intertext Publications, McGraw-Hill.

Chesbrough, H. (2003a). *Open Innovation: The New Imperative for Creating and Profiting from Technology*, Boston, MA: Harvard Business School Press.

(2003b). 'Towards a dynamics of modularity: a cyclical model of technical advance', in A. Prencipe, A. Davies and M. Hobday, (eds.) *The Business of Systems Integration*, Oxford: Oxford University Press, 174–198.

Clark, K. B. (1985). 'The interaction of design hierarchies and market concepts in technological evolution', *Research Policy*, 14, 235–251.

Clark, K. B. and Fujimoto, T. (1991). *Product Development Performance*, Boston, MA: Harvard Business School Press.

Clark, K. B. and Wheelwright, S. C. (1992). 'Organizing and leading "heavyweight" development teams', *Californian Management Review*, Summer, 34 (3), 9–28.

Cleland, D. and King, W. R. (eds.) (1988). *Project Management Handbook*, New York: Van Nostrand Reinhold.

Coase, R. H. (1937). 'The nature of the firm', *Economica*, 4, 386–405.

Cohen, W. M. and Levinthal, D. A. (1989). 'Innovation and learning: the two faces of R&D', *The Economic Journal*, 99, 569–596.

Cohen, W. M. and Levinthal, D. A. (1990). 'Absorptive capacity: a new perspective on learning and innovation', *Administrative Science Quarterly*, 35, 128–152.

Collins, T. and Bicknell, D. (1997). *Crash*, London: Simon & Schuster.

Cook, S. D. N. and Brown, J. S. (1999). 'Bridging epistemologies: the generative dance between organizational knowledge and organizational knowing', *Organization Science*, 10 (4), 381–400.

Coombs, R. and Hull, R. (1997). 'Knowledge management practices and path-dependency in innovation', Centre for Research on Innovation and Competition (CRIC) Discussion Paper No. 2, Manchester.

Cova, B., Ghauri, P. and Salle, R. (2002). *Project Marketing: Beyond Competitive Bidding*, Chichester: Wiley & Sons Ltd.

Crichton, M. (1997). *Airframe*, Arrow Books.

Cringely, R. X. (1992). *Accidental Empires: How the Boys of Silicon Valley Make their Millions, Battle Foreign Competition, Still Can't Get a Date*, London: Penguin Books.

Culver-Lozo, K. (1995). 'Software process iteration on large projects: challenges, strategies and experiences', *Software Process: Improvement and Practice*, 1, 35–45.

Cusumano, M. A. and Nobeoka, K. (1998). *Thinking Beyond Lean: How Multi-Project Management is Transforming Product Development at Toyota and Other Companies*, New York: The Free Press.

Cyert, R. M. and March, J. G. (1963). *A Behavioural Theory of the Firm*, Englewood, Cliffs, NJ: Prentice-Hall.

D'Adderio, L. (2001). 'Crafting the virtual prototype: how firms integrate knowledge and capabilities across organisational boundaries', *Research Policy*, 30 (9), 1409–1424.

(2002). *Bridging Formal Tools with Informal Practices: How Organisations Balance Flexibility and Control*, Edinburgh: Research Centre for Social Sciences (RCSS).

Davenport, T. H. (1993). *Process Innovation: Reengineering Work Through Information Technology*, Boston, MA: Harvard Business School.

(1996). 'Why reengineering failed: the fad that forgot people', *Fast Company*, Boston, MA: Premiere Issue, 70–74.

Davies, A. (1996). 'Innovation in large technical systems: the case of telecommunications', *Industrial and Corporate Change*, 5 (4), 1143–1180.

(1997a). 'Ericsson CME R5A Project', SPRU-CENTRIM CoPS Working Paper.

(1997b). 'The life cycle of a complex product system', *International Journal of Innovation Management*, 1 (3), 229–256.

(2003).'Integrated solutions: the changing business of systems integration', in A. Prencipe, A. Davies and M. Hobday (eds.) *The Business of Systems Integration*, Oxford: Oxford University Press, 333–368.

(2004). 'Moving base into high-value integrated solutions: a value stream approach', *Industrial and Corporate Change*, 13 (5), 727–756.

Davies, A. and Brady, T. (2000). 'Organisational capabilities and learning in complex product systems: towards repeatable solutions', *Research Policy*, 29, 931–953.

Davies, A., Brady, T. and Tang, P. (2003). *Delivering Integrated Solutions*, Brighton: SPRU-CENTRIM, 1–34.

Davies, A. and Tang, P. (2003). 'Ericsson Vodafone 3G systems services project', SPRU-CENTRIM CoPS Working Paper.

Davies, A., Tang, P., Hobday, M., Brady, T., Rush, H. and Gann, D. (2001). *Integrated Solutions: The New Economy Between Manufacturing and Services*, Brighton: SPRU-CENTRIM, 1–43.

Davis, S. M. and Lawrence, P. R. (1977). *Matrix*, Reading, MA: Addison-Wesley.

DeFillippi, R. J. (2001). 'Introduction: project-based learning, reflective practices and learning outcomes', *Management Learning*, 32 (1), 5–10.

DeFillippi, R. J. and Arthur, M. B. (1998). 'Paradox in project-base enterprise: the case of film making', *California Management Review*, 40 (2), Winter, 125–139.

(2002). 'Project-based learning, embedded learning contexts and the management of knowledge', paper presented at the 3rd European Conference on Organizing, Knowledge and Capabilities, Athens, Greece, April.

DeMarco, T. (1979). *Concise Notes on Software Engineering*, New York: Yourdon Press.

DeMarco, T. and Miller, A. (1996). 'Managing large software projects', *IEEE Software*, July, 24–27.

Department of Trade and Industry (2002). *The Value Added Scoreboard*, London: DTI Business, Finance and Investment Unit.

Dickens, L. and Watkins, K. (1999). 'Action research: rethinking Lewin', *Management Learning*, 30 (2), 127–140.

Domberger, S. (1998). *The Contracting Organization: A Strategic Guide to Outsourcing*, Oxford: Oxford University Press.

Dosi, G. (1988). 'Sources, procedures, and microeconomic effects of innovation', *Journal of Economic Literature*, 26, 1120–1171.

Dosi, G., Hobday, M., Marengo, L. and Prencipe, A. (2003). 'The economics of systems integration: towards an evolutionary interpretation', in A. Prencipe, A. Davies and M. Hobday (eds.) *The Business of Systems Integration*, Oxford: Oxford University Press, 95–113.

Doty, D. H. and Glick, W. H. (1994). 'Typologies as a unique form of theory building: towards improved understanding and modeling', *Academy of Management Review*, 19 (2), 230–251.

Drucker, P. F. (1977). *Management*, New York: Harpers.

Dvir, D. and Lechler, T. (2004): 'Plans are nothing, changing plans is everything: the impact of changes on project success', *Research Policy*, 33, 1–15.

Eden, C. and Huxham, C. (1996). 'Action research for the study of organizations', in S. R. Clegg, C. Handy and W. R. Nord (eds.) *Handbook of Organization Studies*, London: Sage, 526–542.

Eisenhardt, K. M. (1989). 'Building theories from case study research', *Academy of Management Review*, 14 (4), 532–550.

Emam, E. El and Madhavji, N. H. (1995). 'The reliability of measuring organisational maturity', *Software Process: Improvement and Practice*, 1, 3–25.

Engwall, M. (2003): 'No project is an island: linking projects to history and context', *Research Policy*, 32, 798–808.

Ericsson (1990). 'Your guide to PROPS', Ericsson Publication EN/LZT 101 1020 R1.

Fairburn, A. G. (1995). 'A systems approach to ventures', *IEE Review*, September, 195–198.

Fleck, J. (1988). 'Innofusion or diffusation? The nature of technological development in robotics', ESRC Programme on Information and Communication Technologies, Working Paper Series, University of Edinburgh.

Flowers, S. (1996). *Software Failure, Management Failure: amazing stories and cautionary tales*, Chichester: Wiley.

Flyvbjerg, B., Bruzelius, N. and Rothengatter, W. (2003). *Megaprojects and Risk: An Anatomy of Ambition*, Cambridge: Cambridge University Press.

Follett, M. P. (1918). *The New State*, London: Longmans.

Foote, N. W., Galbraith, J. R., Hope, Q. and Miller, D. (2001): 'Making solutions the answer', *The McKinsey Quarterly*, 3, 84–93.

Frame, J. D. (1994). *The New Project Management: Tools for an Age of Rapid Change, Corporate Reengineering, and Other Business Realities*, San Francisco: Jossey-Bass Publishers.

Freeman, C. (1974). *The Economics of Industrial Innovation*, Harmondsworth: Penguin.
  (1994). 'The economics of technical change', *Cambridge Journal of Economics*, 18, 463–514.

Freeman, C. and Soete, L. (1997). *The Economics of Industrial Innovation*, 3rd edn, London: Pinter.

French, W. L. and Bell, C. H. (1973). *Organization Development: Behavioural Science Interventions for Organization Improvement*, 2nd edn, New York: Prentice Hall.

Gaddis, P. O. (1960). 'The project manager', *Harvard Business Review*, May–June, 89–97.

Galbraith, J. R. (1971): 'Matrix organizational designs – how to combine functional and project forms', *Business Horizons*, February, 29–40.
  (1973). *Designing Complex Organizations*, Reading, MA: Addison-Wesley.
  (1982). 'The stages of growth', *Journal of Business Strategy*, Summer, 70–79.
  (1983). 'Strategy and organization planning', *Human Resource Management* (reprinted in H. Mintzberg and J. B. Quinn (eds.) *The Strategy Process*, 2nd edn, Upper Saddle River, NJ: Prentice Hall, 1991, 315–324.
  (2002a). 'Organizing to deliver solutions', *Organizational Dynamics*, 31 (2), 194–207.
  (2002b). *Designing Organizations: An Executive Guide to Strategy, Structure, and Process*, San Francisco: Wiley.

Gann, D. M. (1993). 'Innovation in the built environment: The rise of digital buildings', PhD thesis, SPRU, University of Sussex.

(2000). *Building Innovation: Complex Constructs in a Changing World*, London: Thomas Telford.

Gann, D. M. and Salter, A. J. (1998). 'Learning and innovation management in project-based, service-enhanced firms', *International Journal of Innovation Management*, 2 (4), 431–454.

(2000). 'Innovation in project-based, service-enhanced firms: the construction of complex products and systems', *Research Policy*, 29, 955–972.

Gardiner, P. and Rothwell, R. (1985). 'Tough customers: good designs', *Design Studies*, 6 (1), 7–17.

Garvin, D. A. (1993). 'Building a learning organization', *Harvard Business Review*, July–August, 78–92.

Gerstner, L. V. (2002). *Who Said Elephants Can't Dance? Inside IBM's Historic Turnaround*, London: HarperCollins Publishers.

Gessler, F. (2002). 'The development of wireless infrastructure standards', doctoral dissertation, Industrial Economics and Management, Royal Institute of Technology (Kung Tekniska Högskolan, KTH), Stockholm, March.

Geyer, A. and Davies, A. (2000). 'Managing project-system interfaces: case studies of railway projects in restructured UK and German markets', *Research Policy*, 29, 991–1013.

Gholz, E. (2003). 'Systems integration in the US defence industry: who does it and why is it important?' in A. Prencipe, A. Davies and M. Hobday (eds.) *The Business of Systems Integration*, Oxford: Oxford University Press, 279–306.

Gibbs, W. W. (1994). 'Software's chronic crisis', *Scientific American*, September, 72–81.

Goode, H. H. and Machol, R. E. (1957). *System Engineering: An Introduction to the Design of Large-Scale Systems*, New York: McGraw-Hill.

Grabher, G. (2001). 'Ecologies of creativity: the village, the group, and the heterarchic organisation of the British advertising industry', *Environment and Planning A*, 33, 351–374.

(2002a). 'Cool projects, boring institutions: temporary collaboration in social context', *Regional Studies*, 36, 205–214.

(ed.) (2002b). 'Fragile sector, robust practice: project ecologies in new media', *Environment and Planning A Theme Issue*, 34 (11): 1903–2092.

(2003). 'Hanging out, staying in, logging on: Learning in project ecologies', paper presented at the Academy of Management Meeting, Symposium on 'Knowledge spaces: Multiple contexts for knowledge creation', Seattle, 1–6 August.

Graham, P. (1995). *Mary Parker Follett – Prophet of Management*, Boston, MA: Harvard Business School Press.

Granstrand, O., Patel, P. and Pavitt, K. (1997). 'Multi-technology corporations: why they have "distributed" rather than "distinctive core" competencies', *California Management Review*, 39 (4), 8–25.

Granstrand, O. and Sjölander, S. (1990). 'Managing innovation in multi-technology corporations', *Research Policy*, 19, 35–60.

Grant, R. M. (2002). *Contemporary Strategic Analysis: Concepts, Techniques, Applications*, Malden, MA: Blackwell Publishing.

Grieve, A. and Ball, D. F. (1991). 'The role of process plant contractors in transferring technology', Paper presented at the R&D conference 'External acquisition of technological knowledge', Kiel, 8–10 July.

Hamel, G. (2000). *Leading the Revolution*, Boston, MA: Harvard Business School Press.

Hamel, G. and Prahalad, C. K. (1994). *Competing for the Future: Breakthrough Strategies for Seizing Control of Industry and Creating Markets of Tomorrow*, Boston, MA: Harvard Business School Press.

Hammer, M. and Champy, J. (1994). *Reengineering the Corporation: A Manifesto for Business Revolution*, London: Nicholas Brealey Publishing.

Handy, C. (1993). *Understanding Organizations*, 4th edn, London: Penguin Books.

Hansen, M. T., Nohria, N. and Tierney, T. (1994) 'What's your strategy for managing knowledge?', in *Harvard Business Review on Organizational Learning*, Boston, MA: Harvard Business School, 61–86.

Hax, A. C. and Wilde, D. L. (1999). 'The delta model: adaptive management for a changing world', *Sloan Management Review*, Winter, 11–28.

Hayes, R. H. and Wheelwright, S. C. (1984). *Restoring Our Competitive Edge: Competing Through Manufacturing*, US: John Wiley and Sons.

Hedberg, B. and Wolff, R. (2001). 'Organizing, learning, and strategizing: from construction to discovery' in M. Dierkes, A. B. Antal, J. Child and I. Nonaka (eds.) *Handbook of Organizational Learning and Knowledge*, Oxford: Oxford University Press, 535–556.

Henderson, R. M. and Clark, K. B. (1990). 'Architectural innovation: the reconfiguration of existing product technologies and the failure of established firms', *Administrative Science Quarterly*, 35, 9–30.

Hill, T. (1993). *Manufacturing Strategy: The Strategic Management of the Manufacturing Function*, 2nd edn, London: Macmillan.

Hilmer, F. G. and Donaldson, L. (1996). *Management Redeemed: Debunking the Fads that Undermine our Corporations*, New York: The Free Press.

Hirshman, A. O. and Lindblom, C. E. (1962). 'Economic development, research and development, policy making: some converging views', *Behavioral Science*, 7, 211–222, reprinted in F. E. Emery (1969) *Systems Thinking*, Harmondsworth, London: Penguin.

Hobday, M. (1994). 'The limits of Silicon Valley: a critique of network theory', *Technology Analysis and Strategic Management*, 6 (2), 231–244.

(1995). *Innovation in East Asia: The Challenge to Japan*, London: Edward Elgar.

(1998). 'Product complexity, innovation and industrial organization', *Research Policy*, 26, 689–710.

(2000). 'The project-based organisation: an ideal form for managing complex products and systems?', *Research Policy*, 29 (7–8), 871–893.

Hobday, M. G. and Brady, T. (2000): 'A fast method for analysing and improving complex software processes', *R&D Management*, 30 (1), 1–21.

Hobday, M., Davies, A. and Prencipe, A. (2004). 'Systems integration: a core capability of the modern corporation', submitted to *Industrial and Corporate Change*.

Hobday, M. and Laursen, K. (2003). 'International trade in high technology capital goods: an empirical assessment', mimeo, Complex Product System Innovation Centre, SPRU, England.

Hobday, M. and Rush, H. (1999). 'Technology management in complex product systems (CoPS): ten questions answered', *International Journal of Technology Management*, 17 (6), 618–638.

House of Commons (1998). 'Environment, transport and regional affairs committee, "Air Traffic Control"', Fourth Report, Vol. 1, Report and Proceedings of the Committee, 27 March.

Huber, G. P. (1996). 'Organizational learning: the contributing processes and the literatures', Chapter 6, in M. D. Cohen and L. S. Sproull (eds.) *Organizational Learning*, California: Sage Publications.

Hughes, T. P. (1983). *Networks of Power: Electrification in Western Society, 1880–1930*, Baltimore: Johns Hopkins University Press.

(1998). *Rescuing Prometheus*, New York: Pantheon Books.

Humphrey, W. S. (1989a). *Managing the Software Process*, Reading, MA: Addison-Wesley.

(1989b). *A Discipline for Software Engineering*, Reading, MA: Addison-Wesley.

Iansiti, M. (1995). 'Technology integration: managing technological evolution in a complex environment', *Research Policy*, 24, 521–542.

(1998). *Technology Integration: Making Critical Choices in a Dynamic World*, Boston, MA: Harvard Business School Press.

Iansiti, M. and Clark, K. B. (1994). 'Integration and dynamic capability: evidence from product development in automobiles and mainframe computers', *Industrial and Corporate Change*, 3 (3), 557–605.

Iansiti, M. and Khanna, Y. (1995). 'Technological evolution, system architecture and the obsolescence of firm capabilities', *Industrial and Corporate Change*, 4 (2), 333–361.

IBM (2002). 'A history of IBM Global Services', IBM Corporate Archives 2405SH01.

Johnson, S. B. (1997). 'Three approaches to big technology: operations research, systems engineering, and project management', *Society for the History of Technology*, 891–916.

Jones, C. (1996). 'Our worst current development practices', *IEEE Software*, March, 102–104.

Kanter, R. M. (1985). 'Supporting innovation and venture development in established companies', *Journal of Business Venturing*, 1, 47–60.

Kay, J. (1993). *The Foundations of Corporate Success: How Business Strategies Add Value*, Oxford: Oxford University Press.

Keegan, A. and Turner, R. J. (2001). 'Quantity versus quality in project-based learning practices', *Management Learning*, 32 (1), 77–98.

   (2002). 'The management of innovation in project-based firms', *Long Range Planning*, 35 (4), 367–388.

Kellner, M. I. (1996). *Business Process Modeling: Lessons and Tools from the Software World*, Software Engineering Institute, Carnegie Mellon University.

Klein, B. (1962). 'The decision making problem in development', in 'The rate and direction of inventive activity: Economic and social factors', Conference of the Universities-National Bureau Committee for Economic Research and the Committee of the Social Science Research Council, Princeton University Press, Princeton.

Klein, B. and Meckling, W. (1958). 'Application of operations research to development decisions', *Operations Research*, 6, 352–363.

Klepper, S. (1996). 'Entry, exit, growth, and innovation over the product life cycle', *American Economic Review*, 86 (3), 562–583.

Kline, S. J. (1990). *A Numerical Measure for the Complexity of Systems: The Concept and Some Implications*, Report INN-5, Thermosciences Division, Department of Mechanical Engineering, Stanford University, California.

Knight, K. (1976). 'Matrix organization: a review', *The Journal of Management Studies*, May, 111–130.

Kotler, P. (1976). *Marketing Management: Analysis Planning and Control*, 3rd edn, London: Prentice Hall.

Kusunoki, K., Nonaka, I. and Nagata, A. (1998). 'Organizational capabilities in product development of Japanese firms: a conceptual framework and empirical findings', *Organization Science*, 9 (6), November–December, 699–718.

Lake, J. G. (1992). 'Systems engineering re-energized: impacts of the revised DoD acquisition process', *Engineering Management Journal*, 4 (3), September, 8–14.

Landau, R. and Rosenberg, N. (1992). 'Successful commercialization in the chemical process industries', in N. Rosenberg, R. Landau and D. Mowery (eds.) *Technology and the Wealth of Nations*, Stanford: Stanford University Press.

Langlois, R. J. (1992). 'External economies and economic progress: the case of the microcomputer industry', *Business History Review*, 66 (Spring), 1–50.

Langlois, R. J. and Robertson, P. L. (1989). 'Explaining vertical integration: lessons from the American automobile industry', *Journal of Economic History*, 49, 361–375.

Larson, E. W. and Gobeli, D. H. (1987). 'Matrix management: contradictions and insights', *Californian Management Review*, Summer, 29 (4), 126–138.

(1989). 'Significance of project management structure on development success', *IEEE Transactions on Engineering Management*, 36 (2), 119–125.

Lawrence, P. R. and Lorsch, J. W. (1967). *Organization and Environment: Managing Differentiation and Integration* (revised edn 1986), Boston, MA: Harvard Business School Press.

Lemley, J. K. (1992). 'The Channel Tunnel: creating a modern wonder-of-the-world', *PMNetwork, The Professional Magazine of the Project Management Institute*, July, 14–22.

Leonard, D. (1995). *Wellsprings of Knowledge: Building and Sustaining the Sources of Innovation*, Boston, MA: Harvard Business School Press.

Leonard-Barton, D. (1988). 'Implementation as mutual adaptation of technology and organization', *Research Policy*, 17, 251–267.

(1992). 'Core capabilities and core rigidities: a paradox in managing new product development', *Strategic Management Journal*, 13, 111–125.

Lindblom, C. E. (1959). 'The science of "muddling through"', *Public Administration Review*, 19, 79–88.

Lindkvist, L. (2004) 'Governing project-based firms: promoting market-like processes within hierarchies', *Journal of Management and Governance*, 8, 3–25.

Lindkvist, L., Söderlund, J. and Tell, F. (1998) 'Managing product development projects: on the significance of fountains and deadlines', *Organization Studies*, 19 (6), 931–951.

Linx (1997). *ETL Internal Newsletter*, Issue 28, Ericsson.

Lipschitz, R., Popper, M. and Oz, S. (1996). 'Building learning mechanisms: the design and implementation of organizational learning mechanisms', *Journal of Applied Behavioural Science*, 32 (3), 292–305.

Littlewood, B. and Strigini, L. (1992). 'The risks of software', *Scientific American*, November, 38–43.

Lundin, R. A. and Söderholm, A. (1995). 'A theory of the temporary organization', *Scandinavian Journal of Management*, 11 (4), 437–455.

Lyytinen, K., Mathiassen, L. and Ropponen, J. (1995). 'A framework for software risk management', Paper Presented at the Third European Conference on Information Systems, Athens, Greece, 1–3 June.

MacCrimmon, K. R. (1993). 'Do firm strategies exist?', *Strategic Management Journal*, 14, Winter, 113–130.

March, J. G. (1991). 'Exploration and exploitation in organizational learning', *Organization Science*, 2 (1), 71–87.

March, J. G. and Simon, H. A. (1958). *Organizations*, New York: Wiley.

Marquis, D. G. (1969). 'Ways of organising projects', *Innovation*, 5, 22–33.

Marshak, T. A. (1962). 'Strategy and organization in a system development project', in 'The rate and direction of inventive activity: Economic and social factors', Conference of the Universities-National Bureau Committee for Economic Research and the Committee of the Social Science Research Council, Princeton University Press, Princeton.

Mayntz, R. and Hughes, T. P. (eds.) (1988). *The Development of Large Technical Systems*, Frankfurt am Main: Campus Verlag.

Metcalfe, J. S. and de Liso, N. (1995). *Innovation, Capabilities and Knowledge: the Epistemic Connection*, University of Manchester, Department of Economics, mimeo.

Meurling, J. and Jeans, J. (1994). 'The mobile phone book: The invention of the mobile phone industry', Ericsson Radio Systems AB, Communications Week International, London.

Middleton, C. J. (1967). 'How to set up a project organization', *Harvard Business Review*, March–April, 73–82.

Miles, R. E. and Snow, C. C. (1986). 'Organizations: new concepts for new forms', *Californian Management Review*, Spring, 28 (3), 62–73.

Miller, R. and Cote, M. (1987). *Growing the Next Silicon Valley: A Guide for Successful Regional Planning*, Massachusetts: Lexington Books.

Miller, R., Hobday, M., Leroux-Demers, T. and Olleros, X. (1995). 'Innovation in complex systems industries: the case of flight simulation', *Industrial and Corporate Change*, 4 (2), 363–400.

Miller, R. and Lessard, D. R. (2000). *The Strategic Management of Large Engineering Projects: Shaping Institutions, Risks, and Governance*, Cambridge, MA: The MIT Press.

Mintzberg, H. (1979). *The Structuring of Organizations*, Englewood Cliffs, NJ: Prentice Hall.

(1983). *Structures in Fives: Designing Effective Organizations*, Englewood Cliffs, NJ: Prentice Hall.

(1989). *Mintzberg on Management: Inside Our Strange World of Organizations*, New York: The Free Press.

(1996). 'Crafting strategy', in H. Mintzberg and J. B. Quinn, *The Strategy Process: Concepts, Contexts and Cases*, 3rd edn, New Jersey: Prentice Hall International, Inc., 101–110.

(2004). *Managers not MBAs: A Hard Look at the Soft Practice of Managing and Management Development*, London: FT Prentice Hall.

Mölleryd, B. G. (1997). 'The building of a world industry – the impact of entrepreneurship on Swedish mobile telephony', *TELDOK*, Stockholm.

Morgan, G. (1986). *Images of Organization*, London: Sage.

(1996). *Images of Organization*, 2nd edn, Thousand Oaks, CA: Sage Publications.

Morgan, F., Brady, T. and Davies, A. (1997). *The Turnkey Project Start-up Guide*, Ericsson publication EN/LZTG 501 R1.

Morris, P. W. G. (1994). *The Management of Projects*, London: Thomas Telford.

Morris, P. W. G. and Hough, G. H. (1987). *The Anatomy of Major Projects: A Study of the Reality of Project Management*, Chichester: John Wiley.

Moss, S. (1981). *An Economic Theory of Business Strategy*, Oxford: Martin Robertson.

Mowery, D. C. and Rosenberg, N. (1982a). 'Technical change in the commercial aircraft industry, 1925–1975', in N. Rosenberg, *Inside the Black Box: Technology and Economics*, Cambridge: Cambridge University Press, 163–177.

Mowery, D. C. and Rosenberg, N. (1982b). 'The commercial aircraft industry', in R. Nelson (ed.) *Government and Technical Progress: a Cross-Industry Analysis*, New York: Pergamon Press.

(1989). *Technology and the Pursuit of Economic Growth*, Cambridge: Cambridge University Press.

Mueller, D. C. and Tilton, J. E. (1976). 'Research and development costs as a barrier to entry', *Canadian Journal of Economics*, 2, 570–579.

Mullins, L. J. (1994). *Management and Organisational Behaviour*, 3rd edn, London: Pitman Publishing.

Nelson, R. R. (1991). 'Why do firms differ, and how does it matter?', *Strategic Management Journal*, 12, 61–74.

Nelson, R. R. and Rosenberg, N. (1993). 'Technical innovations and national systems', in R. R. Nelson (ed.) *National Innovation Systems: A Comparative Analysis*, New York: Oxford University Press.

Nelson, R. R. and Winter, S. G. (1982). *An Evolutionary Theory of Economic Change*, Cambridge, MA: The Belknap Press of Harvard University Press.

Nightingale, P. (2000). 'Economies of scale in experimentation: knowledge and technology in pharmaceutical R&D', *Industrial Corporate Change*, 9 (2), 315–359.

Nightingale, P., Brady, T., Davies, A. and Hall, J. (2003). 'Capacity utilisation revisited: software, control and large technical systems', *Industrial Corporate Change*, 12 (3), 477–517.

Nightingale, P. and Poll, R. (2000). 'Innovation in investment banking: The dynamics of control systems within the Chandlerian firm', *Industrial Corporate Change*, 9 (2), 315–359.

Nonaka, I. and Takeuchi, H. (1995). *The Knowledge-Creating Company*, New York: Oxford University Press.

Obeng, E. (1995). 'The role of project management in implementing strategy', in *The Financial Times Handbook of Management*, London: Pearson Education, 178–193.

Oliva, R. and Kallenberg, R. (2003). 'Managing the transition from products to services', *International Journal of Service Industry Management*, 14 (2), 160–172.

Orlikowski, W. J. (2002). 'Knowing in practice: enacting a collective capability in distributed organizing', *Organization Science*, 13 (3), 249–273.

Orr, J. (1987). 'Narratives at work: story telling as cooperative diagnostic activity', *Field Service Manager*, June, 47–60.

   (1990). 'Talking about machines: An ethnography of a modern job', doctoral dissertation, Cornell University.

Owen, D. (1997). 'GEC Alstom in career discussions', *Financial Times*, 19 November.

Packendorff, J. (1995). 'Inquiring into the temporary organization: new directions for project management research', *Scandinavian Journal of Management*, 11 (4), 319–333.

Parnas, D. L. and Clements, P. C. (1986). 'A rational design process: how and why to fake it', *IEEE Transactions on Software Engineering*, SE-12, February, 251–257.

Paulk, M. C. (1993). 'Capability maturity model, version 1.1', *IEEE Software*, 10 (4), 18–27.

   (1995a). 'The evolution of the SEI's capability maturity model for software', *Software Process: Improvement and Practice*, Pilot Issue, 3–15.

   (1995b): 'The rational planning of (software) projects', Proceedings of the First World Congress for Software Quality, San Francisco, CA, 20–22 June, Section 4.

Pavitt, K. (1990). 'What we know about the strategic management of technology', *California Management Review*, Spring, 16–26.

(1994). 'Key characteristics of large innovating firms', in M. Dodgson and R. Rothwell (eds.) *The Handbook of Industrial Innovation*, Cheltenham: Edward Elgar.

(2003). 'Specialization and systems integration: where manufacture and services still meet', in A. Prencipe, A. Davies and M. Hobday (eds.) *The Business of Systems Integration*, Oxford: Oxford University Press, 78–91.

Pavitt, K. and Rothwell, R. (1976). 'A comment on "a dynamic model of process and product innovation"', *OMEGA, the International Journal of Management Science*, 4 (4), 375–377.

Peltu, M. (1992). 'Project process management', *Integration*, September, 51–55.

Penrose, E. (1959). *The Theory of the Growth of the Firm*, Oxford: Oxford University Press.

(1960). 'The growth of the firm: a case study: the Hercules Powder Company', *Business History Review*, 34 (1), Spring.

(1995). 'Forward to the third edition', *The Theory of the Growth of the Firm*, Oxford University Press.

Peters, T. (1987). *Thriving on Chaos: Handbook for a Management Revolution*, London: Macmillan.

Petroski, H. (1996). *Invention by Design: How Engineers Get From Thought to Thing*, Cambridge, MA: Harvard University Press.

Pinto, J. K. and Covin, J. G. (1989). 'Critical factors in project implementation: a comparison of construction and R&D projects', *Technovation*, 9, 49–62.

Pinto, J. K. and Kharbanda, O. P. (1995). 'Lessons for an accidental profession', *Business Horizons*, March–April, 41–50.

Pinto, J. K. and Prescott, J. E. (1988). 'Variations in critical success factors over the stages in the project life cycle', *Journal of Management*, 14 (1), 5–18.

Piore, M. J. and Sabel, C. F. (1984). *The Second Industrial Divide*, New York: Basic Books.

Pisano, G. (1997). *The Development Factory*, Boston, MA: Harvard University Press.

Popper, M. and Lipschitz, R. (1995). *Organizational Learning Mechanisms: A Structural/Cultural Approach to Organizational Learning*, Haifa, Israel: University of Haifa.

Porter, M. E. (1980). *Competitive Strategy: Techniques for Analyzing Industries and Competitors*, New York: The Free Press.

(1985). *Competitive Advantage: Creating and Sustaining Superior Performance*, New York: The Free Press.

(1990). *The Competitive Advantage of Nations*, London: Macmillan Press.

(1996). 'What is strategy?', *Harvard Business Review*, November–December, 61–78.

Potter, S. and Roy, R. (1996). 'The development of high speed trains', 5–76, *Innovation: Design, Environment and Strategy: Block 4 Case Studies*, Milton Keynes: The Open University.

Prahalad, C. K. (1993). 'The role of core competencies in the corporation', *Research/Technology Management*, November–December, 40–47.

Prahalad, C. K. and Ramaswamy, V. (2000). 'Co-opting customer competence', *Harvard Business Review*, January–February, 79–87.

Prencipe, A. (1997). 'Technological competencies and product's evolutionary dynamics: a case study from the aero-engine industry', *Research Policy*, 25, 1261–1276.

(2003). 'Corporate strategy and systems integration capabilities: managing networks in complex systems industries', in A. Prencipe, A. Davies and M. Hobday (eds.) *The Business of Systems Integration*, Oxford: Oxford University Press, 114–132.

Prencipe, A., Davies, A. and Hobday, M. (eds.) (2003). *The Business of Systems Integration*, Oxford: Oxford University Press.

Prencipe, A. and Tell, F. (2001). 'Inter-project learning: processes and outcomes of knowledge codification in project-based firms', *Research Policy*, 30, 1373–1394.

Pulford, K., Kuntzmann-Combelles, A. and Shirlaw, S. (1996). *A Quantitative Approach to Software Management*, Wokingham, England: Addison-Wesley.

Quinn, J. B. (1980). *Strategies for Change: Logical Incrementalism*, Homewook, IL: Irwin.

(1992). *Intelligent Enterprise: A Knowledge and Service Based Paradigm for Industry*, New York: The Free Press.

Ramo, S. (1969). *The Cure for Chaos: Fresh Solutions to Social Problems Through the Systems Approach*, New York: David McKay Company.

Rich, B. R. and Janos, L. (1994). *Skunk Works: A Personal Memoir of My Years at Lockheed*, London: Warner Books.

Richardson, G. B. (1972). 'The organisation of industry', *Economic Journal*, 82, 883–896.

Robertson, D. and Ulrich, K. (1998). 'Planning for product platforms', *Sloan Management Review*, Summer, 19–31.

Rosenberg, N. (1963). 'Technological change in the machine tool industry, 1840–1910', *The Journal of Economic History*, 23 (4), 413–443.

(1976). 'Marx as a student of technology', *Monthly Review*, 28, 56–77.

(1982). 'Learning by using', in N. Rosenberg (ed.) *Inside the Black Box: Technology and Economics*, Cambridge: Cambridge University Press, 120–140.

Rothwell, R. (1992). 'Successful industrial innovation: critical factors for the 1990s', *R&D Management*, 22 (3), 221–239.

Rothwell, R. and Gardiner, P. (1989). 'The strategic management of re-innovation', *R&D Management*, 19 (2), 147–160.

Rout, T. P. (1995). 'SPICE: a framework for software process assessment', *Software Process: Improvement and Practice*, Pilot Issue, 57–66.

Rumelt, R. (1974). *Strategy, Structure and Economic Performance*, Boston, MA: Harvard University Press.

Sage, A. P. (1981). 'Systems engineering: fundamental limits and future prospects', *Proceedings of the IEEE*, 69 (2), February, 158–166.

Sahal, D. (1985). 'Technological guideposts and innovation avenues', *Research Policy*, 14, 61–82.

Sahlin-Andersson, K. and Söderholm, A. (2002) *Beyond Project Management: new perspectives on the temporary-permanent dilemma*, Malmö: Copenhagen Business School Press.

Sako, M. (2003). 'Modularity and outsourcing: the nature of co-evolution of product architecture and organization architecture in the global automotive industry', in A. Prencipe, A. Davies and M. Hobday (eds.) *The Business of Systems Integration*, Oxford: Oxford University Press, 229–253.

Sandberg, R. and Werr, A. (2003). 'The three challenges of corporate consulting', *MIT Sloan Management Review*, Spring, 59–66.

Sapolsky, H. M. (1972). *The Polaris System Development: Bureaucratic and Programmatic Success in Government*, Cambridge, MA: Harvard University Press.

(2003). 'Inventing systems integration', in A. Prencipe, A. Davies and M. Hobday (eds.) *The Business of Systems Integration*, Oxford: Oxford University Press, 15–34.

Sapsed, J., Gann, D., Marshall, N. and Salter, A. J. (2005). 'From here to eternity?: the practice of knowledge transfer in dispersed and co-located project organisations', Special Issue of *European Planning Studies* on 'Location, innovation and knowledge management', 13, 6.

Sapsed, J. and Salter, A. J. (2004). 'Postcards from the edge: local communities, global programs and boundary objects', *Organization Studies*, 25(9), 1515–1534.

Schön, D. A. (1983). *The Reflective Practitioner*, New York: Basic Books.

Schumpeter, J. A. (1947). *Capitalism, Socialism and Democracy*, Cambridge, MA: Harvard University Press.

Senge, P. M. (1990). 'The leader's new work: building learning organizations', *Sloan Management Review*, 7, Fall, 7–23.

(1999). *The Fifth Discipline*, New York: Doubleday.

Shenhar, A. J. (1993). 'From low- to high-tech project management', *R&D Management*, 23 (3), 199–214.

(1994a). 'Systems engineering management: a framework for the development of a multidisciplinary discipline', *IEEE Transactions on Systems, Man, and Cybernetics*, 24 (2), February, 327–332.

(1994b). 'A new conceptual framework for modern project management', in T. M. Khalil and B. A. Bayraktar (eds.) *Management of Technology, IV*, Institute of Industrial Engineers.

Shenhar, A. J., Dvir, D. and Levy, O. (1994). 'Mapping the dimensions of project success', in T. M. Khalil and B. A. Bayraktar (eds.) *Management of Technology, IV*, Institute of Industrial Engineers.

Shepherd, C. and Ahmed, P. K. (2000). 'From product innovation to solutions innovation: a new paradigm for competitive advantage', *European Journal of Innovation Management*, 2, 100–106.

Simon, H. A. (1955). 'A behavioural model of rational choice', *Quarterly Journal of Economics*, 69, 99–118.

(1993). 'Strategies and organizational evolution', *Strategic Management Journal*, 14, Winter, 131–142.

Slywotzky, A. J. (1996). *Value Migration: How to Think Several Moves Ahead of the Competition*, Boston, MA: Harvard Business School Press.

Slywotzky, A. J. and Morrison, D. J. (1998). *The Profit Zone: How Strategic Business Design Will Lead You to Tomorrow's Profits*, Chichester: John Wiley & Sons.

Smith, D. J. (1994). 'Software quality and reliability', in D. Lock (ed.) *Gower Handbook of Quality Management*, 2nd edn, Hampshire: Gower.

Starbuck, W. H. (1983). 'Organizations as action generators', *American Sociological Review*, 48, 91–102.

(1985). 'Acting first and thinking later: theory versus reality in strategic change', in M. Pennings and Associates, *Organizational Strategy and Change: New Views on Formulating and Implementing Strategic Decisions*, San Francisco: Jossey-Bass, 336–372.

Stata, R. (1989). 'Organisational learning – the key to management innovation', *Sloan Management Review*, 63, Spring, 63–74.

Stinchcombe, A. L. and Heimer, C. A. (1983). *Organization Theory and Project Management*, Oslo: Norwegian University Press.

Sturgeon, T. (2002). 'Modular production networks: a new American model of industrial organization', *Industrial and Corporate Change*, 11 (3), 451–496.

Summerton, J. (ed.) (1994). *Changing Large Technical Systems*, Oxford: Westview Press.

Sydow, J., Lindkvist, L. and DeFillippi, R. (2004). 'Project-based organizations, embeddedness and repositories of knowledge: editorial', *Organization Studies*, 25 (9), 1475–1489.

Taylor, F. W. (1911). *Principles and Methods of Scientific Management*, New York: Harper and Row.

Teece, D. J. (1986). 'Profiting from technological innovation: implications for integration, collaboration, licensing and public policy', *Research Policy*, 15, 285–305.

(1996). 'Firm organization, industrial structure, and technological innovation', *Journal of Economic Behavior and Organization*, 31, 193–224.

Teece, D. J. and Pisano, G. (1994). 'The dynamic capabilities of firms: an introduction', *Industrial and Corporate Change*, 3, 537–556.

Teece, D. J., Pisano, G. and Shuen, A. (1997). 'Dynamic capabilities and strategic management', *Strategic Management Journal*, 18 (7), 509–533.

Teece, D. J., Rumelt, R., Dosi, G. and Winter, S. (1994). 'Understanding corporate coherence: theory and evidence', *Journal of Economic Behavior and Organization*, 23, 1–30.

Tidd, J., Bessant, J. and Pavitt, K. (1997) *Managing Innovation: Integrating Technological, Market and Organizational Change*, Chichester: John Wiley & Sons.

Toffler, A. (1970). *Future Shock*, New York: Bantam Books.

(1985). *The Adaptive Corporation*, London: Pan Books.

Turner, R. J. (1999). *The Handbook of Project-Based Management: Improving the Processes for Achieving Strategic Success*, 2nd edn, London: McGraw-Hill.

Turner, R. J. and Müller, R. (2003). 'On the nature of the project as a temporary organization', *International Journal of Project Management*, 21, 1–8.

Tushman, M. and Anderson, P. (1986). 'Technological discontinuities and organizational environments', *Administrative Science Quarterly*, 31, 439–465.

Tyson, S. and Jackson, T. (1992). *The Essence of Organizational Behaviour*, New York: Prentice Hall.

Utterback, J. M. (1994). *Mastering the Dynamics of Innovation: How Companies Can Seize Opportunities in the Face of Technological Change*, Cambridge, MA: Harvard Business School Press.

Utterback, J. M. and Abernathy, W. J. (1975). 'A dynamic model of process and product innovation', *OMEGA, The International Journal of Management Science*, 3 (6), 639–656.

Utterback, J. M. and Suarez, F. F. (1993). 'Innovation, competition, and industry structure', *Research Policy*, 22 (1), 1–21.

Vernon, R. (1960). *Metropolis 1985: an Interpretation of the Findings of the New York Metropolitan Region Study*, Cambridge, MA: Harvard University Press.

(1966). 'International investment and international trade in the product cycle', *Quarterly Journal of Economics*, 80, 190–207.

Vincenti, W. G. (1990). *What Engineers Know and How They Know It, Analytical Studies from Aeronautical History*, Baltimore: Johns Hopkins University Press.

von Hippel, E. (1988). *The Sources of Innovation*, Oxford: Oxford University Press.

Walker, W., Graham, M. and Harbor, B. (1988). 'From components to integrated systems: technological diversity and integration between the military and civilian sectors', in P. Gummett and J. Reppy (eds.) *The Relations Between Defence and Civil Technologies*, London: Kluwer Academic Publishers.

Welch, J. with Bryne, J. A. (2001). *Jack: What I've Learned Leading a Great Company and Great People*, London: Headline Book Publishing.

Wernerfelt, B. (1984). 'A resource-based view of the firm', *Strategic Management Journal*, 5, 171–180.

Williamson, O. E. (1971). 'The vertical integration of production: market failure considerations', *American Economic Review*, Papers and Proceedings, 61, 112–123.

(1975). *Markets and Hierarchies*, New York: The Free Press.

Winch, G. (1997). 'Thirty years of project management. What have we learned?', presented at the British Academy of Management, Aston University.

Wise, R. and Baumgartner, P. (1999). 'Go downstream: the new profit imperative in manufacturing', *Harvard Business Review*, September–October, 133–141.

Womack, J. P., Jones, D. T. and Roos, D. (1991). *The Machine that Changed the World*, Cambridge, MA: MIT Press.

Womack, J. P. and Jones, D. T. (1996). *Lean Thinking: Banish Waste and Create Wealth in Your Corporation*, New York: Simon & Schuster.

Woodward, J. (1958). *Management and Technology*, London: Her Majesty's Stationary Office.

(1965). *Industrial Organization: Theory and Practice*, 2nd edn, Oxford: Oxford University Press.

Yourdon, E. (1978). *Structured Walkthroughs*, 2nd edn, New York: Yourdon Press.

Zuboff, S. (1988). *In the Age of the Smart Machine: The Future of Work and Power*, Oxford: Heinemann.

Index